The War After

Anne Karpf is a journalist and sociologist. The radio critic of the *Guardian*, she has contributed regularly to many other national newspapers and magazines, and irregularly to many radio and television programmes. She has been a columnist on the *New Statesman* and a contributing editor to *Cosmopolitan*. Her first book was *Doctoring the Media: The Reporting of Health and Medicine*, and she has taught medical sociology at the University of London, as well as lecturing widely on medical and sociological subjects and the mass media. She lives in London with her partner and their two daughters.

Also by Anne Karpf

**Doctoring the Media:
the Reporting of Health and Medicine**

THE WAR AFTER

Living with the Holocaust

Anne Karpf

Minerva

A Minerva Paperback
THE WAR AFTER

First published in Great Britain 1996
by William Heinemann
This Minerva edition published 1997
Reprinted 1997

Random House UK Limited
20 Vauxhall Bridge Road, London SW1V 2SA

Random House Australia (Pty) Limited
20 Alfred Street, Milsons Point, Sydney
New South Wales 2061, Australia

Random House New Zealand Limited
18 Poland Road, Glenfield, Auckland 10, New Zealand

Random House South Africa (Pty) Limited
Endulini, 5a Jubilee Road, Parktown 2193, South Africa

Random House UK Limited Reg. No. 954009

A CIP catalogue record for this title
is available from the British Library

ISBN 0 7493 2009 5

Phototypeset in 11pt Baskerville
by Intype London Limited

Printed and bound in Great Britain
by Cox & Wyman Ltd, Reading, Berkshire

For Bianca,
and in memory of
Josef Karpf

I did not manage to save
a single life

I did not know how to stop
a single bullet

and I wander round cemeteries
which are not there
I look for words
which are not there
I run

to help where no one called
to rescue after the event

I want to be on time
even if I am too late

Jerzy Ficowski
(translated from Polish
by Keith Bosley)

Contents

Acknowledgements

This book's long gestation was eased by two grants. Thanks to the Authors' Foundation and the K Blundell Trust for a very useful early award, and to the British Academy for a Thank-offering to Britain Fellowship (endowed, appropriately, by refugees from Nazi Germany) which proved invaluable. A travel grant from the British Council in Warsaw helped make possible my trip to Poland.

Juliet Spitzer, whom I met at the first International Jerusalem Conference of Children of Holocaust Survivors in 1988, generously sent me a large, extremely useful batch of journal papers on the second generation. Sylvia Paskin also kindly supplied me with many papers and articles on the subject. Linda Rozmovits, in a brief, chance meeting, suggested some choice historical readings. Thanks are due to the Wiener Library and the Library of the Anna Freud Centre for allowing me the run of their holdings, and to Jerzy Ficowski for permission to reprint his poem 'I did not manage to save/a single life' from his collection *A Reading of Ashes* (The Menard Press, 1981).

I'm grateful to my parents, Natalia and Josef Karpf, for their willingness to be interviewed in detail and over many months about often traumatic events. Thanks also to Recia Herschdoerfer and Józik Rozewicz in London and Bianka Karpf in Israel for their help in confirming facts and details of my parents' stories. Rafael (Felek) Scharf invited me to Poland, helped me gain a sense of pre-war Polish Jewish life, and responded good-humouredly to my constant fact-checking phone-calls. Joachim Russek and the Centre for Jewish Culture were generous with their time and resources in Kraków. Zygmunt Rozewicz was a stimulating guide to Tarnów, Jasło, and other Polish towns which figured prominently in my parents' past.

David Fainman, Alfred Garwood, and Tanya Gutter have been crucial in sharing their ideas, insights, and feelings about the second generation, and helping me through difficult times. Fellow mothers Beth Noakes and Sarah Walker have provided essential emergency childcare in the book's final stages. Among many supportive friends, Corinne Pearlman, Caroline Pick, and Lennie Goodings helped convince me that this book would somehow get finished. Barbara Rosenbaum sustained me through many of the experiences described in it; her perceptiveness has been enriching.

My former agent Anne McDermid's enthusiasm for the project saw me through the faltering first years of writing. Her recent successor Felicity Rubinstein has already been an equally responsive and enthusiastic reader. With only the slenderest proposal to go on, Dan Franklin made an impressively speedy decision to commission the book. Tom Weldon was an ideal, patient early editor, leaving me in (guilty) peace while reacting encouragingly to the odd chapters which arrived every few years. His successor Victoria Hipps has been discreetly more interventionist: her gentle enquiries as to my progress, thoughtful suggestions for changes (which I haven't, needless to say, invariably taken up), and warm commitment to the book have greatly aided its completion.

Esther Green accompanied me on most of the journey which this book sketches. She sat with me through dreadful dark, stuck days, contained my rage, acknowledged my every tiny breakthrough, and helped bring me to life.

Thanks to Bianca Lewis Karpf for (just about) tolerating my absences over the last five months of most intensive writing. Together with Peter Lewis, she has dragged mè (kicking and screaming) into the present tense. It might seem far-fetched to thank a baby *in utero*, but since almost two-thirds of this book was written between the sixteenth and thirty-seventh weeks of pregnancy thanks are due to an obliging baby who didn't sap my energy (even if it partied relentlessly in my stomach each night).

Peter M Lewis is acknowledged in the text itself, and over eighteen years has shared in the struggles and break-throughs it charts: in the culture he comes from, to receive more praise would be embarrassing and generate the risk of 'a big head' (there's no Gentile equivalent of 'kvell', only the pejorative 'to boast' or 'to show off'). Too bad. His (almost) unwavering support for the book (despite the inevitable pall it sometimes cast over our lives), along with his sense of humour, energy, and the vast quantities of child-care and housework he has shouldered over the past six months, have been critical. He is a mensch and a half.

London
January 1996

Glossary

Aktion	'an action' – a rounding up of Jews by the Nazis, prior to a Selektion, where it was decided who would work and who would die
bimah	raised platform on which the reading desk stands in the synagogue
Chanukah	The Feast of Dedication, also known as The Feast of Lights, which often falls in December, near Christmastime
charoseth	a paste of raisins, nuts, wine, apple and cinnamon, eaten as part of the Seder meal, symbolising the bricks the Jews made to build the Pharoahs' pyramids
gefilte fish	fish balls
gemütlichkeit	cosiness
gewalt!	a cry of fear, amazement, or for help
golem	an imaginary, magical creature, most famously the Golem of Prague, supposedly made by a rabbi to protect the Jews
haimish	homely, homeliness
Kaddish	a prayer glorifying God's name, recited at the end of synagogue prayers; a mourner's prayer
kasha	roast buckwheat
kayn ayn hore	magical phrase uttered to ward off the evil eye

klezmer music	music traditionally made by an informal group of musicians in Eastern Europe
knadel, knaidlach	dumplings
kvell	to beam with immense pride and pleasure
landsman	someone who comes from the same home town
Lebkuchen	a biscuit, usually containing honey and spices
matzo	unleavened bread, eaten during the Passover festival. When the Jews fled Egypt in Exodus they did not have time to wait for their bread to rise, so took unleavened bread, or matzo, with them
menorah	candelabra
mensch	a man; an honorable, upright human being; a person of consequence
mezuzah	a little oblong box, containing a parchment with verses from Deuteronomy, which is affixed to the door jamb in Jewish homes
mikvah	a ritual bath for Jewish women
mitzvah	a commandment; a meritorious act, good deed
nebech	an interjection, similar to alas, expressing dismay, regret or sympathy; a fool, an ineffectual, helpless or hapless person
nudniky	from nudnik: a pest, prat – hence irritating
Rosh Hashanah	Jewish New Year
Seder	the Passover meal
Selektion	see Aktion
shiva	the seven solemn days of mourning for the dead
Shoah	Hebrew word for destruction; the Holocaust

shtetl	small town or village, particularly in Eastern Europe
Simhat Torah	a festival honouring the Torah (the first five books of the Bible)
stolat	phrase meaning 'may you live for a hundred years', 'may it be so for a hundred years'
tallis	prayer shawl
Talmud	the debates, dialogues, conclusions and commentaries of the scholars who for over a thousand years interpreted the Torah
tefillin	phylacteries; a slip of parchment, inscribed with certain passages of scripture, in a box worn by Jewish men on the left arm or forehead during morning prayers
Yad Vashem	the Holocaust Museum in Jerusalem
yarmulke (also known as kippe or kappel)	skull cap
yeshivah	a rabbinical school or seminary
Yiddish	Yiddish is the language of East European Jews, based on German. Yiddish is not Hebrew, which remains the Jews' language of prayer and official ceremony. In Israel, modern Hebrew is spoken
Yiddishkeit	'Yiddishness' – like haimish. A longing for Yiddishkeit can be a nostalgic longing for an Eastern European-style Jewish home
Yom Kippur	the Day of Atonement

Part One

1

My family was big on coats. Throughout my adolescence and well beyond we'd spontaneously combust into spectacular rows about them. My parents, always convinced I was a season behind (dressed for summer in the autumn, autumn in the winter), would 'tsk', then openly lambast me for the thinness of my coat: 'You can't go out like that, you'll freeze.' I'd deny that my coat was inadequate with as much vigour as if my very self had been called into question, while strangling my own doubts about whether I'd be warm enough. They'd plump up their attack with medical warnings – 'You'll catch pneumonia'. I'd counter with a furious adolescent assertion that I could look after myself. It would end either in screams or a fraught expedition to buy a new coat.

Virtually none, in their view, was thick enough. How many sheep gave their fleeces for my parents to be satisfied that I was sufficiently warm I couldn't say. And despite my protests, I too secretly subscribed to the belief that the only way to avoid refrigeration was by wearing bulk. When, at fifteen, for the first and only time I made a skirt, I used a fat felt – the kind of material that lines roofs in blustery places. The seams required industrial needles, and the hem was like a sandwich.

I never really understood what lay behind their obsession with trussing me in wool – one which seemed to go far beyond normal, even normal Jewish, parental concern – until many years later when I was going out with a friend. It was winter and cold, and she wore a thin shirt and an even thinner jacket – on my parents' scale its warmth rating would be somewhere near that of a bikini. I found myself asking her if she wasn't cold. Apparently this hadn't ever occurred to her. I learned that her father was a military man, and saw his children less as a family than as a squadron: he believed in toughening them up. It wasn't quite Basic Training, but they were expected to learn to survive without complaint. As a consequence, feeling cold had never been included in her alphabet of sensations. I, on the other hand, as a result (I'm sure) and not a cause of my parents' concern, felt constantly cold or, if I didn't, was anxious that I might.

And so it dawned on me that cold wasn't just a meteorological fact but also a psychic state. My parents experienced the post-war world as cold, both in their bodies and minds. Cold for them was life outside the home, cold represented what awaited you when you went out. They could control the temperature in their own place (and rightly considered the English, in their freezing houses, barbarians); but if the *gemütlichkeit* of a Jewish home signified safety, anything in the icy beyond could make you ill. The air outside was a polluting miasma, a kind of alien non-chicken soup, and you needed to take a little Jewish warmth out with you. You had to take inside out.

About the dangerous outside my sister and I learned early. I can't remember when we were first told about the war. I sometimes think that maybe we were never told; it just seeped into our home, like some peculiarly mobile fog, and took up residence. The house and our parents seemed layered with a kind of subcutaneous sadness. The large, old, heavy pieces of furniture shipped from Poland contributed

4

to the sense of gloom which schoolfriends much later confirmed. This was not a home to which you invited loud or uncomplaisant playmates. Or where several children simultaneously squealed. This was a serious house. Our social lives unfurled largely at the homes of our schoolfriends.

We were told stories about the war, and saw the number inked into my mother's arm. I remember little: both my sister and I have almost no memory of our childhoods – our remembered lives began properly at about the age of thirteen. Before that it's all gummed up, with only the odd sensation or incident showing through, like fragments of newsprint in papier mâché. Or a dream maddeningly just beyond recall. It's as if we never really had a childhood, and perhaps in some sense this was so.

But I do know that death was alive and present in our home. My parents had a few rescued pre-war photo albums containing group pictures of chillingly merry people. They would point out who was who and how they died. With so few living relatives dead ones had to suffice, so my sister and I heard countless stories about the Jóseks and Jadzias, the Mileks and Natans. They were spoken of vividly, as if they might walk through the door at any moment. But these reminiscences only confirmed the deep caesura in the family's continuity. Looking back, it sometimes seems as if we'd been cast adrift in Britain, or abandoned on one bank of a river with all our necessaries on the other. But if we felt a profound sense of erasure, we strenuously tried to busy it away. So I was never able to identify the lack, to name it let alone meet it, since all of our energies went into stopping and plugging it.

It seemed as if from birth I was obsessed with death. My parents tried to assuage this but almost certainly fuelled it by lying about their ages. It wasn't vanity so much as anxiety that made them lop off a few years, and their confession to the subtraction when I was around eight or nine only persuaded me that there was something risky in being the age they now admitted to. My sister Eve was charged with breaking the news of the death of a large neighbour to me: because of my preoccupation with death she was told to stress the woman's obesity as the cause of her drowning in the bath. Both my father's age (fifty when I was born) and my parents' past made them seem fragile: in rows Eve's trump card was 'You'll give Daddy a heart-attack'. (If I'd known he'd live to ninety-three, I might have won more of them.) So pervasive was our anxiety about our parents' dying that when the fairies we dreamt up reached 100, they began the life-cycle all over again but now in reverse, returning to nought. An incidental effect of this was that, at certain stages in their lives, the child fairies found themselves to be older than their parents.

Outside began in earnest when I started school, a grimy building smelling of boiling cabbage and bleached toilets, and utterly alien to the mittelEuropean knädel-and-strudel atmosphere of home. I was like an astronaut stepping out on to the moon, but it was a small step for humankind, and a vast one for me. In my first week, the teacher distributed a malt tablet to each child. I didn't know what it was but already I doubted my ability to ingest it. I tried and gagged. I got permission to go to the cloakroom to try again. To my horror in my fumbling the pill dropped down the sink, leaving behind a terrible moral dilemma: should I confess to the teacher? I didn't, and after school rushed home to persuade my mother to give me a note excusing me from further pills.

This is my earliest and one of my most resonant memories; I recoiled from those malt pills like a kosher child first tasting pork. I think going to school felt like abandoning my parents (or being abandoned by them). The pills were part of a frightening foreign culture, little pellets of Englishness; refusing them was a rejection of that alien world beyond my parents' house.

In fact, until I was eleven, school was a digestive night-

6

mare. My policy seemed to be nil by mouth. I couldn't abide milk and had to be excused from this too. And school dinners were beyond the pale. For years I remembered one of the earliest as a fried egg on top of a rice pudding – unlikely even in the culinary ruin that was a mid-1950s London state primary school. But the very preposterousness of the memory is eloquent: they were giving me absurdly dissonant things to swallow. I found a simple way of refusing. I would go home for lunch – a brief return visit to the safe place. And so I did: while my friends and peers were gulping down their school dinners unperturbed – for them it was just a prelude to playground handstands – I, until the age of eleven, made a daily extra journey to and from home. I think I was trying to reassure myself that it was still there.

School was alien not just nutritionally but also linguistically: in those days there was no conception of encouraging a pupil's mother tongue. So I went from a home where, between them, my parents could get by in eight languages (Polish, English, German, Russian, French, Italian, Hebrew, and Spanish, with a smattering of Yiddish), to a resolutely monolingual world, one where my parents' foreign accents, inaudible to me, were regularly remarked upon. My mother was often asked if she was French – presumably because this was the nearest foreign country, and so could conveniently stand for Abroad.

Leaving home was always frightening and felt wrenching: it wasn't so much a leaving as a forcible extraction. My anxiety invariably announced itself in my feeling sick, and this became a shameful insignia of childishness. Parties, picnics, holidays, outings of any kind – all were marked, to the exasperation of my sister and parents, by my feeling (and sometimes being) sick. If the outing involved leaving my parents for any length of time, the sickness would be all the less resistible. Family reminiscences are still scattered with the reproachful refrain 'and then you were sick'. They put a high premium on coping, and disapproved of these gastric displays of fragility.

I, for my part, was deeply ashamed of my inability to go robustly into the world, and tried to bludgeon my anxiety away. In fact, once I was out there, I always managed remarkably well. But the adhesiveness of my fears at that time doesn't surprise me now. We'd been raised on stories about the fractures in our parents' lives and the hiatus in their history. (Even my mother's embrace – fervent, enclosing, but abruptly concluded – was articulate, like being held and suddenly dropped.) Other families' lives seemed oiled by an extraordinary continuity and natural momentum in comparison.

Out of doors on a fine day, my parents would inhale extravagantly and exhort us to do the same. 'Breathe, breathe,' they'd urge, as if anxious that we might somehow forget to, and as though fresh air were a scarce commodity, which had to be seized while stocks lasted.

My mother's most common phrase was 'stolat', a Polish word meaning 'may you live one hundred years'. She'd wish it on us after anything from a sneeze to the mention of a pleasurable future event – rather hurriedly, the way Catholics cross themselves. Its very frequency of use conveyed the fear that a normal duration of life couldn't be assumed. It was an incantation against death.

Parenthood is probably intrinsically fearful, but our parents' fears were based not on an imagined future but their actual past. They'd lost so much that they were naturally frightened of losing more. So our daily activities were strewn with injunctions to be careful, as well as my mother's 'Oh my God' and 'I'll have a heart-attack'. Along with the normal socialisation of girls (and the Jewish emphasis on bookish learning) this meant that, although I was naturally athletic and excelled on sports day, my leisure activities never entailed leaving the ground or developing too close an acquaintance with it. Dive? You must be mad. And I never learned to ride a bike, I never climbed, I never camped. Looking back I see how extremely provisional and temporary all places and people seemed to them and then to me. We never learned to take the existence of the world and our place in it for granted.

The most violent extraction from home occurred when I was six, and Eve was nine. Our parents couldn't afford a family holiday, but stinted to send us to a summer school in Dorking. Dorking to others; to me, Hades. I had never been away from home without my parents before and here I was, not just torn from it and them, but abandoned into a dormitory with at least ten others, where group rules applied. Sick was entirely inadequate to express my terror and rage, so one morning early on I awoke with some discomfort to find, oh God, the shame, a large, angry turd lying in my bed.

My sister, enthusiastically cultivating the older girls, barely forgave me. But then I went further. I was struggling again with the alien food: the gravies and dripping, the blue plastic crockery which bequeathed its smell to everything in or on it. It all seemed so strange and un-Jewish, as though I were being made to eat the host. And so at lunch, surrounded by the whole school, like an inverted Oliver Twist I stood and announced that I'd have none of it. They all came running, the teachers, the head teacher, entreating, imploring. But I was resolved. Every day, I declared, I'd eat a buttered piece of white bread, cut into two triangles. And so it was. As the others ate their regulation food, I'd go into the kitchen to collect my triangles.

The bargaining over food didn't just take place away from home. I was that common bane of parents' lives, the child who won't eat. But in our house the mutinies mundane to other children seemed almost sinful, as if they'd only add suffering to our parents' already considerable stash. My refusals to eat were probably a well-aimed act of rebellion: I was rejecting the very thing they'd been forcibly deprived

9

of. To them it must have seemed as if their anxieties about their own survival, only just quelled, were now being reprised with their child. My mother finally, despairingly, brought me to a paediatrician, who soothed her with a phrase which released us all from food struggles: 'The child's not a fool; when she's hungry she'll eat.'

Have I made us sound a lugubrious lot? Oh, would that we had been. Lugubriousness was among the proscribed sentiments – along with sadness, rage, and depression. 'Depressed, what's depressed?' my father would ironically ask if my sister reported one of her schoolfriends to be low (vicarious depression being probably the closest we dared get), 'Her life isn't endangered, she has enough to eat.' If you weren't in a concentration camp, life must be a carousel. There was a hierarchy of suffering and normal, common-or-garden depression, teenage disaffection, or the faint bothersome feeling that all wasn't well with your world came incontestably bottom. When, decades later, a friend asked me if I'd actually felt unhappy as a child or only retrospectively imputed it, I didn't understand why I couldn't answer until I realised that being unhappy simply hadn't been contemplatable. It wasn't a permissible emotion and I wouldn't have known what it meant. If the Eskimos need lots of words for snow, no wonder I had none for unhappy.

My outlawed feelings found their own egress, largely through my body. I was an eczematous baby. At six weeks old my skin erupted into a hot, livid rash; apparently I spent my first year scratching. I couldn't be bathed, so my father oiled and soothed me instead. Though the eczema diminished as I got older, it would return years later, always a reliable bugle of distress.

I also wept through my nose: I had chronic sinusitis from an early age – my primary school years were full of large quantities of snot. Thank God for the invention of the tissue. With only the handkerchief to depend on, I wouldn't have had an education: I couldn't possibly have left home each day with just a couple of hankies to dam up my torrential mucus. Even so, I never managed to estimate correctly the number of tissues to take. Though I packed a fat wadge, they'd invariably run out by mid-morning, leaving the problem not only of what to do with the used ones, now plump and moist, but also of the mucus-in-waiting. I was forever having to exit from lessons to snort it down the wash basin.

All kinds of medicinal solutions were tried and failed, including a strange rubber bulb my parents had to insert into my nose while I lay on the bed with my head dangling off. It was meant to vacuum the mucus out – a sort of nasal enema – but was excruciating.

My demons must have tried to make their exit during the night, for my sister and I had a phrase which we imbued with an almost totemic power, without which we would never drift off to sleep. It had to be the last thing we said before we went to sleep, and needed repeating if some stray chat had intervened after we'd spoken it. 'Goodnight sleep well dream of nothing,' we would say, eliding it at full speed so that it sounded like one word.

Nevertheless, I woke up in the night many times feeling sick from some inexplicit but powerful fear, which must have worked itself loose while my vigilant self was asleep. I became so worried about its possible recurrence that I decided to keep a metal jug by my bed. It remained there reassuringly for years.

My primary source of comfort was the telly. As a narcotic it has no equal: sit before it for five hours on end, watch two consecutive old Hollywood movies, followed by an episode of a cowboy series and a sitcom, and you can be absolutely sure that your inner and outer worlds will evanesce, replaced by a universe which expects and demands nothing.

Our parents, desolate at our addiction, did everything they could to reduce it. They tried to suffuse us with a love of English literature: my father would reverently unfold the almost threadbare piece of paper on which he'd written the titles of the English classics, many of which he'd read in translation. He would repeat their titles, as if their greatness, their very Englishness, would somehow migrate to us, and their names alone seize us with the desire to read them. But my sister stuck to hardback romances, and I read almost nothing until I was seventeen – books were for studying. They were part of the problem, not the solution.

Our parents also tried taking away the television adaptor and hiding it. But the moment their car pulled away from the house, we'd rush down to my father's work-room and find another, so that we could sit transfixed for the whole time they were away. When we heard the car in the drive, one of us would hurriedly return the filched adaptor to his bench while the other turned the chairs in towards the table. On entering they'd go straight over to the television and touch it. It was always incriminatingly warm.

One day we were playing in the garden when a tall woman with long hair and wearing trousers materialised by the dustbins shouting, 'Stop talking about Mrs Wilkinson.' My parents protested their innocence. 'We don't even know a Mrs Wilkinson. Who is she?' 'I'm Mrs Wilkinson,' she announced. She was shooed away, dismissed out of earshot as mad, but her paranoiac outburst had disturbed our fine pellicle of normality. Some days later, hearing a commotion in the road, we went out and saw Mrs Wilkinson at her third-floor window. She was throwing milk bottles at the congregated neighbours and ambulancemen, who were entreating her to come down. Finally, she was carried away and probably confined somewhere, but she escaped regularly into my dreams to leak her craziness.

It must have been around then that my mother hired a Frenchwoman to come to our home to teach her and me French. I was probably about eight, and came to dread the regular sessions with the shiny red-and-white covered Berlitz book. I struggled with formal French lessons without any formal knowledge of English grammar: tormented by 'y' and 'en', which I could never distinguish, I relied instead on wild hazard. What remains for me beyond these sparse memories of childhood is the feeling evoked by those lessons – one of disorientation and floundering, as if I were mapless in a strange place, or trying to function while sedated, yet quite unable to say 'I don't understand', 'I don't want to', 'I can't'. I had no 'no's.

To look at us, you wouldn't have thought anything was wrong. We were loved with abandon. My parents were warm, engaging people, with an expansive European charm (which sometimes embarrassed me in its un-Britishness – I knew how much the English disliked excess). Yet my father's painterly appreciation of female beauty, the boundless praise he often offered, and the Viennese way he'd tip his hat and acknowledge those he knew and liked with a half-bow, disarmed and attracted people. And so did my exuberant, musical mother.

About surviving in England we absorbed a double message. Our parents depicted the world as so unsafe that we gathered it was best to lie low and hold back: if you avoided attracting attention, you might escape a backlash. (This had probably been the best way of surviving in Kraków or Lvov, twenty years earlier.) When my sister's primary schoolteacher called her a dirty Jew, my father wrote anonymously to the headmaster (who subsequently removed the teacher), but only told us about his intervention decades later. When, in my twenties, in a diary for the *Sunday Times*, I wrote about Yom Kippur (the Day of Atonement) and being Jewish, my parents expressed a mixture of pleasure and anxiety at this public coming out. (In the event, a passage about shaving my legs which was misread as an admission that I shaved my pubic hair attracted far more public interest.)

On the other hand we were encouraged to excel. From a very young age I knew that through achieving I could bring something very special to my parents. I took them my feats.

I wasn't one of those who needed to be cajoled, threatened, or bribed into studying. On the contrary, sometimes I had to be urged to stop. School and extracurricular success was something with which to nourish them, an infinite balm. Our achievements, our very existence, had a triumphal feel: they were an assertion of life, a victory against an (unnamed) enemy. But the enemy needed constant revanquishing and life had to be endlessly reasserted. And so I came to believe quite viscerally that without doing one might actually cease to be.

Success and achievement also promised exemption from the common fate: it was as if, through an unstinting effort of intellect and will, you could separate yourself from the mass and survive. We were a family characterised by energy, attack, vehemence. Diffidence was foreign to us and passivity frightened us. We stoked up our life-force. We animated each other and ourselves.

We were weaned on stories of my mother's success as a rallier. How she buoyed up friends and relatives during the war with her unsinkable optimism. Somehow my parents seemed to derive from the fact of their survival not a sense of powerlessness, victimhood, or even luck, but of the possibility of control. All of life seemed purposive, actuated by choice or behaviour; nothing was down to chance. Despite the counter evidence presented by his life, my father would quote to us in Latin that 'omnis homo sui fati auctor est' (every man is the author of his own fate).

With choice came blame. If you got a cold, it was your fault: you weren't dressed warmly enough, you'd consorted with germy people. If others let you down, your judgement in trusting them was impugned. Human agency was paramount; nothing was random or unforeseeable. It was as if they'd had to armour themselves against the terrible serendipity of their survival.

But although our parents seemed invincible, we also

sensed their fragility: they were like mended figurines liable to rebreak. We knew we played a critical role as their glue.

My sense of responsibility for them was exacerbated by a minor car accident when I was about ten. We were returning from a motoring holiday in France, with a roof-rack full of luggage. My mother was driving, and she took the corner too fast. We swerved and the car left the road, propelled by the now winging roof-rack. The road was deserted, and the damage to car and passengers minimal. But when we'd recovered from the shock, refixed the rack, and set off again, I found myself scanning the road and participating in the driving as if I were in the driver's seat and my intense concentration was required to guide the car, to will us to safety. This feeling never left me. Thereafter I was never able to leave the driving to others and assume the car's automobility: I was always a back-seat navigator and invisible rear engine.

The compulsion to supplement and galvanise was at its most acute when my mother gave a concert. She played regularly, giving recitals or as a soloist with orchestras, in all the leading London concert halls. We always attended. Her playing excited and moved audiences, often even the notoriously steely London music critics. But on one occasion, in a Wigmore Hall recital, she briefly mixed up a passage. It's not an unusual experience for performers and she quickly found her way back. Almost no one seemed to notice, except my father, sister and I, who'd heard the piece so often – her music was our Muzak, the background to our study and play.

But as with the car accident, this sign of fallibility had a major effect on me. I never told anyone (least of all my parents) but after this I found her concerts an endurance test. I would mentally accompany her from the audience, straining for any wrong note real or imagined, which would then induce a state of panic. When the concert was over, admiring friends and fans would gather in the green room and invariably ask my sister and me if we were proud of my mother. I could never say that my predominant emotions had been a) terror, and b) relief.

My identification with my mother was total, and yet I was hardly able get beyond the opening bars of 'Für Elise'. It was as if the success of the concert depended on me even though I could barely play. No wonder my favourite record was 'Sparky's Magic Piano' in which a child without musical skill sits down at the piano and discovers that he's suddenly mutated into a virtuoso.

In reality, my mother taught me music and not the other way round. The day before my Grade Three piano exam, I was fooling around on the piano with my best friend, also about to take the exam. She was playing the F-sharp minor scale, but quite differently from me. She insisted her way was right, I insisted mine was. As we sat there contemplating our two different versions, all my confidence ebbed away: I was sure that my mother had taught me wrongly, that – though she'd been a soloist with the Berlin Philharmonic Orchestra at eighteen – she *didn't know* the F-sharp minor scale. In the event, we discovered that there were two scales, melodic and harmonic: my friend had learned one and I'd learned another. Yet even here, in my mother's field of eminence, I hadn't felt able to deliver myself into her hands and trust her ability.

With my mother's music and my father's art, the house dripped with European culture. Her playing was central to our family's life. The Chopin and Beethoven, Brahms and Schubert must have provided her with her only sense of continuity from her pre-war life, while her professional success (which my father tirelessly fomented) confirmed that she'd robustly re-entered the world. But her music was also plaintive, with a grief that was rarely referred to.

I loved being enfolded in her playing. I particularly relished, after recovering from a temperature, having to spend a day at home but out of bed. While she practised, I'd play cosily on the bulky, red Polish sofa in the lounge near the piano, moving the bolsters so as to make myself a little house. But a sadness always hovered over that comforting scene, and I still find certain melodies which she used to play instantly evocative and unbearably poignant. The Paganini-Liszt Studies are my madeleine.

Though my parents' English was thickly accented they were trilingual and, despite his quirky word-order, my father could compose an elegant English business letter. And yet, in an inversion of the generational norm (and like all children in immigrant families) we soon became linguistically more competent than they – our mother tongue was not our mother's tongue. We were also, in the way of all first-generation British, more confident at finding our way around.

Our parents were proud of their children's ease and familiarity with their adopted country. There's a much-repeated family story about how, at around the age of two and a half, I accompanied my father to the food department of John Barnes store where, on the instructions of my mother, he was to buy a packet of chocolate blancmange. But when he couldn't find his way around the labyrinthine shelves and counters, I took him by the hand and led him to the right one.

Why did my parents remember and repeat this molecule of incident so often down the years? Family stories are a kind of DNA, encoded messages about how things are and should be, passed from one generation to another. This story wasn't just about culinary preference or infant precocity – they had other, more telling tales for that. This story said that I was their guide, mediating an alien culture to them. This story said I already knew my way around.

I think we understood from a very young age that we must look after them, or something bad could happen. We tried to keep them alive.

A much older, but no less anxious, me sat down in 1983 and 1984 with each of my parents to record their stories. In some sense I wasn't yet ready to hear them, but was increasingly scared that they'd die and take them with them. I wanted their stories in the bag, stored away for future perusal, every detail elucidated – in case, when I was ready, they wouldn't be around to do it. On the tapes I'm uncharacteristically (for my then self) pernickety about facts. On the other hand, I'd just begun seeing a therapist, and was clearly quarrying my parents' lives in search of material. I had my own agenda, I was on a fishing trip.

So the accounts we produced are a combination of what I was then ready and able to hear, and they were then ready and able to tell. What's more they've been edited and shaped by a later self, one with a different perspective and its own preoccupations.

JOSEF KARPF: My father came from a large family of thirteen. My grandfather lived in Ulanów, on the border of Galicia and the Russian part of Poland: he established himself as a big businessman, buying timber and floating it down the river to Danzig. Almost three-quarters of the town's population worked for him – he was very wealthy. He gave his children a Jewish upbringing, but he was also one of the so-called 'Enlightened' – in the 1860s and '70s they already took an interest in and studied European culture. My maternal grandfather was also very enterprising – a merchant who later bought an estate with more than 2000 acres and a mansion. He established a spirit refinery where raw spirits, about eighty or ninety per cent proof, were refined to ninety-six per cent proof and sold for liqueurs. This was under the Habsburgs and the Austrian regime was very liberal, so there were many wealthy Jews. My father's family had been given the name Karpf: after Poland was partitioned, Jews in the Austrian part were given for the first time names by law under the Emperor Josef II [Before that they were given patronymics. Many of the new names were based either on professions (e.g., Schneider for tailor) or trees (the Greenbaums and Rosenbaums, Baum meaning tree) or otherwise lifted from nature – the names of birds, flowers, animals or, as in the case of Karpf, fish. A spiteful official might give a particularly bad name: rumour had it that if you handed over a bribe, you could choose a better one.] German and Polish were the official languages, and my parents spoke both. After my parents married, my father worked on his father-in-law's estate near Jasło. I was born there in 1900: I had two sisters and three brothers, I was the third oldest.

I spent my first few years on the estate, in the stables and among the cowsheds – I ate in the canteen with the horsemen, there was a staff of about thirty on the estate. I was very happy, very free, I ran about with the son of the administrator. In the evening, when the horses came from the field, I was waiting, and rode aged three or four to the pond. We were left to our own devices, though the girls were more closely watched, not so free.

When I was six, my father expanded – he built a house in Jasło and we moved from the estate into a five- or six-roomed apartment, though we returned to the estate for the summer. Jasło had a population of 11,000, and about ten per cent were Jewish. [According to the Museum of the Jewish Diaspora in Israel, the total Jewish population of Jasło in 1900 numbered 1,524, 23.2 per cent of the population. In 1921, they note, among the sizeable enterprises owned by Jews in the town, were food-processing workshops, chemical works, and timber firms.] My father traded in land and forests. He was also a great scholar – he was a very authoritative.Talmudist, but he was also educated in German and Polish literature. People came to him for advice and to arbitrate in disputes. Our house was always open, the door was never locked – whoever wanted could come at any time, people were never turned away. For Christmas, my father would always send two carts of coal for poor people, for Easter he sent two carts of potatoes. My mother could speak fluent French, she was beautiful and bright, but she was very traditionally brought up, and when she married she had children almost every year. It was easy for her, because there was plenty of help.

I went to the local primary school, where we mixed with the sons of local tradespeople. We learned both in Polish and in German. We felt no anti-Semitism. My grandfather built a big school to teach Hebrew, and my father imported a Hebrew teacher who already read more modern Hebrew, which was very rare at that time. We all learned Hebrew from the age of six or seven, and all the 160 Jewish children in the town spoke within a year or two fluent Hebrew.

When I was fourteen, in 1914, the war came, and we fled, because the Russians were coming. We took a coach with two horses and a cart covered with a tarpaulin with four horses for the children and the main things – we left the estate, everything, and went through the Carpathians south to Hungary. (There were millions of gallons of spirits left in huge tanks and, when the Russians came, they were afraid that their army would get drunk, so they let the spirits out. The spirits flowed for a few days from these tanks, and the peasants ran to collect it – they remembered for many years what a good time they had.) And then we went to Vienna by train. For us children it was exciting.

We rented a very modest flat, my mother cooked, we had no servants. We stayed in Vienna for a year and a half. I went to the Polish gymnasium there – we read *Macbeth* in Polish translation. Vienna was so interesting, it was my first time in such a big town, we had a lovely time. I would

20

buy the evening edition of *Neue Freie Presse*, and read it in
the park. I began drawing portraits: I bought a postcard of
Beethoven and drew a large life-sized version of it. And
at least twice a week on my way home from school I'd stop
off near the Imperial Palace at a shop where there were
automatic record-players, and I'd put ten pence in and
listen for half an hour to *Aida* and the various operas.

At the end of 1915 when the Russians were repulsed we
decided to go back to Jasło. The town was intact, only our
factories were burnt and the estate buildings were all burnt.
The house in Jasło was completely empty. But it wasn't a
terrible shock – I remember the feeling of absolute security
that I got from my father. He was very clever and rebuilt
everything – the refinery, the distillery, and the liqueur
factory – in two or three years without any outside help,
but nearer to the town, and built a railway-line leading to it.

A teacher at school stuck on the walls reproductions of
all the great Renaissance works of art – this was unusual
in a small town. I'd started drawing, but nothing serious,
and I was also very busy after school in the Jewish scouts,
Hashomer, where I was the head. It was a Zionist
organisation and from the age of sixteen I was a Zionist.
We went on excursions and camps, sleeping in tents, we
learned Jewish history, had lectures and gave them. We
didn't mix only with Jewish children – one of my best
friends, who lived opposite, wasn't Jewish.

At eighteen I decided to go to Vienna – it was our capital,
in Galicia – to study law at the university and economics
at the Export Academy, which trained you to be the
manager of a big enterprise (I was already familiar with
this from my father's estate). I was very happy there; a year
later my first cousin, also called Josef Karpf, came there –
he was very brilliant, very decent and modest, he was my
best friend. In 1920 I joined the art school in Vienna,
and managed to combine it with the university and Export
Academy. I drew mainly in charcoal, and then began to

21

paint. I got my doctorate – on agrarian reform in Poland – in 1923.

I returned to Jasło and began helping in my father's business. Then in 1925 he became very ill. He'd always been very optimistic and great fun – he was very witty and liked. But he made a mistake and I might have been the indirect cause: with his son in business with him, he wanted to enlarge his scope. He went to the eastern part of Galicia and bought the wood – oak – of a large forest, at a high price, but it was supposed to be suitable for the manufacture of veneers. It turned out that the trees weren't sound – the whole lot had some sort of rot inside. This mistake completely cut him down – he lost confidence, he could not forgive himself for this mistake and he got a terrible depression. It was for me the beginning of the greatest tragedy of my life. I saw him standing against the wall, saying 'Such a happy, lovely family and what have I done to them?' If I'd been more mature at the time I would have told him to sell other businesses he had, but I didn't prevail upon him: he was still a rich man, he had the estate, the factories, everything was still there though he wasn't liquid any more, but he'd already lost his faith in himself. He lost the lust for life, and contracted typhoid – he didn't want to recover. It was 1926, he was fifty-four. And then he died. I remember when the doctor came from his bedroom and said 'Gone', I threw myself on the sofa, face down, nobody could lift me from there. I reproached myself terribly, that I didn't show him enough patience when he was in such a state – I couldn't forgive myself. For eleven months I went twice a day to the synagogue to say Kaddish.

I didn't have much time to cry because I had to take care of everything. My sisters were married. I did what I had to do. I stayed in Jasło because of my mother – possibly, were it not for her, I would have left: I wanted to go to London, to Paris – I might have started painting seriously.

But I wanted my mother not to feel any change. I saw to it that she was looked after. I had occasional girlfriends, short and uncommitted relationships, but no one serious. I was busy – with sport, for instance. From our house to the ski-slopes was ten or fifteen minutes – in winter, after lunch, I went for an hour's skiing. I had witty and interesting friends in Jasło – a brilliant lawyer, a painter, and a mathematician. I had friends in Kraków, I went to Warsaw very often, I had friends there, highly intelligent and nice friends. I spent a year in Lemberg [Lvov] with my cousin, I had to look after my sister in Wieliczka, and I spent three months in Spain in 1935, organising the export of eggs, and learned Spanish – I returned to Poland just a few months before the outbreak of the Civil War.

My mother wanted me to get married, but I didn't want to. A matchmaker from Kraków heard about me and sent particulars about Natalia Weissman to my mother, and by chance I saw them in the safe. I said, 'What's this – Natalia Weissman, a pianist?' But I wasn't interested in music.

In 1937 I met a woman called Roma – I would have married her eventually, I believe, if not for the war. My mother liked her.

We knew that war was inevitable – like a gale or a storm, an event of the elements. We had instructions in sealed envelopes from the authorities because we had great stores of alcohol which is, after all, an important raw material in a war. About Hitler, we knew he was a terrible monster; but there was a monster in the East, Stalin, also. But we didn't know what was going to happen to the Jews – we knew about Kristallnacht, these things that had happened in Germany, but we didn't know of course there would be extermination, gas chambers.

My mother died two weeks before the outbreak of war: she'd got cancer of the stomach in 1937. I was prepared for it – it wasn't as tragic for me as my father's death. She was sixty-two. My mother died just in time, so that she could have a normal funeral – all the people came, as it should be. Because later started this hell: when I came after the war to the cemetery, all the tombstones had disappeared.

Now it was the turn of my mother, Natalia Karpf. We sat together in her living-room, and I tried to pin down what hitherto had always seemed a butterfly of a story: I wanted dates and details, to net those experiences which had proved perpetually beyond my retention.

NATALIA KARPF: I was born in Kraków, Poland; my father, Isidor Weissman, had various businesses. First he imported Chinese hair to sell to wig manufacturers (people wore wigs a lot then, and religious Jewish women all wore them). It was a good business until the 1920s when the fashion changed, and everyone wanted short hair. My parents were affluent: I remember all my childhood living in a very large apartment which we owned. We had servants for as long as I remember. I had an older sister, Regina, who was born with a deficiency of the thyroid – she couldn't hold anything, and couldn't write, and mentally she wasn't 100 per cent developed. We all loved her. Later I had a younger sister, Hela [Hela and Helunia are both diminutives of Helena], five years younger than me, and a brother Natan, seven years younger. They sometimes teased Regina because they didn't understand. Regina died when she was fifteen, in a special school in Germany. I was very shocked.

I was very grown-up always: as I was the oldest I was made to be responsible for the younger ones, though we also had a nanny, Mania, who was illiterate, and came to us in about 1916 when she was twenty. She converted to Judaism when I was about ten or twelve. The Catholics didn't want to let

24

her convert: she was so terrified that when she saw a
policeman she thought he was going to arrest her beause
she wanted to become Jewish. We took her to the Chief
Rabbi, Dr Thon, who was very learned and progressive,
and he told her, 'Look, don't be frightened, put your foot
down.' She said she felt Jewish and at last she was accepted:
she had to go to a mikvah, and they gave her a new name,
Sarah, and we gave a big reception for fifty people from
the synagogue, with lunch and drinks, to celebrate and
she was very, very happy. But we kept her original birth
certificate; it was very strange because it wasn't until
eighteen or sixteen years later that the war broke out: then
I told her, now you must hide or tear up your Jewish birth
certificate and use this because that can save you and us.
After she'd converted my mother wanted to introduce
her to some man, but she ran away to a loft because she
didn't want to marry. She was more kosher and observant
than we were, and she stayed with us until she died during
the war in 1943. My mother was even jealous of her, and
when we were crying we never cried Mummy, we cried
Maniu [the vocative form of Mania] – she was like our
second mother.

My parents were kosher (although my mother bought
ham for us because they said it was healthy for the
children, but she didn't put it on our plates!), but we
travelled a lot and when we went abroad we didn't
observe, we ate in restaurants. We didn't speak Yiddish at
home – my mother and father sometimes, and my
grandfather spoke Yiddish, but we spoke Polish to our
parents. I had a very happy childhood. Kraków was lovely
– a very cultivated place, with beautiful concerts,
exhibitions, lectures, social life, we went very often to
cafés in town, although we never mixed with Gentiles, we
knew very few Poles. There was a large Jewish
intelligentsia – lawyers, doctors, engineers, professors, and
we all mixed. There were a lot of orthodox Jews in Kraków,

but also a lot of secular Jews. We were observant, but not orthodox.

But in Poland when it gained independence after the First World War there was terrible anti-Semitism and pogroms. The first thing I remember was when I was six or seven years old: we had a caretaker in our house, and I remember my father calling out, 'Wojciech, shut the gates quickly and don't let anyone in,' because we heard screams in the street how they cut Jews' beards off, with skin, and there were terrible riots all with Jews. And that I remember as a little, little child. I was never ashamed of being Jewish but I was angry that something like this could happen.

Even at school – I had to go to school when I was five years old because I started playing the piano when I was four and a half and they wanted me to be able to read and write, but the compulsory age of schooling was seven and no school accepted a five-year-old. The only school which accepted me was the Evangelische Schule which was a German school where the most important language was German. And there I heard many times 'bloody Jew', towards other Jewish children and towards me. We reacted so that when I was thirteen I went to a Hebrew grammar school because I didn't want to mix with them. But before that I always answered back, I screamed or I pushed them.

There were some people in our house, our tenants, who, during the First World War, went to live in Vienna, and they had an old piano and left it with us in our flat. I was four and I started playing on my own. I just went to the piano and whatever I heard I could play. There weren't any radios but there were concerts and operettas and I heard a bit. My mother used to sing, she knew every aria from every opera and used to sing them, my father used to play the violin but very badly, my mother's brother and sister played the accordion – always there was music. I could play on the keyboard but I couldn't reach the pedals.

I played everything by ear and made up the harmonies with the left hand – I was thrilled because I could do it, but it came to me so naturally that I didn't think it was strange. One day, it was a hot summer when I was nearly four and a half, the bell rang and a young lady called. She said she'd heard that my mother had a child prodigy, would she want her perhaps to teach me piano. Until today I don't know who sent her. My mother called me and asked, 'Would you like to have some piano lessons?' and I looked at this young woman with very, very thick spectacles but she looked kind so I said yes, so it was arranged that she would come to us twice a week to give me piano lessons.

She was a very well-known teacher, and a pupil of a famous Polish pianist who lived in Vienna. Later on when I was nine and he came to Kraków she took me to him for a test: he gave me a book of Beethoven sonatas to sight-read, and I played it straight away because sight-reading was always for me the easiest thing – I could read music like a book or a paper from the very beginning.

At the beginning I didn't like practising, I wanted to play what I wanted to play, I was lazy. I was expected to practise two or three hours a day by the age of seven. They bought a very big portrait, a wood-cut of Beethoven's head, and they threatened me that if I won't practise he will be very angry with me, so for a couple of days I was terrified and started practising. But one day I thought I'll try not to and see what he does with me, and nothing happened, so I always had an excuse. My teacher arranged for me to play in concerts for gifted pupils from the age of seven, although I didn't want to and she forced me – I wanted to play for myself and my family.

So after a while I left her and went to the brother-in-law of Artur Rubinstein, and stayed with him for two years. At school I was always chosen to play or to accompany. But then when I was nine I did agree to give two concerts, proper ones, my first, sharing them with a famous singer.

At the second he lost his voice and couldn't sing so I filled the whole evening for him, playing Mozart, Beethoven, in front of 700 or 800 people. I wasn't at all nervous, it was a pleasure. I got a fantastic reception.

In 1920 my parents were invited to Berlin for a very big wedding of my father's first cousin. As my mother wasn't very well, my father took me. At this wedding was Nahum Sokolow, who was one of the most important men in the history of Zionism, the poet Bialik, and Leonid Pasternak, the father of Boris Pasternak, with his wife. She'd been a well-known pianist who couldn't play any more because she had a heart condition. I played at the reception, and Boris Pasternak's mother came and kissed me and said she had tears in her eyes when she heard me play.

My father then had a knitted goods factory, and some other businesses, and properties in Berlin. He did very well and started to make a lot of money, though he also trusted people and gave credit to people. He never listened to the warnings of my mother and later he lost it all.

When I was thirteen I went to the Hebrew gymnasium, where I learned Hebrew – Hela and Natan went there too. The standard was very high, the atmosphere was wonderful, we had excellent teachers and learned Latin, Hebrew, German, and Polish. I was very happy there.

It was about that time too when I decided that I wanted to be a pianist. My grandfather, to whom I was very close, had a most beautiful tenor voice, if he'd been trained he would have been a second Caruso. He was a very orthodox Jew, a learned Talmud 'chacham' [wise man], but also spoke and wrote beautiful German. Only because of him I studied music because he pressed and he suggested to my parents to send me away to study the piano. When I was fifteen my then teacher said to me that he can't teach me anything more – now I should leave and go abroad to have lessons with someone famous. So my parents arranged that I should leave school and go to Berlin, where my father had properties, and go into a so-called Mädchen Pensionat, which was a sort of finishing-school with part-time classes. I was terrified to be away because I was very attached to my parents, to my home and I was frightened and the first few weeks I was crying all day long. In such a big town on my own. I already spoke fluent German because of school. The Mädchen Pensionat was the most horrible place I can remember. The headmistress was an old spinster with five dogs and false teeth falling out all the time who starved us – my parents paid a lot of money, but she didn't give us anything to eat. I sent the meat she gave me for lunch once in an envelope to my parents to show them where they put me up – it was so thin and so dry already that it couldn't rot in the post! After four weeks I ran away from there to the administrator of our properties, a man with children, and he put me up opposite them with a high-school teacher who gave me a room in his flat and I hired a piano and I could practise. The teacher and his family treated me like their own daughter.

We knew about Artur Schnabel and, as one of our tenants was his pupil Maria Zweig, a sister of Arnold Zweig and cousin of Stefan Zweig, the well-known writers, and herself a well-known pianist, I went to her and she prepared me and said, yes, she thought I was advanced enough to be taken by him. When I was sixteen, she made an appointment for me, and I went with her. It was 1927. I was terrified because he looked very serious, but he could be also cynical and funny. He must have been nearly fifty, and he had five pianos in his house. I had to play for him: I played a Beethoven sonata, a Scarlatti sonata, and some Rameau pieces and he said straight away, 'Fine, you can come to me.' I sent a telegram home, I was so overjoyed, because it was such a great honour to be accepted by Artur Schnabel, world famous pianist and teacher.

They were private lessons and they were very expensive – they were 100 marks, then £20 a lesson, so I only went once a week but they were always much longer than an hour, sometimes even up to two hours. And if he had an interesting lesson with somebody, the secretary, who was his sister-in-law, phoned me to say could I come and listen – we were allowed to listen to other lessons and that was the most wonderful experience. His son Carl Ulrich Schnabel (Ruli) taught me harmony and theory. Schnabel had many other pupils – Clifford Curzon was his pupil for twenty-nine years. Schnabel could be very unpleasant and I was scared of him. He thought I was very gifted but he knew that I was lazy. I also had ballet lessons and he learned about it and so his secretary phoned our administrator and said would Miss Weissman choose either to be a ballet dancer or a pianist. So I stopped the ballet lessons – he thought if one wants to do something well one has to do just one thing.

Every Sunday he gave sonata recitals and played all the thirty-two Beethoven sonatas. I went to every concert, he was one of the greatest Beethoven executants, marvellous. I had lessons with him for only two years, because I thought musically he was fantastic but he didn't care about my technique, and I felt that I need somebody who will help to still make it easier with my technique, and there was Georg Bertram, a very well-known pianist. I played to him and he said I needed a lot of work on technique. I never explained to Schnabel, I just disappeared which wasn't very nice. I said I'm leaving and going home, and just didn't book another lesson.

I was very homesick, and went home for all the holidays – Jewish holidays and non-Jewish ones. And my father came every month to Berlin and stayed a few days, for business. I couldn't sleep the whole night before I was so excited, because first of all I was so happy to see my father and then I knew that he'd book tickets every night somewhere else, and take me out to musicals, to opera, to theatre. Otherwise I only went to concerts. But Berlin before the war was very exciting – I had many friends, young men who wore capes and top hats, and had a wonderful time. For four years in Berlin I never experienced any anti-Semitism – there were so many mixed marriages – in Poland yes, but not in Germany.

After a while Bertram decided that it was time to give a big concert. He booked one of the biggest concert halls, which seated 1500 or 2000 people, for a concert with three pianists – one American, a German (the niece of Rathenau, the famous German-Jewish Foreign Minister who was assassinated in Germany), and me – in Berlin. I played the Chopin E Minor First Concerto with the Berlin Philharmonic, conducted by Heinz Bongartz, on 14 December 1929. I was eighteen and the youngest of the three. It was a very big success, and I had marvellous reviews, it was thrilling.

Then my cousin in Berlin called me and told me that my mother was ill, they didn't know what was wrong with her, but I had to leave the next day. I went to tell Bertram, and he said to me, 'Natalia, if I was twenty years younger, I wouldn't give you to anybody, I would marry you straight away.' I was amazed, I never expected that he, my teacher, would fall in love with me. I was terribly embarrassed. He was an old bachelor, and he lived with his sister. I left everything behind, and took the train – it was only a ten hour journey from Berlin to Kraków.

My mother, who was forty-seven, was in a terrible state, she had such attacks of pain. At last a professor came from Berlin and said she had kidney trouble and she would have to have an operation, so we decided she would have to come to Berlin. She was brought there by ambulance because she was so ill.

I went to the hospital to stay with her. They operated on her kidney stones on one side, and she recovered completely – I brought my gramophone with records into the hospital and we played and she sang and we were happy. But then they thought that her other kidney wasn't working well, and they decided to operate on it. She had a kidney infection and there was no penicillin: they put a catheter into the kidney because she had terrible pain the day after the operation. The doctor came to change the dressing and the catheter fell out, and instead of putting in a proper new one he put in a short one which didn't clear it properly and caused a general uraemic infection, and she died three weeks later, in terrible pain. The professor wasn't there because he went to Rockefeller in the States whom he'd operated on before. I was there all the time, my father was also there but the last few days his passport was expiring and he had to go back to Poland to get it renewed, so I was alone with her when she was dying.

That was a Catholic hospital: the nuns came and started praying and I threw them out. I said, 'What are you doing here?' And they said, 'We are praying for your mother because she's dying.' I said, 'No, she's not dying, she can't die.' But one day, it was so lovely, it was May, the sun was shining, and there were such beautiful trees and everything was blooming and she said, 'Oh, how sad, I shall never come out from here any more, I will never see it again.' I said, 'What are you talking. Nonsense.' She said, 'No, my dear. And your father is making such mistakes, he's giving credit to people who can't pay and he will make you beggars,' she was crying, 'You won't have anything.'

And that's what happened. She died on 22 May 1930: I was screaming, screaming, so the sisters phoned my cousins, who came to collect me and take me to them for the night, because my father was arriving the next morning – too late: he never saw my mother again. He was shocked by her death, but ten months later he married again – a horrible woman.

I came home after the funeral in Berlin. (It's better now that she's buried there because I could visit her, but many Jewish graves in Kraków were destroyed during the war. That's why I later went and played in East Berlin – to be able to visit my mother's grave.) My mother's death changed my life a lot: I finished with my studies in Berlin because I had to look after my younger sister and brother, and also something died in me together with my mother. I was always as a young girl full of life – I could sing, I could entertain, I could dance, I was joking, I was so lively – and after that, I was never, never the same again, that was such a shock for me and I shall never forget it.

I came home and I took charge of my brother and sister. My father had decided to go back to Berlin and stay there – he lived there until 1937 – and we were on our own, though Mania was still with us. When I came back from the funeral I had to be strong, because those two poor children, fourteen and twelve, they were lying on the bed crying, 'Yesterday I had a mother and today I haven't got one any more.' And Natan was just one year before the barmitzvah. And this boy, twelve years old, who nobody told to do it, from the next morning after the shiva, this boy before school got up at six thirty and went to the synagogue to say Kaddish for a whole year.

I didn't touch the piano for six months. Then my grandfather came to me, such a religious Jew but with his thoughts so emancipated: the Jews are meant to mourn for a whole year, not to go out to the cinema, not to listen to any entertainment, and my grandfather came to me after two or three months and said, 'But this is your profession, you're a musician, you don't do it for entertainment or pleasure, you have to practise, you have to play.' And only because of him I started practising again. My grandparents were heartbroken at my mother's death.

33

My grandfather with this long beard, and with this little cap on his head which they used to wear in Russian Poland, stood and looked at her photograph which was hanging on the wall, and cried bitterly, 'Why did I survive you?' She was his only married child, she was doing well and had children. When she died, people used to come to me and say, 'We are crying for her, she used to give us coal for the whole winter' – and I'd never known about it. She never told us a thing, that she was supporting poor people. And she was active in perhaps twenty charities, for blind people, poor people, children.

Six months after she died I started to practise again, and then I started teaching. I was left without money. Sometimes our father sent us some money. He was suing the people who wanted to take away all our houses, which he'd mortgaged when people didn't repay the credit he'd given them. I had to provide money to live on, sometimes I didn't have money for the next day to live. Sometimes he sent me £5 in an envelope – just enough for two or three days. As well as teaching I started making cushions and crochet gloves which were fashionable at that time and selling them, or I sold some Persian rugs or silver from the house. I'd worshipped my father as a young girl but my relationship with him suddenly changed after he remarried. He and his wife came back and took valuable things like silver and jewellery from the house. Then he saw that she was a bitch and he divorced her in 1932. But he stayed in Berlin, even when Hitler came – I was wondering how he could be there.

Finally, when he returned, he got some knitting machines and started up a workshop again – Hela worked for him – and it was developing quite well. Had the war not come, he probably would have made quite a lot of money again because he was a clever businessman.

In the summer of 1930 I took my sister and brother to the seaside, to Sopot. I rented two rooms with my best friend, Jadzia, and there I met my first husband Julius Hubler – we'd met when I was a little girl and I played the piano at the house of some friends, and he remembered me. He was eight years older than me, I was nineteen. He was a lawyer, a music critic, and a wonderful pianist. When I returned to Kraków, he invited me to his parents' home. I thought I was too young to get married, but I felt very lonely, because my father had left us and my mother was dead. His mother said, 'I'll be a mother to you.' She thought I was very rich, but when she discovered we'd lost all the money, she wanted him to break off our engagement. I wanted to break up with him and he threatened me: he stood at the corner of our street and said, 'If you break us up I'm going to shoot you and shoot me.' I was so naïve – I thought when he'd touched me and kissed me (though I never slept with him until we were married) it was a terrible thing to break off an engagement. I phoned my father to tell him that I was getting married and he was very upset because he thought Julius wasn't good enough for his daughter.

We married on 24 December 1933. My grandfather had died four days before, and I didn't know. We went on a honeymoon to Zakopane: Julius's aunt, Jelinek, lived there. She was the most beautiful woman I ever met, and already had her first son, Jerzy. Hela and Natan lived with us after we got married – they were my children, they didn't have a mother, I was their mother. In the late 1930s, Natan wrote to Leslie Hore-Belisha, the Jewish British Secretary of State for War, saying that he was Jewish and he'd heard so much about England and he'd love to come here, would he help him? He got a reply saying that they couldn't deal with this matter. Then he wanted to go to Israel and I didn't have the money so I went to my father-in-law and asked him to lend me 500 złoty because I wanted to give it to my brother, and he said he hasn't got it and he was such a rich man. They were such stingy people. Hela, Natan, and

Mania lived with me and my husband between 1933, when I got married, and 1938, when my father returned. My husband resented it.

Julius was also jealous of my playing in public: he said, 'You're a very good pianist but sit at home' – he didn't encourage me to give concerts, completely contrary to my second husband who encouraged me and helped me to pursue my career. But Julius, no. So I only gave concerts in Kraków, but I didn't travel abroad any more, though I still had lessons.

Natan was in engineering college – he did very well, and got a job with a firm, and bought himself a big Buick. When I sold a ring and got the money for him to go to Israel, the ship had already left: that was one of the ships which were either turned back or arrested by the British. But in the end they got there because his schoolfriends got there, some of them, and he would have been alive today.

I got pregnant and felt very well and excited – I always wanted to have children. In August 1938, when I was eight months pregnant, I went to a resort with a friend of mine who was also pregnant. One day I woke up and I said to my friend, 'You know, I felt such terrible kicking and suddenly it stopped, I don't feel anything since yesterday.' She said, 'Oh it happens.' And another day and another day and another day and I felt nothing, and I phoned Julek [Julek is the diminutive of Julius] and he said, 'You're coming home straight away,' and I went to the doctor and she didn't realise that I had a dead baby inside me, three weeks I was walking like this. I felt something had happened and I was very upset. The baby was born dead, soon after. The placenta had become detached and the baby had died of hunger. I was heartbroken. It was a girl and I'd wanted to have a daughter and call her Eva.

In July, August 1939 there was already talk of war. We

36

knew Hitler was in Germany, we were terrified that something can happen, but nobody could believe that there could be such a Holocaust and such disasters. In 1939 they were in Austria and Czechoslovakia, so we were the next ones, and the Polish army wasn't equipped at all and we knew what was happening there. We thought there would be a war and people would fight on the front but nothing would happen here – we didn't think we'd be affected. In July 1939 I met a friend's mother who told me that her daughter was going to the World Exhibition in the States. I came home and said to Julek, 'You know what? Let's go to the World Exhibition in the States.' And he said, 'It will cost 2000 złoty,' and I said, 'So we'll have 2000 złoty less in our bank, we can afford it, let's go.' He didn't want to, he would have survived . . .

Hating one's parents is a necessary stage of childhood, like becoming potty-trained. We bypassed it. How could you hate those who'd already been hated so much? Any hatred we felt could never be comfortably aired, so it remained largely covert, a hidden pocket of sedition to which I was virtually oblivious for decades. What little peeped out seemed to me completely illegitimate, and I immediately tried to stuff it back into its hiding place. When my sister or I ventured criticism of my mother – in the way that children do of their parents – our protective father would invariably pitch in with a 'Remember what she's been through'. I came to abominate what she'd been through no longer on her account, but on ours. Was everything she said and did beyond reproach because of her past? Apart from our coat rows, one of the only ways through which, as an adolescent, I felt able to assert my values against theirs was in political arguments. So the normal, but to us intolerable, acrimony of teenage–parent conflict was siphoned off into politics, and at mealtimes I could be heard fiercely arguing socialism with my parents as if my life depended on it.

For my parents the war was the yardstick by which all other bad experiences were judged and thereby found to be relatively good. Frustration, irritation, anger, disappointment – to them all these seemed trivial and indulgent, and so never could be freely vented. My repertoire of tolerable emotions became so minimal that when, much later, I went into therapy, I had to ask the therapist 'What is a feeling?'

Our parents desperately wished us a wonderful life, free of the darkness which had stained theirs – my mother often supplicating out loud that we should have only good things. Our lives were heavily symbolic: we were meant to tip the family scales towards happiness. They seemed almost angry if things didn't turn out so. We knew, almost intravenously, that if negative emotions weren't rebutted they might overwhelm positive ones and collapse the liveable life our parents had so energetically reconstructed. With resolve, obstinacy and hope our parents had assembled for themselves a new world. An enormous amount of mutual effort was expended in reassuring ourselves that (almost) all was well with it.

My love for my parents, as anxious and prodigious as theirs for me, was a kind of bandage – yards and yards of it. Its impulse was definitely restorative. The birthday cards I made for them, even by the time I was grown-up, were shrines to the superlative: the most wonderful, amazing, extraordinary mother/father, with all my love and more, etc. No injuries from the world, or from me, could penetrate there.

Of course I did also shout, scream, and rant at them through childhood and adolescence. But these outbursts always seemed – to them and to me – deviant, almost delinquent, so that I was constantly promising better behaviour, and vowing to 'turn over a new leaf'. (My father used to quip that there were no more leaves to be turned.) My mother in particular seemed to experience me as *permanently* cussed, and for decades I thought she was right, until I learned what it really was to be defiant, and then I couldn't fathom how such a trickle of dissent could have been mistaken for the real chute of rebellion. Perhaps like some dowser she'd divined the existence of my unconscious rage? (It was more likely, I concluded later, that my parents, having experienced such a surfeit of evil, craved perfection from their children. Their world had been split into good and bad: if you weren't one, you must be the other.)

At home and school I was a gushy confection, perpetually enthusiastic, dependably fulsome. The family mode was one of manic jollity, a kind of irresistible mild euphoria. Even when I was as old as twenty-four, my reports of life outside, my postcards home, were all about validating this shared amniotic sac – my parents' values. As a teenager I assumed a ghastly second-hand contempt for the youth culture which my contemporaries were embracing with relish. I disdained to go to Beatles or Rolling Stones concerts, I was the last into mini-skirts. None of the paraphernalia of adolescent rebellion was available to me. I never even stuck posters on the wall of my room, so anxious was I not to deface their culture, or threaten their homeostasis.

How can I write all this? It will surely kill. My parents' friends will read it, my mother will be crushed and my father disgusted. So here I am, into my fourth decade, still persuaded that perpetual jolliness is demanded and that anything other will crack their well-being and endanger their lives, that my reality cannot sit alongside theirs without obliterating it and them. As if, having survived the Nazis, they could not weather their children's dissension. ('Nebech,' I can hear my mother responding saltily. 'You don't think we've put up with it for forty years already?' Go away, mother. Stick to your part of the book.)

Since I hosed away most bad feelings as soon as they appeared, it's perhaps not surprising that I was sometimes left with a curious sense of not being real. This took several forms. One was a passing sensation – it could strike on the school staircase or in the middle of a conversation – of being outside my body, on a different plane of reality from my incarnated self. I would hover overhead, like a tacky seaside repertory theatre Peter Pan, while me simulated normal everyday life; some recalcitrant speck of psyche had truanted. Being drunk or stoned can make one feel this way, but experiencing it without stimulants must have hinted disturbingly at the existence of a whole class of fugitive emotions.

Yet it wasn't more reality I was after, but less. In my fantasy I was Toni (with all the longed-for cuteness of that final 'i'). She was an actress, in the style of Mary Tyler Moore or those cartoon-strip flawless females (abundant obliging hair, pert nose, mathematically symmetrical nostrils). Unwittingly (and many years before I ever saw one), I had redesigned myself as a Barbie doll. Of course, Toni was then the shared female ideal of most teenage girls in our culture. She had another great attribute. My Toni seemed to have circumvented adolescence – she was virtually unembarrassable. And along with all this I'd rid her of one more particularly unwanted characteristic: she contained no cell of Jewishness.

Reimagining myself as Toni, I had a rich parallel fantasy life with a strong erotic dimension. Whenever I wanted I could tune out of my daily world and into this alternative one, which seemed much more immediate and had such a compelling narrative momentum that, like the original readers of Dickens when his works were first serialised in the periodical press, I couldn't wait to find out what would happen next.

But perhaps my most pervasive sense of unreality was evoked by a phrase which would turn up uninvited in my head with increasing frequency until my late thirties: I wasn't 'a proper person'. Sometimes this just manifested itself in intense self-hatred about how I looked or sounded – a sort of pathological variant of normal teenage discomfort. (It was as if years of accumulated negative feelings, denied expression, had turned inward, leaving me certain that my whole self was bad. Only my academic and professional achievements provided respite.) At other times it produced a terror of being seen by people – as if my precarious sense of self couldn't tolerate any kind of objective appraisal, and would disintegrate beneath others' necessarily punitive gaze.

A memorable moment of relief came one day when I was about twenty. Lying on my sister's bed, I opened R.D. Laing's *The Divided Self* and to my astonishment read an absolutely vivid account of what it was like not to feel like a proper person, summed up by the phrase 'primary ontological insecurity'. I stored away this term as a potentially useful source of comfort. Never mind that Laing was describing schizophrenics and their false selves – for some reason I felt quite unstigmatised, so profound was the sense of recognition and (passing) relief. And that perpetual gush? Why, it was nothing but my own false self! I luxuriated in the jargon, walking around cheerfully announcing – to my family's disgust – that I was a schizophrenic.

My sense of not being a proper person mainly revealed itself socially. Away from home and school I was excruciatingly shy. Worse, I had no boyfriend when at least one was mandatory, and even the pimpliest schoolgirls seemed to have no difficulty acquiring several. But pimples weren't my problem. In fact, after my initial resistance to the emerging youth culture gave way, I'd begun to look like a genuine 1960s teenager. I'd always been almost Twiggishly thin, and now I embraced some of the other impedimenta (clothes, make-up, musical tastes) of the day. I yearned to have a boyfriend but at the same time shrank from anyone showing interest in me, amplifying their flaws: the very idea of allowing them close enough to glimpse the badness was vile. So I had to make do with Toni's adventures, though my desire to be like everyone else once became so desperate that I lied to my schoolfriends and pretended to have met an attractive young man of my own (in the most 'B' movie circumstances) until my deception was shamefully unmasked.

As my A' levels approached so did an extended panic

attack; I felt dreadfully anxious and couldn't eat. What was taken to be a fear of failing was probably terror at the imminence of leaving home. It continued after A' levels: at home or school, on the tube or in the theatre, I kept feeling the urge to scream and run.

I found even a temporary break with home unimaginable, but at the same time I was battling with the sheer shamefulness of my timidity, for this was the 1960s: eighteen-year-olds, not to speak of fourteen-year-olds, were throwing off the parental yoke with relief, while here was I petitioning for bondage. Being tethered to home and elders was not something one flaunted.

I couldn't countenance the idea of rebelling, and was sure it would devastate my parents too. (My sister *had* managed a rebellion of sorts, making it all the more imperative for me to remain the good child.) But this was a decade in which teenagers who deferred to their parents were regarded as Harijans and scorned by their peers; freedom was now compulsory. These were ideal conditions for the proliferation of shame, and indeed I did feel deeply ashamed of my nervous attachment and dependency. Yet shame itself was then presumed dead: laid-back was the thing, and you couldn't be laid-back and ashamed, only laid-back *or* ashamed. Or ashamed of not being laid-back.

For me the sixties were characterised by this powerful mix of shame and anxiety, though I had no idea of its origin, other than a conviction that it was a sign of deep personal inadequacy. I'd react very physically to shame, involuntarily holding my breath and clenching my buttocks, as if trying to choke those feelings inside my body by plugging all their exits. For my aim was to extinguish and not scrutinise: my inner life was opaque.

And trying to reconstruct it now, all I have to go on are fragments of memory and recollected feelings – psychological fossils. But archaeologists can never be sure quite how authentically they've reconstituted the past. And the unconscious has no gazeteers: some of it is irrecoverable – even millennia on the couch can't change that.

All I know for certain is that, until an indecently advanced age, I was unable to imagine myself surviving away from my parents, or them without me. So chronic was this fear of separation and rupture (to me they were equivalent) that I balked at endings of any kind: for decades I found it hard to leave shops or the bath, finish phone conversations or evenings with friends. I was never parted from my belongings either: I marvelled at the casualness of my friends, most of whom seemed quite happy to leave possessions of theirs stored or loaned or even strewn around for months on end in the rooms and flats of their mates and ex-mates. I had no notion of ebb and flow, or trust in reunion, only a recurring presentiment. I treated all partings as if they were final: wherever you were going, you might never come back.

When people packed during the war, they rarely did come back: my parents' lives were full of such sudden fractures. In my life, though, no one had left and hardly anyone I knew had died: in its external reality, my world was preternaturally constant. It was as if my parents' experience had become my own; I'd soaked up their fear of loss. For all of us, separation had become symbolically equivalent to death.

But I did leave, albeit briefly. I went to Florence for three months with two schoolfriends to study art and Italian. And there, away from family, I began to concoct some sort of social self – it was easier in another language. I also finally had boyfriends – three even (though not all at the same time).

The following year I went up to Oxford, driven there by my parents at the start of my first term. On arrival we went to the Kardomah Coffee House for a snack; I had a Welsh rarebit with an unusual tang that I couldn't identify. I tried over and over to reunite the flavour and its name. As my parents helped me unload my luggage into my college room, my need to identify the mystery Welsh rarebit ingredient became obsessive, blasting away any other sensation – I wasn't inside an Oxford college, I was barnacled to the roof of my mouth – though I was faintly aware of a sense of sheer disbelief that I could have been evacuated from my safe home into a boxy room in a grid of institutional corridors in this English town. By the time I had finally solved the rarebit conundrum – it was paprika – my parents had long departed, and I was left in what seemed like an inescapable spume of unreality, certain that I'd fetched up somewhere quite arbitrary, to which I had absolutely no affiliation. I felt as if I'd exiled myself to Oxford.

The Oxford of my imagination was a place of Jewish intellectuals – Hampstead with spires, a yeshivah of the arts. This real Oxford was more like a Roedean and Harrow annexe. Its very stones gave off continuity and lineage, custom and practice, and its languid punters and sweeping lawns – so comely, so peaceful – seemed like the imperious marks of a world which recognised nothing beyond itself: you either submitted or remained a perpetual outsider.

My college had its gymkhana girls and sylphine debs, Northern chemists and rowing blues, but very few Jews. This wasn't something that I was conscious of minding, and, if I had, there was undoubtedly a Jewish Society somewhere. But the Jewishness I knew – my family's – was largely secular, and it was cultural rather than theological familiarity I craved. I wanted *haimish*. I found a friend with some of it, and she had a friend in one of the men's colleges with a little more, but most of the time I simply broke off my Jewish bits and dispatched them to my least accessible recesses, where so much else that was unwanted was already stored.

It's only now that I realise I wasn't alone in finding the university an inhospitable place to be a Jew. An Oxford-based rabbi was quoted recently saying, 'In the past it wasn't easy to be Jewish here in Oxford. Think about it, colleges called Corpus Christi, Christ Church, Jesus. Jews felt like guests here.'

My time in Oxford was spent acting, in every sense. In my second year, with OUDS (the Oxford University Drama Society), I played Masha in Chekhov's *Three Sisters*, disintegrating vicariously for one week, nightly, on the stage of the Oxford Playhouse. Off-stage, meanwhile, I was developing another new talent: I discovered how to banter and joke, acquiring social skills so proficiently that they were later to prove hard to jettison. But back then I busied myself shamelessly plundering other people's personalities to reconstitute a new one for myself – a little bit from him, a little bit from her: everyone was doing it, I just did it better. From the merest trace – a few words or a half-gesture – I could apprehend another person's style and mood and adjust mine accordingly. Almost imperceptibly, but with perfect mimetic skill, I took on their views, voices, and values.

I remember little else of Oxford: it's just another misted-over period of my life, during which I was either stoned or as if stoned. After graduating, I moved back in with my parents and got my first job, as a BBC television researcher. I entered this new world with such a perpetual smile on my face that people would often comment admiringly on its broadness, unaware that I was sunny in inverse ratio to my feelings: the angrier I felt, the more charming and compliant I appeared. The women's liberation movement was then gaining ground and, while I was sympathetic, I also found it terrifying, another potential instrument to prise me from my parents and home; it was no place for a chameleon.

Yet at the same time I also had my first serious relationship, with a married, non-Jewish man. Intensely sympathetic to other cultures (including mine), he made me feel – for the first time – as if being Jewish might be potentially enriching rather than embarrassing, something I might volunteer, instead of hoping it would pass without mention. It was like emerging from a bunker. At school Jewish had connoted clever but hardly stylish. Many of the Jewish girls (though not all) had a natural tendency to the babushka look which wasn't then considered covetable; I wanted to dissociate myself totally from their ample hips and unfashionable curls. About frizz we, the trying-to-assimilate, were phobic, willing to go to almost any lengths to induce, no *compel* our locks to uncoil. To do this we had, above all, to keep them dry. Swimming was a trichological ordeal (even when done the Jewish way, with head perpendicular, as if the water might singe it). The rain was our enemy, the hairdryer our aide-de-camp. Some (although – and this was a matter of some pride – not me) even had recourse to the iron. When Vidal Sassoon was quoted in *Vogue* as saying that he loved to cut his favourite, dead-straight mop (and he a nice Jewish boy), it plunged like a knife through my heart. And the Cathy McGowans, whose hair fell in sheets, were the object of immoderate envy and loathing.

It never occurred to us to flaunt our curls, much less cultivate them. Fashion had declared that this wasn't the look, even if it was (regrettably) ours. When, in my early thirties, I went to see the film *Sophie's Choice*, in which a Nazi tells the heroine admiringly that she looks 'so Aryan, so beautiful', I recognised that this was what I'd always believed: Jewish couldn't be beautiful – it occupied a lower rung in the hierarchy of looks; 'You look Jewish' never could or would be said as a compliment.

Proudly parading difference was done in another decade by another ethnic group, who wore their Afros as a mark of consciousness and whose politics reached down into their follicles. They realised that ideas of beauty aren't natural but cultural: WASP wasn't intrinsically more marvellous, it only appeared so. To accord non-WASP looks and styles equal standing required a shift in consciousness. But to us in the mid-sixties going proudly, Jewishly curly would have seemed equivalent to wearing a yellow star. And the irony, the pitious irony of it was that when finally, in my early thirties, I triumphantly decided to revert to naturally curly,

I discovered that I wasn't, and underneath all my struggles with the hairdryer had languished only the merest wave.

Being Jewish in England, unless you chose to live mainly or exclusively among Jews, was a little like being gay. You didn't so much meet other Jews as detect them by sonar. You gave off discreet clues, but never vaunted. Making contact provided the pleasure of mutuality, but it was also an ambivalent, potentially exposing act: you might lose your cover. In a 1991 television programme the playwright Bernard Kops described how, when he'd moved from the East End to West Hampstead in the 1950s, a Jewish neighbour on Rosh Hashanah had greeted him by silently mouthing the words 'Happy New Year'. A few weeks after I'd seen this programme a Jewish woman serving in one of my local shops wished me a 'Happy NY'.

The sense of being an alien was enhanced at Yom Kippur. At around six o'clock, when the rush-hour traffic was at its thickest, we'd make our way to the synagogue. We walked down familiar streets, but carrying our prayer books and in formal clothes which felt as though they gave off a whiff of stigma, like a prison uniform; we seemed cordoned off from the returning commuters and pedestrians for whom it was just another day. Seder night was a less ambiguous occasion, not only because Passover was a more celebratory festival, but also perhaps because it took place in the privacy of the home, without the possibility of unsympathetic onlookers.

If you did steel yourself to declare openly your Jewishness, you couldn't assume a sympathetic hearing. Once, in my mid-twenties, a few years after the Yom Kippur War, at a gathering in a private house for a group of non-Jewish writers who'd just returned from Israel, I heard the journalist Jill Tweedie expounding her views on the country, and I tentatively suggested that in some ways it was harder to be a Jew in Britain than in Israel. 'Nonsense!' replied Tweedie peremptorily. And I hadn't the confidence to gainsay her (thereby proving my point).

48

I think I experienced a permanent struggle between Jewish and English, inside the home and outside, partly because of my parents' wartime experiences, but also for another reason which only became clearer much later, when I heard Philip Roth in a radio programme talking about America. He argued that America had so many immigrants that everyone was an outsider: outsiders were insiders – it was the experience of the majority. And I understood that in England this wasn't so: in England, an outsider was an outsider. Britain had an identifiable in-group, and palpable indices of Englishness. (Later I came to see how idealised was this notion of the 'melting-pot', a part of American mythology which black people and other disenfranchised groups were now angrily contesting. Later still, I realised that Englishness too wasn't as monolithic and homogenous as it appeared to me as a child, and there were many others who felt equally excluded. But to me then only my own sense of exclusion was apparent.)

Even as children – especially as children – we realised that parts of the culture were effectively out of bounds. Brownies, for instance. Some of my classmates would periodically come to school in brown garb, but I didn't really know what Brownies were – some kind of junior freemasonry, perhaps, and a little churchy too – yet I knew for sure that Jewish children didn't join them. (And maybe – unconsciously, who knows? – there were unhappy associations with brown shirts, not to mention all those sewn-on stars and badges.)

I did yearn to participate in Christmas, but on this my parents were adamant. Turkey was the limit of their compromise, a tree out of the question. One year I nagged so hard that an eighteen-inch high orange plant was conceded. For my parents, Christmas must have been the apotheosis of Christianity and an essential plank of anti-Semitism; to them it meant the birth of that Jesus whom the Jews were accused of murdering. They never understood that in England

49

Christmas wasn't just a Christian festival but was threaded through the culture – in television and radio, the shops, and institutionalised in the long British Christmas holiday. Our inability to take part felt like being culturally disenfranchised and Christmas became for me – as for many British Jews – a miserable time until much later when, with a home and child of my own, I was able to do it my own way, back-to-back with Chanukah. (The first year that my partner and I had a Christmas tree, notwithstanding the Star of David on top, my parents refused to visit. And behind my childlike delight at my first tree, I felt just a little as if I were wearing a cross.)

The sense of exclusion from the dominant culture was aggravated by the fact that as observing but not orthodox Jews we had little visible alternative public secular culture of our own. There was no significant Anglo-Jewish literature to speak of. There were Jewish authors, sure, prominent ones too, but no body of work matching the American-Jewish authors in prestige and confidence. The American-Jewish novel was coterminous with the American novel. You couldn't even say there was a British-Jewish novel. There were rather more Jewish dramatists – Wesker, Kops, and others – but the leading Jewish playwright, Harold Pinter, seemed more like a playwright who happened to be a Jew (although he's recently traced the menace in his plays back to the anti-Semitism of his East End background. And does a Jewish writer have to write only about Jews? A Muslim writer about Muslims? Are only the male WASPs free to write about anyone?). Frederic Raphael and Jack Rosenthal later became rare exceptions among Anglo-Jewish writers, writing for television about Jews the way WASPs wrote about WASPs, in the assumption that everyone would be interested. (Though it was left to an American novelist – Philip Roth in his marvellous *The Counterlife* – to address British anti-Semitism, in all its politeness and covertness, in fiction, and that only in 1986.) The lack of an identifiable British-Jewish literary canon reflected just how marginalised and unconfident British Jews were – in some sense under sufferance.

People criticised the *Jewish Chronicle* for being parochial – photos of smiling Jewish businessmen and charities, and almost any Jewish attainment uncritically applauded. But that was how it was for us: unorthodox though we were, we did scan the culture for the tiniest reference to Jews, and pathetically eked them out.

As a child and young adult I'd always found it maddening when my mother asked if someone was 'English' – her euphemism for non-Jewish – partly because I felt she was withholding judgement on their worthfulness as a person until she knew. And partly also because it implied you couldn't be simultaneously English and Jewish – you weren't *really* English. But she was right all along. (Only about this, mother.) I've always automatically said 'they' about the English.

Being Jewish in North London was one thing; when you receded from this epicentre it was quite another. On the rare occasions in my twenties and early thirties when I ventured out of London and into English country villages, whose fulcrum was the church and where Jews were biblical figures, I felt as if I'd pupated into a rabbi, like Woody Allen in *Annie Hall.* My difference was hanging out.

Once, when I worked at the BBC, I went to research a major who lived in a bungalow with a crazy paving path in Budleigh Salterton. This configuration – major, bungalow, crazy paving, Budleigh Salterton – furnished me with absolute proof that I was an alien, who'd feel more at ease in Paris, Rome, or even Mars, though the major and his wife were most charming and, as we swapped stories, appeared intrigued by the piece of exotica in their parlour.

English Jews – the second, third, and fourth generations – provided no refuge either: they weren't anxious enough. Compared to American Jews they may have lacked self-assurance, but compared with us they seemed to have a confidence, a frictionlessness, an unproblematic sense of entitlement which I found unattractive (and probably envied). They lacked the film of melancholy to which, despite my parents' best efforts, I'd evidently become habituated.

English Jews' point of reference was also different: theirs seemed to be Israel, while mine (if any) was Poland, and where I felt a nostalgic sense of loss for the Yiddishkeit of the shtetl, they appeared to connect more with the pioneer spirit of the kibbutz. They also seemed to revolve around the young, whereas my most powerful, though mixed, feelings were about old Jews: both an inadmissible sense of shame about my family and our house compared with the bright contemporary homes and young parents of my non-Jewish friends, and an almost irresistible pull towards the elderly, thickly accented, sometimes stooping Jews in the Finchley Road. If I overheard them in a shop or restaurant (they congregated in the Dorice and the Cosmo, little bits of Vienna or Warsaw transposed), I had to fight the urge to strike up a conversation, tell them that we were landsmen, and above all look after them.

Looking after was my thing. I was indiscriminate: hairdressers, milkmen, shop assistants – I gave great beaming smiles, boundless affirmation, and multi-thanks to them all. There was a sequence in *The Godfather Part II* (whose Mafia seemed to me like a big, boisterous, besieged Jewish family) where Michael (Al Pacino) discovers his injured father Don Corleone (Marlon Brando) alone and unprotected in hospital. The son fiercely defends the father against an attempted violent attack. No matter how often I saw it, the scene always made me sob: it must have played out all the rescue fantasies I had about my parents.

As I got older my compulsion to repair didn't diminish. Just as I'd brought them my academic achievements at school, when I became a journalist I'd render them my articles. My accomplishments seemed earmarked, a direct debit to keep them vital. And on birthdays or Christmas (though they'd pretend it was for Chanukah) I'd buy my parents hugely extravagant gifts, to the limit of my finances. Yet these never seemed to me enough: however lavish I tried to be, I always felt the urge to give more, or again.

Looking after them entailed staying with them; we would only survive as one. When my sister or I went away on holiday, my mother would always mutter, 'I'd like to see you back already.' Still does, *stolat*.

My flight is delayed. Returning home, as always before I've unpacked or even peed I phone my mother. 'I was *so* worried,' she says. 'I thought God-knows-what had happened.' But god-knows-what hadn't.

I would have gladly taken over some of my parents' bodily functions – eaten for them, breathed for them. Or, failing this, suffered for them. (But, even here, it wasn't enough: I would never be able to match them in suffering.)

When I left the BBC at the end of the day, I'd often find myself draped in guilt. I never knew why. It seemed wrong to have time without burdens, freedom without limitation. On the rare occasions I did taste them, I immediately tried to avert the evil eye (kayn ayn hore). And if any current or possible future good fortune was mooted, I'd always say superstitiously 't,t,t' (just like my mother used to say, with a mock-spit) so that it shouldn't be taken away. (But here I surpassed her: I'd say it even about *past* happiness.)

As for leaving home, I couldn't imagine it happening other than surgically. My friends by now had their flats, squats, and (this was the 1970s) communes; I still had the nursery. (My sister had left home only when she got married.) To keep face, I simulated independence and rented a room in West London. I stayed there sometimes with my lover, but otherwise it was a show flat: I'd arrive before friends came to lunch, and leave shortly after them. Once I even let a colleague drive me from my parents' home to what purported to be my own, only to reverse the journey alone minutes later.

Yet, eventually, at the age of twenty-five and with the encouragement of my mother, I did leave home. Slowly. My move into a flat was carried out like a course of behavioural therapy, spending increasing amounts of time there until I could tolerate a weekend, and then a whole week. But I phoned home every day, to check that they were still alive.

I also left the BBC, to concentrate on journalism. With editors I acted as with my parents: I kept problems (and even expenses) from them, assuming that these were meant to be absorbed by me. And I took instruction well: I was good at shaping myself to other people's design, even if my work was becoming an increasingly important conduit for my own beliefs.

I was now living and working alone, and certain patterns of behaviour emerged. In my attempts to drive myself I was totally indifferent to mood, energy, or rhythm; I pumped myself to produce, overriding any bodily needs and frailties. I would set myself a rigid, minute-by-minute schedule and then, understandably, rebel against it, unable to get out of bed no matter how hard I goaded. Eventually I'd emerge and then immediately introduce another punitive regime – I could sit at my desk for six or more hours without allowing myself even to pee – until the whole cycle began again. The war was now within.

Though my relationship had ended, my professional life flourished. My work vitalised me; it was my plasma. The few times I had articles rejected I'd tip into deep depression. I was grooming myself to be a particular kind of media woman – quick, charming, but never abrasive. I was in training for *Any Questions.*

And throughout all this – my childhood, adolescence, and twenties – I doubt whether my parents had any inkling of my distress. (Why should they have? In some very real sense I had none myself.) It would have appalled them to know of it. If they saw disturbing signs, they attributed them (as most of their generation did) to 'complexes' – some vague and undefined neurotic behaviour. I, on the other hand, felt like someone trying to keep slime from escaping from her fists, and failing; it was now squelching out between my fingers. I was trying to protect them against me, but soon I'd no longer be able to.

JOSEF KARPF: On 1 September 1939 I was sleeping in my room in Jasło next to the open window, and suddenly at five o'clock in the morning I heard bombers flying, I knew something was happening. An hour later, some 30 kilometres from our town, a war materials factory was bombed, so we knew . . . It was frightening but we had so many things to do that there was no room for any philosophical approach – we'd known it was coming, and now it was here.

In the morning after the bombing already on the radio there were coded instructions for people in the reserve to join the army. On the first day the Germans were 100 kilometres away, and we knew there was fighting, though the Polish army from the very beginning was in disarray, but still they had ammunition, aircraft. But there was already complete chaos, becoming worse every day. I opened the instructions in sealed envelopes: they said that we should deliver the copper installations from inside the refinery and distillery to Tarnów – Tarnów was seventy kilometres away, it was stupid. Then we asked for further instructions, what to do? Nobody knew.

We decided to open the tanks and let the spirits flow so that they shouldn't fall into the hands of the Germans – there were hundreds of thousands of gallons of spirits, they could have made energy or petrol out of it. We calculated that it would take at least ten days to empty everything. My two sisters were at the house – one lived there, the other had stayed on after my mother's death, sitting shiva, because we'd known that Hitler was already approaching Kraków. My brother Mundek took the car and my two sisters and their children and went east to Lemberg [Lvov] – about 250 kilometres, and I remained behind to deal with the business. I wasn't sure if I'd ever see them again. It was such a traumatic experience – it made everything which had appeared before seem like the far, far past. You listened to the radio all the time, and read the papers for the first two days. It was all like a nightmare – it *was* a nightmare for me at that time, everything, so unreal that one could not confront it with reality.

On 4 September we knew that Hitler would be already thirty-five kilometres from Jasło. I was one of the directors of the Co-operative Bank of Jasło, and also a judge in the commercial tribunal, so I was vulnerable, apart from being Jewish. So we hired a railway wagon – myself with one suitcase, friends, and relatives – and on 5 September we went in it to Lemberg. When I left, the spirits were still running and the peasants, remembering the First World War from their fathers (we joked with them saying, 'See how lucky you are that there's another war and you'll have a supply of spirits for years'), had a field day.

I took only one book, a Hebrew book from my father's big library, *The Wisdom of Ben Sirah*, because there, on the inside cover, he'd written in Hebrew the birth dates of each of his children. I took this with me, otherwise I didn't take anything, apart from documents. It was not the first experience of leaving the house – during the First World War we also left it. We didn't lock up the house – it was useless to, we knew it was the end of everything.

I arrived in Lemberg, my sisters were already there. They were staying in the flat of a very nice woman where I'd stayed eight years before. The whole Polish army's defence fell to pieces, completely. (My older brother Milek was in Kraków with his wife and they didn't manage to get away: later he was taken to Płaszów and was killed there. I only learned that later, after the war.) We heard already about the pact between Ribbentrop and Stalin. I wanted to get away to Rumania and I hired a cart on September 10 or 12 and took one of my nephews with me and my brother-in-law's brother. When we were driving from the town at night we were stopped by a Polish patrol and, because we didn't have any papers, they requisitioned the cart and the horses, and we had to wait for the tram, and go home. And that was the end of our attempt.

The Russians came on 15 September. For the Russians it was a paradise – with the shops full. They asked us to take Russian passports – we knew enough about the Russians and we didn't want to. I met on the street Roma – she came with her parents and grandparents, aunt, uncle, and cousins, in four cars, and stayed in a hotel. And she told me, 'We're leaving tomorrow for Tarnopol (further east), and from there to Rumania.' They left – two or three days later her grandparents came back from Tarnopol, because they didn't want to be a burden to the family. Roma survived but her grandparents didn't.

One had to queue for hours in the morning for bread. A special atmosphere developed in Lemberg in the unreal world – we'd meet with friends and discuss ways of escaping. We met interesting people, and waited for something to happen. We expected the Russians to start taking prisoners, those who hadn't taken Russian passports. There were rumours that they'd start picking us up, so I spent a few nights in the studio of a painter. Nothing happens. So the last night, it was in March, I stayed at home, and then they came at night, at one o'clock, soldiers, with the concierge and asked me, 'Josef Karpf? Come with us.'

So I took – unnecessarily – a briefcase with all the

documents which I had from my father's estate, and one
or two things, a shirt, pyjamas, and they said, 'Hurry, hurry,
hurry.'

AK: Weren't you terrified?

JK: Terrified? We were terrified all the time, one was
prepared for the unexpected to happen. It was bad luck
that I didn't sleep in the studio that night – not bad luck, it
turned out, because had they not taken me I probably
wouldn't have survived, because single people later were
killed by the Ukrainians. [Single people were treated
more harshly because they thought that they might be able
to escape, unlike families.] The others in my family were
later deported to Russia. They took me to the prison, about
1000 of us were picked up that night. We were searched
and everything taken away from us – documents, watches.
We were put in a cell which was usually for sixteen people,
and there were sixty of us, lying on the floor next to each
other with no room to move. And there we spent about
four to five weeks. We got soup once a day, and water in
the morning, and were led to the loo in parties of fifteen
or twenty – 'Hurry, hurry.' And had a commode in the cell.
We got used to it very soon. My sister Nusia knew where
I was, and they were trying to get me out, but they didn't
manage.

Then one day we were loaded into cattle trucks, which
were sealed, and we started the journey to Russia, to the
camps. Ten days in sealed wagons. We didn't know exactly
where we were going, but among us was one man whose
father had been deported by the Czar to Siberia: he looked
through a small window and said we were going through
forests. We were given bread, water, once a day soup – once
they gave us herrings but not enough water, so it was a
torture! There was a hole in the floor with two boards –
that was the loo.

And so we arrived, we were let out, into the middle of a
forest: it was called Suchabezwodnia, a group of camps in
the Mari republic near the Volga. There were a few
barracks, and they told us, 'Find yourself a place in the
barracks' which were three bunks high. The next morning
they started forming brigades, and we went to the forest
to start felling trees – first four kilometres away, then six
kilometres. Then the rains began, the rainy season – it was
awful, but one got used to it. In the first camp we stayed
six months, until they considered us ripe enough, mature,
for a stricter camp! There were 1100 men in that first
camp out of whom, after the first six months, a few
hundred had died, of hunger and hard work. We got soup
in the morning and soup in the evening, and 400 grams
of bread – I divided it into three parts, and had one part
in the morning, one part at lunchtime, and one part in
the evening. Those who didn't do that, who devoured
everything at once and couldn't refrain, starved and were
dead in a few months.

They started feeding us this so-called soup at five o'clock
in the morning. Then at six there was roll call – I was
called 'You bandit' by a youngster of twenty-one or twenty-
two. Then to the woods again – those who over-fulfilled
the quota got extra soup in the woods. I never got any! In
fact I tried to hide because it was hard work – we had
axes and saws, I'd never done work like that before. So
after a few months, in order not to have to go to the
woods, I managed to get myself into the carpentry
workshop where they made coffins. It was very hard work
to saw with these blunt tools. I was there for a short time,
then I was allowed to work in the kitchen to wash up the
wooden bowls in the terrible water which was already black.
I didn't get ill – the air was healthy!

In September we went at night to another camp in the
same group. We didn't know where we were being taken,
we were waiting at night two or three hours to be put on

to the train. We knew the next morning there'd be a
medical examination, so I started at night – like anyone
who could – inhaling for hours on very strong tobacco so
that my heart should show something. It didn't work! The
next morning I was ordered to go to the group which was
working hard in the forest, loading wood, for the poor
horses to drag – the horses couldn't survive more than
two or three months there. But once, later, I managed to
get some fat from a horse's carcass to use as margarine –
that was the first time we had anything nourishing. I got
ill there – I was swollen from hunger, from the toes to
head. But it was difficult to get let off going to the woods,
until a doctor at the small field hospital – a few rooms –
managed to get me admitted there. I spent two weeks in
this hospital – it was a paradise: I got soup, white bread,
kasha, and sometimes fish – it seemed like an optical
illusion. I would grab it and climb on to my top bunk and
jealously guard it.

I stayed in that camp about six months, until the
beginning of 1941. By now a few hundred more had died
– there were about 600 of us left. If you've read *One Day
in the Life of Ivan Denisovich* then you have an idea of how
it was, life in the camps. They considered that now we were
ripe for an even stricter regime! So we were taken to the
Urals – again by train.

They searched us on the train – whoever had a belt had
it taken away, and got a piece of string instead. I still
had the same clothes I'd arrived at the first camp in,
though they'd also given us quilted overcoats. But I was
only forty-one, I was a young man.

They took us to what was later called Molotov, on a
tributary of the Volga. Then we were loaded into barges,
which were dragged by a motorboat. On these barges there
was also a brigade of prostitutes and thieves (there were
men and women in all the camps). We were a group of
eight and we kept together, we sat on the lower deck in

a circle with our so-called belongings in the middle. The other people who were not so clever were on the deck in the dark, and from time to time we heard 'Oy, gewalt!' because the thief had grabbed somebody's suitcase and run to his prostitute and she put the contents under her quilt and threw overboard the empty suitcase. The journey took about two days upstream, and so it was going on all night – very interesting, I can tell you!

And so we arrived at the harbour, at the foot of the Ural mountains. We walked all day until we arrived in the evening at a place with no name – until today I don't know where it was. Before we'd left the last camp, I'd received my first parcel from Poland, I don't remember from whom – there was sugar, cigarettes, some margarine, and pyjamas (we'd been allowed to write letters, so they'd known where to reach me). So at night I tied myself and the parcel to a post, and fell asleep, but in the morning everything had gone, and I saw the thieves smoking the cigarettes they'd stolen from me!

AK: Didn't you feel a sense of incredible anger?

JK: Anger? We were already immune – things like anger were already so subdued, all these feelings were subdued, these are special conditions. If you want to hear about it, Natalia was the one who experienced it much more than me. I knew that we were helpless – impotent from the day we were taken from Lemberg. You couldn't complain – if you complained it was worse, they took it out on you.

That was the worst camp because soon, in June, it was hot. And we had to go to the forests, and the flies there – you have no idea what a plague there was, it was terrible. Dry, no water, and flies, and so we were waiting for the so-called night – it was not night, at twelve o'clock you could read the newspaper because there were white nights there already. We were there from May until September

1941. Hitler invaded Russia in June 1941 – nothing changed until General Anders concluded an agreement with Stalin to form a Polish army out of the prisoners. And so we were made to go to the Polish army. Before we left we were invited into the office and they tried to persuade us to be spies for them. In vain. And they gave us a few roubles – we were no longer the enemies. We felt some relief. After a few hours I found an inn, had soup with beef and kasha there. So we went again to Molotov, the harbour on the Volga, on foot. There I met friends from other camps. Motorboats came there on the Volga: we wanted to go south, but eventually we came to Stalingrad – the journey took a few days and on the shore on the way there women brought food to sell and we (I and a friend of mine) bought it for the few roubles we had, and we ate and we ate. And when we came to Stalingrad I got ill – I got dysentery, and I was lying there on the floor of the station for two days until I recovered. I didn't know where the rest of my family was – but I knew that families were deported, not as prisoners, but as deportees, into the same area as I'd been in, not enclosed in barbed wire but in settlements where they worked and got food. That we knew, but we didn't know exactly where.

I had call-up papers, and I had to go to a small place between the rivers Don and Donets. I went there, to the secret police, the NKVD, and they told me 'You are going to this and this place in the German republic' (from where the Germans had been deported at the beginning of the war), and they wanted me in this collective farm to be busy with the harvest, because the wheat was so high and thick in the black, marvellous soil. It was terrible there, because the deserted German huts were already being rained in. That was autumn 1941. I was made to go to the fields in the morning and cut the wheat. I saw that I shall perish there, because in the fields it was cold and there was rain – to wait until midday from seven in

the morning until they called us for the soup . . . So I
made a deal with the chairman of this collective farm, that
I shall draw his portrait if he let me go. And so I drew
him a portrait and he said 'All right', he gave me my sixty
kilograms of wheat, my earnings. My friend was allowed
to leave with me. I was allowed to put the wheat on the
cart, which went to Frolovo, which was about thirty
kilometres away, but the horse was so weak and loaded that
I wasn't allowed to sit on the cart so I walked alongside it
on the dirt road.

We arrived at night again, in the dark. We knocked at
the window of a small hut, and an old woman opened it,
and allowed us to sleep on the floor, and gave us tea! So
we ate and drank and slept, and started the next day to look
for a way to get away from there. We went to the station,
and military trains passed, and we weren't allowed in, of
course. We wanted to go to the North, because I knew
already that my sister Nusia and her husband and child
were there – we'd learned that at the harbour at Molotov.
We travelled all day but I was picked up by soldiers to go
and dig trenches, because the Germans were already
approaching from Kharkov in Ukraine – they were about
twenty kilometres away. I was taken with others into an old
cinema to spend the night before leaving for the trenches.
In the morning they formed us into columns to take us:
we got sausage and bread but then I managed to sneak
away behind the corner, and I didn't go.

AK: Were you frightened doing that, frightened you might
get caught?

JK: What else could happen to me? So I stayed there, but
I didn't have any papers. I'd learned Russian in the camps,
so I took a piece of paper and wrote in Russian, and took
a cork and cut out something similar to a rubber stamp,
and stamped it, so I had a document (because most of

63

them couldn't read)! We managed to join a train, which took four weeks to go 1000 kilometres. On the way, with my papers, I got food where the soldiers got food. And most important, there were delousing centres, because I could shake the lice from my head. It was terrible.

Finally I managed to reach Yoshkar Ola, the capital of this small republic, the Mari republic, and I phoned Nusia, and arrived at Nusia's place in Sernur. I knocked at the door, she came out and said, 'Take off everything and throw it out, and wash.' (In the camps we'd had showers, but we had to walk naked from the barracks to the showers sometimes fifty metres, 100 metres away.) And then Nusia put me to bed, and that was really the nicest time – she looked after me, it was heaven, I got to eat, there were no worries, and slept. For two weeks. Exhausted, but living for the first time like a human being again. I was in a state of self-imposed amnesia.

Yet I'd never had the feeling in the camps that my survival was in danger. I was prepared for the worst, but not for annihilation.

Nusia lived in this town with her husband, who was a consultant at the hospital, and her son, Ludek. After a fortnight her husband said, 'If you stay longer in bed, the Russians will say that you're a parasite.' So I had to take a job. There was a job going as an accountant in an agricultural college there: the one who'd done it before was a dentist from Latvia who hadn't distinguished between credit and debit . . . Any mismanagement or mistake, and you could immediately be accused of sabotage, so I was in such a panic when I saw these books which were in such a mess that you could not try to unravel them – it took me two or three weeks and I had suicidal moments. The more so as Ludek was called to the secret police – Nusia and her husband were waiting outside, it took perhaps three hours before he came out. They'd wanted him to spy, on everyone, for them.

Once I'd sorted out the books, I was told I'd have to lecture to the children of the agricultural collective farm. I had to lecture on accountancy in the 'kolhozy', the collective farms, with some economics. I remember, the first time I lectured, behind a screen were two informers from the secret police, listening how this bourgeois man does – whether he does subversive work. But they accepted that I was all right. So I lectured there until 1944 – almost three years. I had a secretary there, I was mentioned in the circulars of the Russian Ministry of Agriculture as an exemplary worker. I lectured in Russian, which I now spoke fluently. I was called Josef Markovich.

I had to submit an Industrial and Financial Plan every year, with everything itemised and how much it cost. It was a fiction because you couldn't get things – so I made it up, and how! For instance, according to the Plan we were meant to have six or eight cows, but we had only one or two; we were meant to have six horses, we had one. We were meant to cart twenty tons of dung into the fields – but we had perhaps one ton. I wrote as I was told, if one didn't one would have perished.

I lived with Nusia and her family. Nusia had to get up at six in the dark in winter to go to the market of the peasants from the collective farm. She'd take a sheet and exchange it for eggs and butter. We reared a pig and slaughtered it, and hung it in the pantry where it immediately froze. One went every morning with an axe and hacked a piece off that and cooked it in a cast-iron pot with various other things, and that was meat soup. That we ate in the morning, midday, and the evening, and that kept us fit, though Ludek had TB in the settlement. I made friends with nurses and doctors there in the hospital, it was not too bad. I rode twenty kilometres to other communal farms on the Steppes. We didn't know *anything* about the war – there was nothing about Auschwitz and all these things in the Russian papers. My sister Gizia

was in the same republic, and we knew that. My brother
Lonek was in Palestine – he'd gone there in 1931.

In 1944 the Polish Communist leader formed a Polish
Communist army in Moscow to march into Poland, and
they wanted all people of Polish origin to be sent to her.
But the college managed, each time I was called up, to
have me exempted, because they needed me. Until, in late
summer 1944, they said I had to go and join the army in
Minsk.

That was after [the Battle of] Stalingrad, and the
Russians were chasing the Germans already. I didn't want
to go, because I wasn't badly off there, but at the same
time I was curious about what was going on. So I went via
Kiev, and got to Minsk. And was told that the army had
moved already to Lublin, a Polish town. So I went there
via Lemberg and via Jasło. Jasło was terrible, only one or
two houses hadn't been destroyed. Otherwise the whole
town was completely razed – one could hardly find a street
there, the Germans systematically destroyed everything. It
was a great shock, but in the context of all these shocks
which I had had . . . You cannot realise how immune one
becomes in such a situation towards many, many
experiences which otherwise would be difficult to survive.

And then I went to Lublin. I arrived in October 1944
and began to have blackouts (I'd got Ménière's Disease,
a disease of the inner ear, in Russia) and never joined the
army. My sister Gizia was there, she'd come back from Russia
three months earlier, and my brother-in-law said, 'Don't be
silly, who kept records that you came from Russia?'

The Germans were destroying Warsaw, and the Russians
wouldn't let the West defend it – they sat across the Vistula
and watched Warsaw after the Uprising being burnt and
destroyed and bombed.

Two months later my brother Mundek arrived in Lublin.
He'd managed to escape from a concentration camp,
Janowska, in Lemberg, but caught typhoid, and then had

to escape from an Aktion in a Jewish hospital. After that he escaped from a work camp which was being liquidated and hid in the forests in a bunker which he'd dug with some other people. In the bunker about thirteen people hid for five months and they miraculously survived. Six of us – my sister and her two sons, my brother and his wife, and I – lived in a tiny room for a few months. I learned later that my cousin Josef Karpf and his wife had been deported from Warsaw by the Germans and killed, after his son had been killed in front of his eyes.

I joined the Polish Treasury, and they made me soon a Councillor. Then the Treasury and whole government moved to Warsaw, after the Germans had been repulsed, in 1944. Only the left bank of Warsaw survived, and there I got a room. I got myself a pair of shoes and a suit, and made friends. I had mixed feelings on 8 May 1945 when the war ended, because we'd learned already what had happened: I saw a transport of shoes and a transport of ties, which the Russians had taken from the German stores in Auschwitz and other concentration camps. People came back already to a Jewish centre, and left on the wall their names and who they wanted to find. I already started thinking about how I could get out of Poland, because I knew Russia, and that this was already Russian, if not by name by fact.

When I listened to the taped interviews with my mother again, thirteen years after I'd recorded them, I was struck by how reluctant I was to move on from 1936, as if that year was still a safe one and I didn't want to advance to 1939. But eventually we did.

NATALIA KARPF: At the end of August 1939 there were

already committees in every block of flats which organised rotas of people to keep watch – for what we didn't know, bombs or what. Julius and I lived on the fourth floor of a very big building owned by the Polish Savings Bank. On 31 August they appointed me and Julek to keep watch on the flat roof. We were equipped with something on our heads if the bombs started falling; we were frightened of fire. This house was very near the railway bridge, and we were frightened that they would start throwing bombs on the railway bridge and that can hit our house. And the Germans also knew that there was this big Savings Bank. Hela and Natan were not far away, in the same block.

On 1 September at four thirty in the morning the sirens came and they started bombing Kraków. We were in such a terror. But that was nothing. I had a terrible maid who was such an anti-Semitic girl that I was frightened of her, because I knew that when the Germans come, she will be the first one to show me up as Jewish. I was frightened of her and of the caretaker of the house because I knew that he was very anti-Semitic too. When the bombing started, Julek said, 'Let's go to my parents.' So we went there. Polish radio ordered all the men to leave the towns, saying that the Germans won't harm any women but they will do terrible things to the men, so I said, 'You have to go, but I am going with you.' He said, 'No, you stay here with my mother.' So he left with his father and his youngest brother on 4 September. He was killed on the same day in a bombed train and I didn't know. His cousin came and told me after the war. His father and his brother were under German occupation and they were shot and killed. My brother left the same day that they all left and went to Lvov, which was under Russian occupation. He was homesick, so in November 1939 he turned up back at my father's flat with a woman guide. But he said he wasn't staying, he saw what was happening, and he went back to Lvov with the same guide. We had news that he crossed the frontier and arrived there safely. Never heard any news from him again. Except once someone met a young man who had met our brother in 1942 in Guzary in Russia, where there was a terrible epidemic of typhoid, and he must have died. Had he lived he would have contacted us and looked for us. I looked for him twice through the Red Cross, and there was no trace anywhere. I went once to a clairvoyant here in London. I paid 12/6d for it, and she said my brother was with someone called Maria (Mania). That's why I believe that he's dead.

The Germans arrived in Kraków on 5 or 6 September. I saw them in the streets, I saw them everywhere. I was terrified. When the maid saw Germans she went downstairs (they told me later) and said, 'Come upstairs, there is a beautiful flat here.' And they stayed there for about ten days. I went back one day to the flat to rescue some things, and there they were: these young German officers introduced themselves to me and when they learned that I'm a pianist (because I had two pianos) they asked me to play. And they brought me a book with Russian songs, and I played to them and they were singing, and they gave me food, and they were like gentlemen. They told me, 'Look, you have an enemy here in your flat', and they dismissed her for me, and she had to sign that she has no claim against me. I managed to take some personal belongings, a few Persian rugs, linen, that was all, and I went back to my mother-in-law.

One had to queue for everything – for coal, for bread, sometimes at five o'clock or six o'clock, and queue for two or three hours. I had chilblains. I had to clean her flat. One day in 1940 she suddenly lost her sight in one eye. She was terribly ill, and sometimes after the nine o'clock curfew I had to put on my star and go out and run for the doctor – I could have been shot anywhere. (They'd announced a few weeks after they'd arrived that we'd have to put on these white bands with a blue star –

yellow stars were afterwards.) I took into my room
Jelinek's [Julius's aunt] sister and niece, who didn't have
where to go.

I lived like that until there was talk that they were going
to make a ghetto, in 1940, and I didn't want to go into
the ghetto, so I decided to take Helunia and go to Tarnów,
to where my best friend Jadzia was living with her uncle and
aunt, because there was no ghetto there. My father stayed
behind, and he went into the ghetto.

So in November 1940 we went to Tarnów – you had to
wear the armbands and the star but you could still travel
with a special pass, though they were already catching men
like dogs in the street, and arresting them and shooting
them. I went to Tarnów with Hela and Mania to join Jadzia
and her two-year-old son in her aunt's flat, until they
announced one day in 1942 that in this district Jews can't
live and on this side of the road Jews can't walk. Within
one year we moved twelve times – all the time the Gestapo
told us to leave this part of the town, that part of the
town. We had some clothes and bedlinen with us, we used
to sell a little bit and bought food. We started working in
the Jewish community there, collecting things for the
transports from outside.

One day in 1941, before there was the ghetto in Tarnów,
I'd arranged to meet Jadzia at the corner of the street at
two p.m. because a transport of 2000 Jews came from
Hamburg and we didn't have enough cutlery and
crockery in the community so we wanted to go to various
Jewish families and collect. But in the entrance-hall
downstairs, it was a three-storey house and we lived on the
third floor, I saw two men, one tall, one shorter, being
searched, and I recognised that the taller one was my and
Hela's friend Alex Weissberg. I wanted to pass them, I
didn't know that they were being searched by Gestapo men
because they didn't wear any uniforms. So I was passing,
and Alex said in German, 'Wait Natalia, we have come to

you.' And the German stopped searching Alex and looked at me, and kicked me, and said 'Raus from here, Sarah' – they called every Jewish woman Sarah. I looked astonished and said, 'I'm going.' So he let Alex go and he ran after me, this tall good-looking German, called Grunow, with the other one, and said, 'You are arrested, you rude Sarah.' And they took me on the right side of the street, so that the Jews who walked on the left side knew there was something wrong if I walked, with my armband and these two plain-clothed men, on the right side. They took me to the Gestapo building and they started hitting me with enormous rubber truncheons and sticks: 'Du freche Sarah, wo ist dein Mann?', 'You rude Sarah, where is your husband?', and I didn't know where he was. I screamed like an animal because they hit me so terribly for an hour perhaps. I was covering my face, so they hit me on my back and took me into the cellar and locked me up. I was the only one who came out alive from that – other people who came after me who were arrested were beaten to death or shot dead, by this Gestapo in Tarnów. This one man who was called Grunow, he was such a beast that it's indescribable.

I was walking in that cell many hours. I was praying to my mother and to my grandfather either to save me or to have me killed painlessly so that I won't feel again this terrible pain. And suddenly, it must have been very late, I didn't know if it was one o'clock in the morning, two o'clock in the morning, I heard some steps coming again and opening the cellar – I was in such a fright, I can't describe to you. And another man took me upstairs, it was dim light, and he started hitting me again. Then Grunow came in and the man said to him, 'Rudi, you still have your Sarah whom you arrested yesterday afternoon.' Grunow replied, 'Let her out in the street and shoot her there.' A third man said, 'No, I'd like to take her down in the cellar where the rats are' – they were inhuman, they

71

could torture you with words also. But the man who'd brought me up took me downstairs, and said, 'Take your things with you.' And then they kicked me, they kicked me out, and said, 'Thank Jehovah.' It was three o'clock in the morning: do you know what that meant? It meant that if a Gestapo man saw me in the street, he would shoot me. And they shot in the air to frighten me.

Opposite the Gestapo headquarters lived a friend of mine, but I didn't want to go there because I knew that they might be watching me to see where I go. So I ran to the next, parallel, street, where the Birnbaums, parents and brother of a friend of mine, lived. I didn't realise that I was swollen and completely black and blue from top to bottom – there was not one piece of my flesh which wasn't black. I ran as if God gave me wings, floating in the air – in two minutes I was there. Three o'clock in the morning, I knocked at the house door and the porter let me in. I knocked on my friends' door, and they opened straight away: they were sitting in their clothes – they hadn't gone to bed because they heard that I'd been arrested and everybody who knew me was afraid that when they beat me, I would tell. The Gestapo had asked me while they were beating me, 'Where are your friends?' I said, 'I have no friends here.' A few weeks before, Mrs Birnbaum had a telegram that her son had died in Auschwitz. And when she undressed me and saw my back and body, she started screaming, 'Now I know what they did to my son, if they could do such a thing to a young woman.'

There I collapsed and started crying, I broke down. They gave me two sleeping pills, I had to lie on my tummy, I couldn't lie on my back, and she was sitting the whole night and put cold compresses on me. Then they decided to call a doctor and when she saw me, she said, 'The hands who could do such a thing to a human being should rot.' But she couldn't help me – I couldn't lift my leg one inch from the sheets because I was in such pain. But she said it will go. Someone let Mania know where I was, and Hela was away in a small village: when she came back ten days later she nearly fainted when she saw me.

Then they made a ghetto in one part of the town. Our Mania was in Tarnów with us too: she wanted to come and live in the ghetto with us but I said, 'No, why should you come with us, you have your birth certificate as an Aryan, you stay outside and you can help us.' And she did – she was terrified, but she did. She used to sell towels, and sheets, and so on, and buy food and cook it and bring it to us to the factory outside the ghetto where we were taken to work.

On 1 June 1942 I learned what had happened to my father. I'd written to a Jewish friend in Kraków and he found out: he sent me a telegram that my father had been taken from the ghetto on a transport.

AK: Did you know where he went, what camp he was taken to?

NK: What camp? If somebody was taken out from the ghetto, he wasn't going to a camp, only to the oven. I felt absolutely crushed, shattered.

One day, before the ghetto had been established, they started gathering all the Jews of Tarnów in a big square, and shooting them. They didn't take us, but they shot 15,000 people in one day. It was a massacre. We heard the shooting all day long. Before that we had to go to the Gestapo headquarters and get a card with a stamp: those with a stamp didn't have to go to the square.

AK: On what basis did they give you a stamp?

NK: Who knows? Whether their nose was nice, or they wore spectacles, or didn't wear spectacles, or had a beard – who knows? We were so terrified all the time: whenever I

73

heard the sound of bootsteps behind me and 'Halt',
I always thought that I feel a bullet through my head. I
had a stamp, so I didn't have to go to the square, but my
sister didn't have one, so I was in hysterics over what to do
with her. I had some friends who had a stamp but were
working in a clothing factory, and one said that she'd hide
Helunia there, and she took her and hid her there for a
few days.

Three times we went through this and one time, when
we both had stamps and were now living in the ghetto,
we hid 200 people in our flat. Behind a door in the room
where we lived there were steps to a built-in hiding place
which, before the war, had belonged to the illegal Bund
[Jewish socialist] print-workers. We put a cupboard
against this little door, we didn't know about it, but people
came to us and told us about it and they said, 'Could we
come and hide there because the Germans are coming
again and it starts again in a few days, and they will take
us God knows where.' I said to Helunia, 'What will happen?
They will shoot us if they find out', and she said, 'All
right, so we will be killed together with all of them, but we
have a chance to save these people.' So I said, 'Fine, all
right.' So 200 came through this door (among them the
Birnbaums) – they came at night, they knew beforehand
that the massacre was coming, they came with small
children who were drugged so as not to cry or make any
noise, and with buckets to use as toilets during the day. At
night, we pushed the cupboard away and let them out a
little bit, and gave them fresh water, and emptied the
buckets. That was for five days. But on the third day we
heard the Germans marching at about six or seven o'clock
in the morning. So I locked the door from the outside,
and knocked and said to one of the Birnbaums who was
on guard duty, 'Look, the Germans are coming – don't
give yourselves away, even when they call for you to come
out. You must behave quiet and ignore any call.'

So the Germans arrived in our house: they said, 'All raus – all out.' We didn't know where they were taking us. And I asked the one who came, 'Can I lock up my room?' and he said, 'Yes'; 'And can I take the key with me?' and he said, 'Yes.' But when we went out and we locked it, they heard a shot, the Germans were shooting in the air, and all those people hidden there thought that they'd shot us.

So the Germans marched us to the square: we didn't know what would happen to us, or to the people hiding in the house. They held us in that square for many, many hours, until late afternoon, and then we learned that they are opening in the ghetto houses and bunkers and searching for people who are hiding. They told us that we weren't to go back into the ghetto, but on the other side of the town to various houses – for how long we didn't know.

We went there, but didn't undress, we didn't go to sleep – the night was agony because we didn't know what to do: should we creep there or send one of us there and open the room so that they could get out? But my sister and I decided that we'd take the risk and leave them there, because if they weren't discovered they'd be safe and we wouldn't be shot. But the Germans also engaged Jewish policemen who went round the ghetto and were shouting 'Jews, come out – nothing will happen to you', and when people came out they were shot.

But our group, the hidden ones, remembered what I'd said – 'Don't come out and don't believe, stay there.' After twenty-four hours the Germans told us, 'You can go back to your places in the ghetto.' When we came in, all the rooms in the house were ransacked and opened except our little room – nothing had happened to it. I had the key, I opened the door – it was a miracle. But those people didn't know that we were alive, and it was daytime and we didn't want to let them out and talk to them, because we were frightened that the Germans were round there.

So I started calling 'Heluniu' and laughing, and Helunia
said 'Natalko', so that they knew that we are both alive
and well. Afterwards they said that these voices and
laughter sounded to them as if angels were ringing
and singing.

And one man who survived with his family said, 'Because
of that which you did, you will have a happy life.' Poor
Helunia.

We saved them all, but they went at the next: when we
escaped to Warsaw, many of them perished at the next
Aktion.

But after that, Helunia said, 'I can't stand it any more,
we have to escape from here.' It was late 1942, and we
were making plans, because Helunia said we wouldn't
survive the next Aktion, and we didn't want to go into a
camp anywhere. So we bought some non-Jewish birth
certificates and found two Poles who said that they'd take
us by train from Tarnów to Warsaw, for 2000 or 3000 złoty
(about £100 – Mania had brought with her to Tarnów all
the things which my mother had collected for her as a
future dowry. I had money in gold, which, when the war
broke out, I'd had melted down into a key. All these things
helped us to live). We sent a message to Jadzia, who'd gone
on ahead to Warsaw. My name was Anna Bolechowicz, and
I repeated to myself 100 times that I wasn't Natalia Hubler
but Anna Bolechowicz. My sister was Julia Gajevska, and
we were friends. We packed two suitcases with our best
clothes and some bedlinen and towels. We told Mania that
we were going to escape, and she was very frightened and
started crying, and said she wanted to come with us. We
said, 'You can't come with us but we're going to send
someone for you afterwards, you stay here until then.'

On 13 January 1943 we were going in the group to the
factory, and Helunia and I stayed at the back of the line,
and took off our armbands – it wasn't yet very light, it was
dawn – and the guard who was taking us was in front.

They went round one corner and we went the other way and met the men. We were terrified. The men, railwaymen, had already collected our suitcases and bought the tickets and said we could wait in their hut for the train. But they frightened us more because every few minutes they went out and came back saying, 'Oh, there are Germans there.' At the station we saw another friend of ours, also doing the same, and dressed in mourning, as if she had lost God knows whom, because she had a little Jewish nose and she wanted to cover her face, so they told her to wear a black veil, as if she was in mourning [laughs]. But she didn't want to look at us even, and we were in the same train, escaping from the same ghetto to Warsaw.

The journey was a few hours long, and the men accompanied us, joking with us as if they were our husbands. It was the most horrible journey in my life, apart from afterwards in these cattle trains to and from Auschwitz. Absolutely terrifying. We arrived, and the men left us at Jadzia's, but she said we could only stay there one night, because the woman she was staying with didn't know that she was Jewish, and if she saw two more women she'd suspect. When we opened one of the two suitcases, instead of the beautiful dresses and our clothes, there were stones and newspapers – they had robbed us, those two men. That's how the Poles were. I was so furious, because we'd paid them handsomely.

With our birth certificates we had to pretend, and learn to live lying all the time, not to be caught and shot. Jadzia had rented for us one room in a flat with a Polish woman, who had a small upright piano. I hadn't played the piano for three years. One day I played and she was amazed how I play. When the sirens sounded, because of Allied bombs, we didn't want to go down into the cellar because we didn't want to be in close contact with other people. Once, there were such long sirens that we had to go down, and there I

77

saw one conductor whom I knew, a Jew who was pretending not to be [laughs], and a very well-known pianist – I didn't let him see me.

We brought Mania over a few weeks after: through a Jewish friend we arranged to give 1000 złoty to someone who brought her to us. We lived a normal life, but always afraid that someone will denounce us. The caretaker, who suspected that we were Jewish, did denounce us, and sent the Gestapo and Polish police to us, and denounced someone else in this house whom I knew and who was killed. One day, in 1943, seven o'clock in the morning, a knock on our door. Come in. The landlady let them in. This caretaker hadn't denounced our Mania, only us two, who he thought were Jewish. These Polish police started questioning us and we showed them the false birth certificates. But they took us to the police station and locked us up there together with thieves. And then they started bargaining with us: 'How much do you give to be let out? If you don't give, you are being taken to the Gestapo.' I said, 'I haven't got any money and why should I give you?' But we knew that the Gestapo would be the end. So I said to him, 'Look, I've got here a silver powder compact, a silver comb, a silver lipstick, and 2000 złoty – I can give you this and let me go.' And they took it and they let us out; after a few hours we returned home.

But we decided that we couldn't live there any more because it was dangerous; we had to move again. So we found in a tiny little house again a room with a tiny little stove, and we were all three in it. That was in April 1943: we knew about the [Warsaw] ghetto, that Jews were defending themselves. The smoke from the ghetto could be seen all over the city. And this Polish woman who lived next door said to me, when the ghetto was burning, 'Oh, how wonderful to see the Jews frying.' And I couldn't say a word, I just looked at her. I felt terrible, that I am outside and I can't help anybody and and mustn't disclose that I am Jewish and have to pretend that I am not.

Helunia worked for the underground movement in Warsaw, and every time she left me and didn't come back for a few hours I was in agony, because she would take false identity cards to political people or Jews. I couldn't have dissuaded her from doing it because she wanted to do something and we couldn't just sit and do nothing.

Mania became ill, with terrible pains, we called the doctor: he said there was something wrong with her liver. They took her to hospital, we visited her every day. Poor woman – the priest visited her every day, and she said to me, 'I don't want him, I'm not a Catholic any more', and I said, 'Shh, you mustn't say it: what you are in your heart nobody knows.' And she died several weeks later, in August 1943. She only wanted to be buried in a Jewish cemetery, but we had to bury her in a Polish one. It was very sad for us, because it was as if a second mother died.

And in the meantime Helunia met her husband, Adam Josefert. He arranged for us to go on a train to a place near the Tatra mountains, and guides would take us through the mountains to Slovakia, where coaches for escaping Jews would be waiting to take people to safe countries. We wanted to get through Turkey to England.

Jadzia and I had decided to split up. I never saw her again: the Gestapo took her away and beat her and shot her and her child.

On November 14, five or six of us got on to the train. And when we arrived at the station where we were meant to get off, we saw the Polish police. Hela and I got off the train, but when Adam saw the police, he said get back on to the train. I already had my foot on the step of the train, but Helunia had a very big rucksack and I saw that she couldn't get on in time, so I thought if my sister stays here, I stay here. And of course the Polish police came straight away, and one of them said, 'These are Jewish people,' and they handed us over to the Gestapo. Adam stayed on the train, back to Kraków, and survived the war hiding. If we'd managed to get back on the train, we'd have done the same.

The Germans took us to Zakopane, the famous ski resort where I'd been for my honeymoon, and held us for three weeks, with Polish women in the cellar of a hotel. They were such fun, those women, they made us laugh. There was one tall good-looking Gestapo man who pitied us, and when no one saw, he brought us an apple. He knew we were terrified, and whenever he came with food he whistled, so that we'd know it was him. Another fell in love with Helunia and brought her all the time something to eat. 'Julia,' he said to her, 'you are so beautiful.'

On 9 December 1943, it was freezing cold, they loaded six of us on to an open lorry. The tall German said, 'Don't be frightened. You're going into a labour camp.' He himself probably didn't know what was going on there. But it wasn't. They took us to Płaszów, a suburb of Kraków, where this camp had been erected on a Jewish cemetery on a hill.[1] The Germans had pulled down all the tombstones and paved the road with them. We arrived in the afternoon: it looked like a military camp with barracks, surrounded by electrified barbed wire, guard towers, and Germans with guns. Helunia and I were locked up in a prison cell. From there they took people up on to the hill and shot them. If someone saved you, you went to work in the labour camp. In the next cell was Jelinek's brother, and from him I learned that Jelinek and her younger son were also there, and they'd got her out of the cell with her child to the labour camp.

It was the birthday of the Commandant of the camp and some of the kapos [Jewish policemen, appointed by the Germans] were from Kraków and knew that I was a concert pianist and that the Commandant of the camp, Amon Goeth, was musical. The kapos went to him and told him that five people had been brought in. So he said, 'What are they?' and this kapo replied, 'One is a klaviervirtuoso, a concert pianist.' So he said, 'Let her come tonight to my birthday party and play.'

The kapo came to me and said I was going to play for the Commandant that night. They took me out of the cell to the hairdresser, and then to a beautiful villa, built by Jewish architects and Jewish workmen on the other hill of Płaszów. There were perhaps twelve or fifteen people, German officers in SS uniform, drinking and eating. Goeth was wearing a white jacket, a uniform – he was over six foot tall and terribly fat, and he had these huge white dogs with black spots with him. But he also had a very beautiful mistress there, who looked a bit kinder.

When I arrived, he addressed me by the familiar form, 'du': 'Sit down and play something for me.' I hadn't played properly for nearly three or four years, so my fingers were stiff. I played a Chopin nocturne – the posthumous C-sharp minor one, because it was a very sad piece and I was sad and I loved Chopin. I heard her, this beautiful woman, whispering something into his ear, and he never said to me 'du' any more. After, he said, 'I agree that you can play well. But will you run away?' How could we run away? We were surrounded by electric barbed wire and armed Gestapo, so he said, 'Sie soll leben – She shall live. You are free now, to come out of the prison, into the camp, to work.' I was numb and don't remember what I said next. But when we were on holiday in Switzerland in the 1980s I met two Israeli women who had been at the same camp. I never knew them but they'd heard of me and my story – everyone was talking in the whole camp about it, the kapos had told them – and apparently I answered Goeth and said 'Not without my sister' and he agreed.

Then he said, 'Let her play something jolly.' So I started playing De Falla Dances, and he said, 'Stop, this is Jewish music.' It was never Jewish. Then he said, 'Let her go into the kitchen and have something to eat.' So there was his Jewish cook, and she gave me plenty to eat, and I asked her whether I could take something for my sister, and she gave me something. They took me back to the prison to Hela, and we were transferred to a barracks the next day. All our friends and people who knew about it said, 'You were born again on 9 December 1943.'

Each barracks must have housed 200 to 300 people. We slept on a bunk – Helunia and I always slept together on one bunk, we didn't want to be separated. In Płaszów we wore our own clothes, but with a yellow star. We got up at six, had our ration of bread and something to drink. There were no toilets, just one barracks with latrines – an enormous board with about fifty holes, and on this you sat. Toilet paper, what? It didn't exist. We went to other barracks to work on torn German army woollen socks – we had to put in new heels and toes, and we got terrible lice. But we learned to darn beautifully, that's why I darn so well.

We got cotton wool for our periods. My periods continued until Auschwitz: the day we got to Auschwitz, my periods stopped until the war ended. It was the same for a lot of women. Three weeks after the war, they started again.

I remember one horrible day that they hung six young men and we had to go round a few times and look at them hanging from the scaffold. And I remember hearing shooting, and once seeing Amon Goeth outside our work barracks with his dog, and a man from another barracks wanted to go to the latrines, and I heard screams because Goeth, when he saw him, said to his dog, 'Mensch' – he called his dog 'Mensch', human being, and us he called dogs – so he said to his dog, 'Mensch, friss den Hund – Man, eat the dog.' And the dog threw himself on this man, and bit off the trousers with the flesh of this man. That's what we saw through the windows. But I don't remember many, many things from Płaszów – that's such a blockage for me.

But one night, after I'd been in the camp a week, at midnight, a kapo came. 'Hubler! Natalia Hubler! The Commandant wants music again.' So I had to get up, get dressed, and to go. And there were the Brothers Rosner playing for him. One was playing accordion, the other the violin, and they played light music. So I said to them, 'I've never played that sort of music.' We decided to play Hungarian Dances by Brahms, but after that I had to improvise with them to accompany them. That was my last 'concert' for Goeth, but they were called many more times.

One day, the woman who was responsible for cleaning the latrines – some of the inmates were very dirty, she had to clean them all, and she was very angry – took this big hard broom, dipped it in this shit, and started hitting me with it and splashing me with it. She let her fury out on me. I didn't scream, but I grabbed this broom from her and started hitting her. And when all the inmates after heard about it, I was the hero of the camp, because nobody dared, they were all terrified of her and terrorised by her.

Recia arrived in March 1944 with Cesia – I'd never met them before. They worked opposite me on the same table. I saw this beautiful woman with these fantastic eyes, and straight away my sympathy went to her. Recia and I felt a deep friendship developing, and from the very first day we were constantly together. Jelinek was in a different barracks, but we decided that when they move us from there, we – Hela, me, Recia, Cesia, Jelinek, and Maria Alexandrovicz – wouldn't part. But Maria was separated from us in Auschwitz.

One of the Gestapo fell in love again with Helunia. Everywhere she went people fell in love with her, because she was so striking, tall and slim and with dark skin. He used to come through our barracks all the time, pretending he was looking for something, just to come in and look at Hela. And one day outside, he approached her and gave her something to eat. We were terrified because it was most dangerous for us – if he was caught admiring some Jews, we would be killed and he would be killed.

We made plans to try and escape, but on the very morning we'd decided to do it, there was an Appel [roll call]. They called us all together at five in the morning: 'March out', into the big square. And our barracks were one of the first, and then they said, 'Stop, and turn round.' So those of us who had been first were now last. And they were being taken into cattle wagons in a train for transport. We were terribly unhappy that in the middle they stopped because there were not enough cattle wagons. But that was our luck, because the whole transport went to Stutthof, by the sea, and they were all drowned.

Jelinek was in a different barracks, and when she saw what was happening, she jumped into a trench, and she saved herself. But that was already after her child was taken. On 14 May 1944 suddenly an Appel again – everyone on this big square. We had to stand there for six or seven hours. They put on the loudspeakers lullabies and songs of children singing 'Mummy', and we heard them taking, on open lorries, all the children, away from their mothers and from the camp – we knew it would be to a gas chamber somewhere. Wojtuc, who was then ten, was taken from Jelinek. We heard the screams of the children, and we had to kneel down and not look up. Can you imagine? Jelinek was in a terrible state, we were all, yet still in August she jumped into a trench.

On another occasion there was a Selektion and we had to undress and file naked past all these Gestapo men outside, and they decided what to do with us: those who were thin were taken somewhere, those who had glasses were sent somewhere else. There were Selektions every few months, when we'd file past them and they'd choose who will live and who will die – they'd say 'Diese, diese, diese.' ['This one, this one, this one.'] Cesia was very thin and I was always frightened that something might happen to her. And when I heard 'diese' behind me and Helunia was behind me, I couldn't look: but it was always someone behind her who'd been chosen. It was pure chance that the five of us survived all the Selektions.

Many people became unbearable to be with – they were fighting for their survival, so they didn't care for other human beings. The Jewish kapos were humiliating us: Jelinek was always late for the Appel – every morning we had to stand there and they counted us – and she was hit, beaten terribly.

The others used to say we'll never survive this, and I was always the optimist. I said, 'Don't talk like this – you will see we will survive, nothing will happen to us.' Sometimes I didn't believe it myself, but I thought, 'Why should I add to it? I'll give them hope.' I only wished I would go to sleep and not wake up any more – that's what I wished.

On Yom Kippur in 1944 in Płaszów I fasted. The others in the barracks laughed at me because they said, 'You fast the whole year here, how can you fast?' But I didn't eat anything that day.

Our last day in Płaszów was 22 October 1944. They were liquidating Płaszów because the front was coming nearer. (In 1943, before we arrived, Schindler took out the group of 1000 or 1500 people whom he had saved, and moved them to his own camp.) They put us on trains – we knew we were going to Auschwitz. We were in a cattle wagon, where there was room for twenty or thirty: we were three times as many, we could hardly breathe. But on the way there they opened it up and let us out – we could actually have escaped, but we were terrified that we would be shot so we didn't. It took a few hours. And when we arrived there, there were so many waiting there. It looked much worse than Płaszów – enormous. We went to Brzezinka [Birkenau], which was just before Auschwitz and was where the gas chambers were. Barbed wire, towers, barracks, many chimneys.

When we arrived there, they brought us into one barracks. They said, 'Wait here', we didn't know for what – we thought that they will take us to the gas chambers. We were there for twenty-four hours and every few hours there was another rumour: one rumour was Mengele is coming. This word Mengele meant the biggest threat to your life, because he destroyed everybody, he sent everybody to gas chambers; when we heard Mengele is coming we knew it was our end, but he didn't come. Then another rumour: they are going to shave our heads. And Helunia said to me, 'If they shave my head, I shall commit suicide.' I said to her, 'You idiot – your hair will grow back but your head will not.' I said, 'Wait, don't anticipate anything.' But our hair was never shaved, only cut very short. Another rumour: we are going to the gas chambers. And so it went on for twenty-four hours.

At last they came to fetch us, and took us to the bath and so-called Entlausung – showers to get rid of the lice. We saw water running in the showers so we knew that they weren't gas chambers. And of course they took everything away from us – whatever we had – our own clothes, our toothbrushes. They took everything away from us. All the guards were armed: how could we resist? With our fists? We were so resigned, and so humiliated, that we really didn't care if they took the clothes or not. When we came out, it was bitterly cold but they didn't give us any towels: we were standing outside for a few hours and shivering so much; we had to dry ourselves by rubbing ourselves and clinging to each other so that we could warm each other with our bodies until we dried. And then they threw us deloused clothes. They gave tall women – like me and Helunia – short black dresses without any underwear,

86

and clogs, and no coat, nothing: it was almost November and we were terribly cold. And Jelinek, who was the small one, got a very long dress and she looked so funny – out of all this we had to laugh.

Then they took us into barracks where we were to sleep, so we knew that for the moment we were saved from the gas chambers. These barracks were huge, bigger even than Płaszów. There was a straw mattress and a blanket. We slept in our clothes, we never undressed for the night. If it was raining when we stood there, we went in those wet clothes to sleep. Yet we never caught any pneumonia or anything – amazing.

I met my aunt Balka, my father's sister, there. She heard that a transport came from Płaszów, so she came to this barracks to see if we were there. And she found us, and what did she bring us? A spoon – to be able to eat the soup they gave us, and not to have to drink or gulp it, because the first day I got terrible stomach cramps. As soon as I got a spoon and ate like a human being, I didn't have these cramps any more. I never saw her again – she must have been taken to the gas chamber.

The next time we went to the shower Jelinek left her clothes on the window sill, and some gypsies stole them and she didn't have anything to put on. So we got from somebody a towel, and she put it round her. Opposite us was a men's barracks, so she went to the fence and in a few minutes they threw over a pair of long and baggy trousers and a long jacket, and two pairs of underpants. She looked like a clown and she gave the white long johns to me and the pink pair to Helunia to wear under these short black dresses. We were the three funniest creatures there: we were all in fits in spite of all this tragedy, because we looked so funny and whoever saw us in Auschwitz walking burst into laughter.

We had to stand at Appel, and they counted us – at five o'clock in the morning, and sometimes in the rain we would stand until eight, and then they took us to work, to carry stones from one place to another part of the camp. In Płaszów we sat and worked in warm barracks; in Auschwitz we worked outside, we were outside from five in the morning until late afternoon, twelve hours. Food was once a day, we got some soup and a piece of bread which was not enough and we suffered terribly from hunger.

A friend of ours from Kraków wore a beautiful knitted woollen suit in Auschwitz, and lovely black boots, so she didn't suffer any cold. We didn't know where she got them from, we don't know what she did to get them. But she behaved well towards me. One day I was standing at Appel and I got such a diarrhoea that I couldn't keep anything in – it was flooding from me, but I couldn't go anywhere. I thought it was my end. Afterwards I was very ill with a high temperature, but Helunia didn't want me to go to hospital, because if you weren't well they might take you straight on to the gas chambers. So Helunia went to this friend and she brought some tablets and an extra blanket to wrap me in and a glass of milk – where she got all this from, we don't know. I don't judge her: I wouldn't do things to gain privileges, at any price, but if as a result maybe she could help somebody . . . She did help me.

At the beginning of the war, before we were in the camps, we heard Churchill on the wireless, and we knew that the war wouldn't end quickly. But we still, then and later, hoped that the West would do something: we were desperate that nothing happened, desperate.

AK: Would you have liked them to have bombed the camp?

NK: Yes, we prayed for it, that they would bomb. We used to say, 'Where is the world? Where is the United States? Where is Russia? Where is Britain?' And sometimes we prayed that we should go to sleep and never wake up, because we were humiliated, we were beaten, we were tortured, we were starved, and we saw such terrible sights that it was unbearable. And I still dream of it: I dreamt the other night again, then I woke up from that bad dream, and then I fell asleep and dreamt the same – that they want to arrest me, that I ran away, and I hid, and I was terrified that they're going to find me.

We weren't in Auschwitz long, because in 1944 the front moved nearer and nearer, and they started talking about liquidating Auschwitz. One day there was an Appel again, and they said they are going to tattoo our numbers. When they said that, we knew that we weren't going to the gas chamber, only they were going to transfer us somewhere else. So we were pleased about the tattoos, although it hurt because they had like a pen: if you look at it, you'll see that it's constructed of many tiny little dots, and every dot went through the skin, and it was red and inflamed after. But we didn't mind. My number is A27407, I think – I forgot already because I don't look at it. [Checking] Yes.

We never saw the gas chambers. They were about half a mile or a mile from us. We smelt them – like burnt skin; we saw the chimneys smoking. No one from our barracks worked there: it was quite separate, but we were conscious of it all the time. Auschwitz was very big – hundreds of thousands of people. We heard of transports from Holland or France and they were taken straight to the gas chambers. Unfortunately Mrs Alexandrovicz was parted from us and she didn't survive. When we were already segregated for the tattoo, we just stuck so together, with our arms, with our hands, we were holding each other, and we didn't allow them to part us: wherever we go, we are going together. They didn't try and force us apart. They loaded us into a cattle train and took us to a small place in Sudetenland (Sudetendeutschland, which was a part of Czechoslovakia which the Germans occupied) to another small camp of 300 women – Lichtewerden, by Jägerndorf.

It was 23 December 1944, the five of us were together, and it took a couple of hours to get there.

There we were in smaller barracks, again surrounded by electric barbed wire. We got up at five a.m., had black water which was meant to be coffee and a very small piece of bread, and after the Appel were taken to the weaving factory, outside the camp in the village, where we worked at big machines. One day they wanted me to carry big sacks with some flax from which they were making rope and cotton wool. The sacks were as wide as this room, and I refused: I said, 'I'm not going to.' I thought I can't do it, and if they're going to shoot me, they're going to shoot me. But we felt that we were not exposed any more to death, as we were in Auschwitz and Płaszów, because they took us out to work every day, and there was only one Commandant and a few other soldiers – no soldiers inside the factory. And there we had information about what was going on in the war every day, because there were German and Czech men and women from the village working in the factory, some of them Communists, and they listened to the wireless and told us.

We had a mop to dust the machine, and one day when I was dusting the machine, my mop fell into it; I wanted to get it out and my fingers got pricked by the machine. So they stopped the machine and my foreman, a horrible German with a big moustache, came to me and asked me in German, 'What have you done?' I said, 'I mopped and the mop fell into the machine.' But I was so furious and so hungry that I was really cheeky. I said to him, 'How long have you been working at this machine?' He said, 'For twenty-five years.' I said, 'And I have been playing the piano for twenty-five years. If you play after a fortnight like me, then I'll work after a fortnight like you do.' After that he had respect for me. All the food, like the potato peel soup, was without salt – it was revolting and we couldn't swallow it. The next day he came to me and asked me

'Have you got a bottle?' I said, 'How can you ask me if I've got a bottle – I haven't got anything.' But the following day he brought me a small bottle of red salt – even the Germans didn't have white salt. And he never behaved to me rudely any more.

I was so hungry – we were given a ration of 100 or 150 grams of bread in the evening for the next twenty-four hours. Jelinek used to cut hers up into tiny pieces so that it would last her the whole day: she lay next to us on the bunk pretending to sleep, and then every fifteen or twenty minutes she'd say, 'I can't. I must eat it now. I can't wait until tomorrow.' And she ate it all, and the next day she was hungry the whole day until the evening, when we got the bread again. There was one woman in our barracks who stole people's bread, so we slept on ours to keep it safe, if we had any left. But mostly the rest of us also ate it at once.

It was cold, it was snowing, we had no stockings, but I had a coat. On Sundays we had to file in front of our Hauptsturmführer, the top Commandant, responsible for the whole camp, and he used to come with a stick and beat us on Sundays, to see if there was any dust from the machines on our black Auschwitz clothes. If there was he beat us: he beat me, and Cesia.

We knew that the war was going badly for the Germans, and that gave us the courage and hope and strength to survive it, although we suffered terribly from hunger. I fell asleep at the machine because I didn't have any strength – I was terribly thin already. Helunia withstood the hunger better than me. I started believing that the war would soon be over, but if it had lasted a few months more I wouldn't have survived it, because I felt so weak.

In this camp when it was Seder, Helunia took a piece of cardboard and drew the Passover plate with charoseth, bitter herbs and eggs and everything and we sat down and she made Seder, with nothing – we had nothing to eat.

And we were singing and rejoicing, and saying, 'Och, the knaidlach, they taste so beautiful.' We were imagining that we eat the most wonderful things, and we were so happy, and we were so hungry.

It was so bad that one didn't want to make it worse. So we made jokes, we sang – Recia had a beautiful voice and every evening she started singing and gave us a concert, and Helunia was reciting, and making up poems. Spring was coming and we had hope, and we had news – radio news every day, and it passed from one person to another, and one machine to another.

Sometimes Helunia brought a raw potato from the kitchen for us to eat – and we were delighted. Getting more food was called 'to organise': Hela organised better than us, she pretended she could tell the future and got food in return. I could never organise. One day she came to me in the factory and brought a small piece of bread with mustard on top. I said, 'Where did you get this?' She said, 'Don't ask, eat.' And I ate it as if it were the best chocolate cake in my life. My dream was scrambled egg made from six eggs, a whole loaf of bread with butter, a pound of potatoes. One can laugh at it now.

Two weeks before the war ended, we were queuing for the soup with our bowls, and a big woman pushed me and kicked me in the heel with the pointed tip of her wooden clog and hurt me terribly. When I woke up I didn't feel well. We called a Jewish doctor and she said, 'I can't take you to the sickbay because you're not ill enough.' So I went to work but when I stood at the machine I fainted. I had to sit there until everyone went back in the evening, and I felt so ill. Afterwards they took me to the sickbay and I had a temperature of 104 or 105 – I had an infected leg. I said to Helunia, 'Don't worry. I'm not going back to the factory. You'll see – the war will be over soon.' They looked at me as if I was delirious. I hadn't eaten for two or three days and my sister and friends were terrified that I was going to die. Helunia asked me, 'What would you eat?' I said I couldn't eat anything. She said 'Would you eat a Kogel-Mogel?' That's a raw egg yolk beaten with sugar – it's fantastic. So I said, 'A Kogel-Mogel? Of course.' It was completely out of reach in the world we lived in – it couldn't happen in real life. In the evening, Helunia came – she looked so funny, with her hair in papers to make it curly: there we were already concerned with our appearance – with a cup. She said, 'Here. Eat this Kogel-Mogel.' So of course I ate it and I said, 'How did you get it?' She said, 'Jelinek took a knife and the whole night did something with the gold crown in her mouth: slowly, slowly, she got it out and sold it to a German or a Polish Catholic woman there, for two eggs and some sugar.' And that was this Kogel-Mogel which they brought me.

I regained my strength, and they used to come to the sickbay every day with better and better news. We heard shooting and we knew that the front was near. There were air raids: you should have seen what cowards the Germans were. They were great heroes towards unarmed, helpless women, but when they saw an airplane which wasn't a German one, the Hauptsturmführer who'd beaten us was so terrified – it was too funny to see. And on May 6 there was an Appel in the big square round which the barracks were built and the Germans said to us, 'We're doomed (verdammt) and have to announce to you that we've lost the war and you are free. You can go where you want.' We felt shivers through us: we were stunned, and started crying, 'We are free to go – where shall we go now?' Nobody knew where to go. And all the Germans ran away.

3

The Holocaust was our fairy-tale. Other children were presumably told stories about goblins, monsters, and wicked witches; we learned about the Nazis. And while their heroes and heroines (I realise now) must have fled from castles and dungeons, the few I remember had escaped from ghettoes, concentration camps, and forced labour camps. Not that our parents' war recollections excluded other stories: we also had our Noddy, Hans Christian Andersen, La Fontaine, Hansel and Gretel, and the rest of the junior canon (I can vaguely recall), along with our father's own delightful invented tales. But no fictional evil could have possibly rivalled the documentary version so often recounted to us and our visitors.

How does a child cope with information about the past brutalisation of its parents? What does it do with such knowledge? How does she process it, render it halfway tolerable? Perhaps it becomes another story. You mythicise it, structure it round the rhetorical devices and narrative features of the other fables you know.

I turned my mother's war into a story I could tell. All families make stories of their lives, at times sharing narratives, at others struggling over whose account will prevail. In my case I used my mother's life to enthral and appal, milking it for drama by underplaying it. And it repaid the compliment by endowing me (in other people's eyes) with a kind of reflected martyrdom. I managed, through my retelling of my mother's Holocaust experience, to secure for myself a second-hand compassion. But it always left me with a slightly sour aftertaste.

Through constant recounting, my mother's story also acquired a kind of mythical quality. It was as if the narrative had taken on a life of its own, detached from the original events to which it referred. I found, curiously, that I could never remember those details of either of my parents' war-time experiences which fell outside my usual account. Right up until I transcribed the taped interviews with them for this book, I knew only the abbreviated drama I regularly told, and if anyone quizzed me, or tried to match it to historical chronology, I could never supply them with further information, and had the awful feeling that what I told might be untrue. It was as if my certainty about the story derived from my own repeated retelling rather than from the events themselves.

This may be because I hadn't experienced it first-hand and was still telling as an adult the version I'd first learned as a young child. Yet even after I'd recorded the taped interviews with my parents in my early and mid-thirties and pinned down precisely the whats, whys, whens, and how-did-it-feels, I soon reverted to the familiar, less detailed version I'd recited down the years. I probably remembered to the degree I found tolerable. But I was also clearly wedded to its storyness. It was as if I knew, somewhere, that the full account wouldn't quite support the version we proffered.

My family's working version of my mother's war was partial. We'd vacuumed everything intolerable from it (all sense of vulnerability and uncontrollable grief), we'd sheared it of helplessness and sorrow. She never depicted herself as abject (perhaps she never allowed herself to be), and admirably refused to be a victim.

Instead she – and so we – described the horror as though it were finite, denying that the war had any consequences beyond its immediate, obvious ones. It was as if we believed that the war could be cheated of its insistence that those who went through it should keep on paying. My mother's extraordinary resilience and exuberance made this seem plausible, with her new, post-war life as the putative happy ending.

My mother's story as told by us was triumphal; its organising principles were heroism and survival. Through the narrative process, we made the Holocaust bearable: we used dramaturgic skills to anaesthetise her trauma.

Whenever, over the past few years, I've gone to conferences and lectures on Holocaust survivors and their families, I've been maddened by the way they so often fetishise talk, as if the key factor determining the psychological health of both parents and children was whether the parents had spoken about their experiences to their children. But there are different ways of talking.

What made it all the harder was the historicity of the Holocaust, the most documented atrocity of the twentieth century (and perhaps all time). Already, by the early 1960s, it was to some – albeit still limited – extent lodged in public consciousness through iconic newsreels and photographs as well as print. But for us it was also biography. The Holocaust had become enmeshed in our parents' personal subjectivity and was part of the family tissue. Verbally or non-verbally it was recruited into arguments, enlisted as a rationale, brought out in admonition. And so it lost its otherness, its status as objective fact: it joined the living matter of our family, where powerful, often wayward feelings inevitably resided. The Holocaust was epic, but for us it was also domestic, and this confusion of the two made any commonplace adolescent cussedness seem monumental, as if we were cocking a snook at anguish.

I lied to my parents when I first met P. The fact that I'd

met an attractive and interesting man would be as nothing, I knew, next to the fact that he wasn't Jewish. I was twenty-seven, but felt as if I were leaching poison into the family milk, or like a law-abiding citizen committing a first burglary – heady but utterly culpable. What increased the sense of danger was that P, though divorced, was available, unlike the married men I'd tended to have affairs with before, whose attachment had relieved me of any need to divorce my parents.

I was nauscous for two days after our first meeting, sick with excitement but also something else. My sister and I had always known that something awful had befallen our parents before we were born, and our unstated mission was to assuage its impact – we were somehow charged with their redemption. But it seemed that I was now about to renege on this duty, to rend instead of mend, and I was certain that it would excite an enormous anger.

So it did, when I told my parents about P, three months later. My mother, apprehending (among what seemed to her a job-lot of defects) his worst, told me I was doing what Hitler hadn't managed to – finishing off the Jewish race. And this only confirmed the desecratory feel of the relationship.

An intense conflict developed, both in me and between me and my parents. I felt as though I was racked between them (whom I was desperate to sustain) in one corner, and in the other the possibility of unprecedented intimacy.

I chafed at my mother's stony disapproval, at her repeated barbs and homilies. My parents often told a cautionary (and possibly apocryphal) tale about a non-Jewish husband, quite happy to go along with his Jewish wife's desire to bring the children up as Jews until one of the kids has a life-threatening fever, whereupon the husband whisks him out of bed and takes him off to a priest to be baptised. When the chips were down, they told us, you couldn't trust them.

At the same time there was my own experience of P, charming, kind, funny, and apparently trustworthy.

I tried repeatedly to reconcile these warring views until, eventually, it all extruded through my hands, unerring somatic proof (the body being an incorrigible punster) that I couldn't in fact handle it. Beads of moisture appeared, trapped beneath the skin, on the palm of one hand, and with them came a compelling urge to scratch. Then I started to claw at my left hand with the nails of my right until the blood ran. This mania of scratching continued until the whole surface of the hand turned raging, stinging scarlet and there came, despite the wound (or perhaps because of it), a sense of release, followed almost immediately by guilt.

This sequence was repeated many times until the palm was florid with yellow and green crests of pus. The other hand also became infected. They seemed like self-inflicted stigmata, visible and so particularly shaming. I hid my hands in public and dreaded social situations, using the healthier hand as far as possible, even if it seemed clumsy and unnatural. And when I resorted to a gauze bandage, I lied about the reason. (But why did people feel entitled to ask? Why did every little plaster need to be publicly accounted for?)

With my parents and P I brooked no talk about my hands or the scratching, insisting (like an alcoholic or drug addict) that soon I'd be able to control it. Eventually, after months of misery, I reached crisis point. I was at a conference, and the effort of avoiding my hands being seen became so overwhelming that I went home and cried and thought that maybe it wasn't all my fault after all, and perhaps in any case I might be helped.

So I went to the dermatologist my parents had been urging me to see, and he looked at my infected hands with horror, and ignored my protestations of guilt, and treated it just like some mechanical failure, and when I tried to draw attention to the underlying distress, he pooh-poohed it, saying, 'How could an attractive young woman have reason to be stressed?'

And I went away with his potions and emollients which did the trick, and I was cured. (I had to soak my hands in purple liquid twice a day, then coat them with greasy ointment and wear white cotton gloves. I couldn't even wash my hair myself, so P did it, gently and without complaint.)

As time passed, my parents' hostility to P diminished. His commitment to me, and his interest in Jewish culture, were apparent. He became assimilated into the family, invited to family events and reunions. My mother even gave him a yarmulke for Christmas. Eventually we decided to live together; we made a home.

But the eczema revisited. This time it couldn't be attributed to parental disapproval. And this time the scratching and subsequent infection of my hands were even more virulent. Once again I tried to hide it. Once more, after a long delay, I visited the dermatologist who prescribed his nostrums. And again he eliminated my every symptom.

Apart from the hands business I relished cohabitation, despite the new problems it ushered in. In the past I'd managed my fear of loss preventively, by not having: you couldn't lose something you'd never had in the first place. But now that I'd admitted an other into my life, I did have something to lose and was convinced that its removal was imminent. If P didn't return at the precise hour that he'd said he would, I'd immediately pace the flat, constructing tableaux of catastrophes. And many times, between the first ring of the telephone and the picking up of the receiver, I buried him, just as I'd buried my parents so often down the years. I dealt with the fear of loss by anticipating it, as if preemptive grief might somehow exempt me from the real thing, or perhaps you could accumulate credit in mourning, to be cashed in in the event of future bereavement. Since I was convinced that, when it came, the pain of losing someone would be intolerable – I assumed all deaths were epic, tragic, and aberrant – I hoped that downpayments might diminish its eventual force.

Winning over my parents to accept P had in some way proved easier than winning over myself. Despite the external changes in my life, there'd been no abating of the sense of exclusion and insufficiency which I'd felt so powerfully in adolescence. I nursed such an unfailing belief that I couldn't have or join that it was almost as if I couldn't tolerate plenitude should it choose to visit, which it now appeared to be doing. After any really good experience I immediately expected a bad one – a swift retributive blow. (If it didn't arrive, I usually supplied it myself.) And long after my parents' initial disapproval of P had evaporated, I often stared at him while he sat reading or watching television, and felt him to be utterly unavailable: he wasn't allowed.

Indeed, whenever too much pleasure threatened, I felt guilty. P was astounded at my capacity for tolerating discomfort, for sitting in unheated rooms or under glaring central lights, perching on the end of the bed for hours on end without back support, and commandeering myself to do things – almost as if I found something reassuring in self-denial, a certain comfort in discomfort. He, by contrast, was a playful person, and exceptionally attuned to his physical needs.

I burdened myself to the limit by embarking on a two-year part-time postgraduate degree, to be done alongside my full-time work. In the summer of the second year when it was almost completed, we took a month's holiday in Italy, but I needed a litre of wine for every few hours of enjoyment. Otherwise, all was inexplicable anxiety, especially first thing in the morning. I also re-experienced the out-of-the-body sensations of my school-days. These reactions seemed so unwarranted that I harangued myself with 'How can you feel bad on holiday?' (a faint, but unwitting echo of 'How could you feel bad if you weren't in a concentration camp?').

We returned and I finished my dissertation with the conviction that life thereafter would finally be perfect. But two things happened instead. One was a growing conflict with my parents. This time there was no obvious cause. My life from the outside seemed far more like that of my contemporaries than at any previous period. I was now in my thirties, living with my lover who was accepted by my family (although, like my sister, I was still phoning home every day). I had my work, my friends. Yet I would get into adolescent disagreements with my parents that left me enraged. The slightest thing would set me off: I ranted, I seethed, and finally I begged forgiveness. The pattern was repeated almost daily, and I was usually the aggressor, exuding belligerence, steaming with bile, as if out to pick fights in the misguided hope that I might, now, at last, win them.

The second thing preventing nirvana came from that eloquent spokesperson, my body, whose protests were once again epidermal. They started off as modest dry patches of skin on the inside of my elbows. But my response was brutal: the venom which had been loosed on my hands was now vented on to the larger canvas of my arms, and I began to attack my body. Paradise was proving elusive.

One day after yet another bruising telephone row with my mother I made an appointment to see a psychotherapist. It seemed an enormously bold step – it was not part of our culture. My parents and their friends prized self-reliance and regarded seeking help as an admission of failure. Plenty of people I knew were in therapy (eventually, in my part of North London, almost everyone I met turned out to be either analyst or analysand) but my fantasies of psychotherapy were wholly punitive – a forbidding, ageing, paternalistic man hovering out of sight behind the couch, exposing undreamt-of badness.

The initial few weeks were a revelation. It had never occurred to me that there could be two different perspectives – my parents' and mine – coexisting in the world and that mine might be perfectly legitimate. I had no inkling of the possibility of, let alone necessity for, psychological boundaries, places beyond which others couldn't enter without invitation, and so naturally it had never dawned on me that I might be entitled to them. To me, private had always been equivalent to secret: my parents were coterminous with me – we were unicellular, an atom. Now fission was being proposed.

But alongside these discoveries, the scratching intensified. It was now turning into some private, shameful, almost erotic release. I tried desperately to police the urge to scratch but it was always stronger. Then, heart throbbing, I would tear at my arms until the blood ran and the carpet was stippled with skin. In its violence it was like the shower scene in *Psycho*, and as it subsided I felt like a murderer after a frenzied, uncontrolled attack. But as yet I had no clear sense of whom I was trying to kill.

Soon, other parts of my body joined my arms as targets, and these sessions of self-injury were taking place every day. As I moved further and further from my previous sense of equilibrium (however precarious and illusory), I tried to coerce myself back to physical and mental health. To no avail.

The therapist talked about anger directed inwards, and tried to get me to empty it over her, even inviting me – symbolically – to scratch her. But while I had some intellectual understanding of the concept of transference, I couldn't recognise any anger in my feelings towards her, nor even in the scratching. In fact I had no idea what frankly faced anger felt like at all; it was a flavour I had never knowingly tasted.

I began to feel uncomfortable almost all the time. My body became a prickly thing, constantly drawing attention to itself. I wanted to divest myself of my skin, slip out of it like a starched dress left standing, while my self crept away to hide. The therapist, arguing that skin marked the frontier between I and not-I, suggested that perhaps for me that frontier had never really existed, and now I was trying to scratch what little there was of it away. Indeed, my skin no longer seemed able to keep what was inside in. I struggled to present an unagitated, unblemished face to the world, but my body mutinied. At night I had dreams of pulling away peeling wallpaper from the walls, exposing cracked and uneven plaster beneath.

My rage towards my parents, interned for decades, began to venture out, and it felt utterly consuming and murderous. The scratching extended upwards, into view, on to my neck. Sometimes even my eyelids and the skin under my eyes turned red and scurfy too, and had to be scoured furiously. But if my unconscious self was trying to articulate its distress, it spoke in a language my conscious self couldn't comprehend, much less converse in. Indeed I invested a lot of energy in hiding what was going on, simulating normalcy despite wearing dark glasses in winter and long sleeves in hot summer. I was usually scarved to the chin, sometimes with my head so immobile because of my now permanently sore neck that I must have looked as if I were frightened of it falling off.

Though convinced of the utter iniquity of my self-mutilation, at the same time I was almost disinterestedly fascinated by the serum and scabs which formed daily and which I daily destroyed. It seemed vaguely fitting that my outside was now beginning to look as scabrous as my inside must have felt for so long, though I was far more aware of the need to prevent any of the inside badness seeping out. Yet it never occurred to me to reduce my work or social activities in any way. On the contrary they intensified: at one time during this period I was writing three weekly columns, as well as doing other freelance work and broadcasting, all between regular bouts of scratching and while feeling almost constantly abject. A runner-up to a journalism award (for work done in Year Two of misery), I attended the awards ceremony with thick pats of make-up to conceal my scarlet, flaky eyes. I permitted myself no respite from going and doing.

But at the same time none of my former palliatives seemed any longer to work. Quite soon after starting therapy I learned that I'd gained a distinction in my M.Sc. In the old days this kind of achievement would have pumped me with confidence and vitality; now it barely registered. I focused entirely on my symptoms – all I wanted was for them to go away. It was as if I'd pressed the piano pedal which shifts the keyboard, and nothing any longer was in the right place.

Yet I was never tempted to return to the dermatologist. I knew that if I did so without facing the underlying reasons for the problem, the symptoms might disappear for a few years but then they would surely reappear. So I went instead to a homeopath. I also realised that, beyond the symptoms, there was no returning to my former self: it would not be able to contain my insistent, dissonant new emotions. Through all my despair (which was considerable, often overwhelming), I maintained some sort of small, vague, but palpable long-term hope that I would eventually emerge healthier.

Although close friends knew what was going on, I managed to conceal it from colleagues and professional contacts. Occasionally, to acquaintances I thought might be sympathetic, I referred obliquely to an 'emotional crisis'. A colleague at a party, after getting me to elaborate, told me that I was the only person she knew who could relay such a tale with a broad beam on her face. (That, of course, was part of the problem.)

In my search for the instant solution I tried a bioenergetics weekend. I'd never had much time for touchy-feely therapies – partly through fear, but also because I was drawn to the more orthodox one-to-one psychotherapy I was now in. Gestalt cushion-bashing and primal screaming in the company of ten other neurotics seemed to me far too embarrassing and parodiable (as well as intolerably un-unique).

But, early on the first morning, when the therapist invited anyone who wanted to work on something particular to step inside the circle, I found myself volunteering. And through carrying out some simple but tiring physical gesture again and again, I began to sob and cry so uninhibitedly about being bad that it must have seemed as if I were an old hand in the self-exposure business. Secretly I was a little proud of myself, and it was genuinely cathartic. Yet it also left me with absurd fantasies of an instantaneous 'cure'. I'd seen so many Hollywood movies about repressed traumas solved after a single dramatic therapeutic revelation that I really believed that my problems too might immediately right themselves. It worked in Hitchcock's *Spellbound*, so why not with me? But it wasn't to be.

My parents, meanwhile, were bewildered by my growing disintegration, and dealt with it by ignoring it. On one occasion we arranged to have lunch in a Czech club in West Hampstead. I arrived grim-faced after a scratching session, bundled in scarves barely hiding a bloodied neck, my arms stiff and purulent. But my parents acted as if everything were quite normal, even trying to quip their way through the lunch, though this only served to inflame my rage, because by now I desperately wanted them to acknowledge my distress.

Yet I craved something they were in no position to give. We were so undifferentiated, so merged that what one felt, all felt: it was as if we held shares in each other's dejection and delight. If they admitted my despair, they would in some sense be experiencing it themselves. And they'd had quite enough of their own.

(Indeed, when, a few years earlier, my sister had lain in a hospital bed, miscarrying her first child at twenty-four weeks, her overriding preoccupation had been not her own distress, but how she was going to tell our parents and how devastated *they* would be.)

In some inadmissible way I think I gained a grim satisfaction from my wretchedness. If children always try to compete with their parents, in this case it had been no contest: we knew, from the first, that our mother's suffering would always exceed, and be more legitimate than, ours – her experience rendered everything else petty. But now I had some misery of my own, and I wanted to force them to acknowledge its existence and authenticity.

After years of my scratching, a close friend asked whether the place on my inside forearm that I was repeatedly injuring wasn't the same place, indeed the very same arm, where my mother's concentration camp number was inked. I was astonished – it had never occurred to me. But I couldn't believe that the unconscious could go in for such crude symbolism, the kind you find in made-for-TV movies – it seemed like a base attempt to endow my own flimsy desolation with historical gravitas and dignify it by reference to my mother's. (I remain unconvinced.)

On the other hand, years later, when my daughter was in nursery and my arms long past healed, a little friend of hers gave her mother a transfer. As we were leaving the nursery the next day, the mother pulled up her left sleeve to reveal laughingly the transfer in that same place on the inner elbow. I gasped, shocked that such a part of the body could be thought innocent, and that a tattoo – however temporary and childish – could be applied in jest.

While the therapy was starting to validate all kinds of states and emotions, it was also freeing a terrible sense of anxiety, which struck most forcibly first thing in the morning when my defences were probably still slumbering. It was a primitive, terrible feeling of unsafeness. I tried to scratch it away.

By now I could scarcely get out of bed, let alone out of the house; I was caught in a spiral of distress. Despite all my attempts to control myself, the scratching came to stand for the recalcitrant part of myself, those particles which refused to comply and which I was no longer able to extirpate. At the same time my attempts to expel my parents from a zone where they had no place to be seemed like a giant act of aggression, which would surely be punished. I was all anger, and simultaneously frantic to protect my parents from my rage. I felt bad about feeling bad, which made me feel even worse.

I had two recurring fantasies. In one I was like a jelly which hadn't set: if you took away the mould I just dribbled away. The jelly mould seemed to embody the rigid, prescriptive side of me – the unyielding bully who kept me in check, myself as Nazi. But without it I felt utterly uncontained, as though I wouldn't cohere. The other fantasy was of being in a vast, dark vat, on to whose sides I was clinging for dear life. If I let go, I would surely drown.

The therapist identified a life-and-death struggle. In some way this was gratifying – it *did* feel as if my crisis was somehow about my ability to survive, and to have her acknowledge this without derision or disapproval (I wasn't in a concentration camp, so how could I possibly be struggling to survive?) was itself extraordinary, and profoundly legitimating. Yet I couldn't help believing that such thoughts were blasphemous. There were no real threats to my life, at least not external, but my mother's life had been full of them.

I became increasingly inert. My posture, which had never been great, deteriorated. My shoulders were now permanently hunched over, as if I wanted to fold myself up into a ball and roll away. Since most of the sensations I was experiencing were so ghastly, I longed to be insensate. It seemed as though I'd receded into a small corner of myself.

I also discovered in myself great sumps of despair, and began to comprehend my old excessive jollity: it must have served as protection against a flood of anxiety and depression.

My parents and I were now mostly locked in combat. My father dismissed any kind of self-scrutiny as 'philosophy', my mother refused to allow that my difficulties might in any way be connected with her experience, as if such a link would constitute some criticism of her. 'I survived the war and I didn't have to see a therapist,' she would sometimes say, sending me delirious with rage.

But very occasionally I saw another side of my mother, what I thought of as her adult mode. It was so unreachably sad that I actually preferred the taunting, battling side, however bad it made me feel.

I also began to see what a talky lot we were, how much we busied ourselves with words and feats, how intolerably empty we found silence.

And I had the odd, astonishing, drunken glimpse of some possible future time when my behaviour might match my feelings, where what I showed was what I thought, not what I thought I should think. I even fantasised about being rude.

Already I was getting slightly bolder in my relationships. I'd always been an affirmer: if somebody in conversation said something foolish, I'd readily join them in their foolishness – I could tolerate my own concealed embarrassment better than open disagreement or the unsupportive role. But about six months into my therapy, at a planning meeting of a TV series for which I was a consultant, a producer came out with the kind of half-baked comment which she made regularly and with absolute confidence. And this time, instead of endorsing her platitude, I found myself feeling detached: she rambled on and I let her travel alone. Of course no one else noticed, but observing my own reaction and fearing that I might lose my nerve, I silently cheered my decision not to accompany her. It was a totally novel feeling and an exhilarating one.

A year later I was at a dinner party with some young people whom I'd met on holiday and hardly knew. I realised instantly that one of the other guests was Jewish. Halfway through the evening another man, who lived in Golders Green, made a comment about the oily people he saw around him on Saturday mornings. My eye caught that of the other Jew, who then looked away. The conversation, after a short embarrassed silence (our hosts knew there was at least one Jew present), started up again, but I felt my heart palpitating and knew that I must speak. I turned to the man directly and asked him what he meant. Before he had a chance to reply I told him that I was Jewish and that his comments had made me feel uncomfortable.

I hardly heard his answer, as he tried to extricate himself; I only knew that I'd confronted someone directly. Later on in the evening, sluiced with drink and dope, I had a panic attack: feeling sick and anxious I glanced round for someone to look after me, but no one seemed suitable. I think my modest little action had terrified me.

But such changes were slow, and overshadowed by something devastating which happened in the meantime: P and I split up, seemingly over an affair he was having.

The real reason, I was convinced, was that what he saw when I finally allowed him close was too terrible – I imagined him like someone in a Ralph Bateman cartoon running for the exit, crying, 'One glimpse of what's in there is enough.' In fact our split, though overdetermined, certainly wasn't due to an excess of intimacy. The opposite in fact: mired as I was in my own misery, I was now no longer emotionally accessible in any way.

After the break-up I felt worse than ever. It was as though someone had pulled away a vital, plump internal organ and left a dessicated hole. My parents, having denounced him for causing me pain, refused to mention his name again. But I wouldn't acquiesce in this symbolic annihilation and, for the first time, allowed myself to feel misery in all its variety. Like a grieving Arab widow, I keened.

J OSEF KARPF: After the war ended I worked hard for the Treasury in Warsaw. In 1946 friends told me that my brother Mundek, who was living in Kraków, knew nice people there. Also, I hadn't seen my brother since Lublin. So I went to Kraków and was introduced to Natalia, and of course I fell in love with her. I saw a very attractive woman: I didn't know what she'd been through, though I heard that her husband had been killed and she'd been in camps. Later, when I learned that she was a musician, it was too late already!

I remember very well how we met. We'd arranged to meet at a coffee house but met on the street on the way there. She was poorly dressed but very good-looking. I thought that I wanted to marry her. I was almost forty-six, but I didn't consider myself old – having survived Russia, I wasn't old. I came back two weeks later, and the third time I went there we became engaged. I went to her concert when she played the Tchaikovsky Piano Concerto in March: it was a great success, a whole crowd of people whom I knew were there, it was a great event.

I was new-born after the war, a new life, it was again self-imposed amnesia. Fortunately, my parents hadn't been alive when the war had started. I didn't meet a lot of people I'd known before the war – most had been killed. From my family 120 people had been killed – aunts and uncles and cousins and children.

Everybody in Poland knew in 1946 that the Russians were there, though they didn't disclose it in so many words, and the government was only pinkish. I wanted to leave, but to stay in Europe – I wanted to come to London.

We were married on April 7. I was no longer alone. Natalia came to live in Warsaw. She had no possessions. I wanted to have children and knew that Natalia wanted it even more than me. Most people who survived the war wanted to have children as soon as they could after the war, when they felt settled. Natalia cooked on one ring there and played the piano.

I got posted to London. We left Poland in April 1947: we were very glad to be leaving, we hoped that it was for ever.

NATALIA KARPF: We didn't know at the time (somebody from the village told us later) that the day before the Germans left, the Hauptsturmführer had wanted to take us all on to the hill and shoot us. But the mayor of this little village was a decent man and he said, 'You can't do it. I'm responsible here for this place, and the front is near: if any harm comes to these women, it's my responsibility.' And he saved our life.

When we realised that the Germans had run away we sat watch in shifts to see if they were going to come back, or the Russians or English would come. Then we learned that not far away there was a train standing full of food, and Jelinek and some other women went to it with buckets and got some meat and other food, because the Germans didn't leave us any food. Otherwise we would have starved.

We ate the food but, though we were so hungry, we didn't eat much because we were frightened. Some women got very ill and some died of diarrhoea, because when you're so hungry and dehydrated and you start eating a lot you can die. We knew that.

At five a.m. on 8 May 1945 a blond officer in a red jacket on a white horse with a Russian flag rode in and when he saw 300 women alive, he started crying: we were the first camp with people left alive in this district – in the others they'd all been murdered. They brought two lorries with masses of clothes, furs, and food, and we warned the women – don't eat much because you'll get sick. But they didn't listen.

I said to Recia, 'I was a very good pianist before the war. We'll go into the village and find a piano and I'll play for you.' When we got there all the houses were unlocked – not one person was in the village. All the Germans had escaped and left their houses open. We went to a doctor's house, and there on the ground floor was an upright piano. So I sat down, but I had stiff fingers and I couldn't play, only a little bit. Recia must have thought, 'Poor girl – she thought she could play the piano.' I was very upset. But while we were there Russian officers came in, and they heard me playing a little bit. They said to us in Russian, 'Tonight we have a very big dinner here, and you are invited to come and sit with us, and we'll give you to eat and drink and you'll play the piano.' We said we'd come.

We went back to the house in the evening: they were laying a big table on the first floor with a white tablecloth, and a lot of food and vodka. I was still wearing the black Auschwitz dress, and the officer who sat next to me paid me compliments, that I'm beautiful – nebech, how I looked, terrible, thin, and pale! Helunia sat next to him, with another officer next to her, and they gave us to drink, and every time they stood and said 'Na Żdorove!' (Cheers!) and 'Stalin!', they didn't notice us pouring it out on the floor. I didn't have a single drink, because I knew if I had a drink I'd be finished – I'd be sick and I didn't know what would happen. At eight o'clock in the evening, they announced that the war had just ended. But there was still curfew, and we told them we had to be back in the camp at ten o'clock. Next to me sat a young, very good-looking officer, and also at the table was the General (a Jew) because here, in that doctor's villa, which was the nicest house in the village, was the headquarters of the Russian party.

I played a little bit and they sang. Helunia and I ate like

a bird because we were so terrified of eating. The officer
asked me if I was married, I said yes, but that I hadn't
heard from my husband since the beginning of the war.
He said, 'I'm sure he's not alive – you come with me to
Russia.' I laughed. And then I said to him, 'Now we have
to go back.' And he said, 'Now? It's half past ten or eleven,
we can't go back, you have to sleep here.' He showed us
into a room and I told Hela quickly to remove the key
from the door so we couldn't get locked in. We heard
some screams from other women in other rooms, but these
two young officers were very decent: they said, 'Go to
sleep' and we said, 'No, we are going to sit the whole night,
we're not going to sleep.' So they said, 'You don't want
to sleep? We'll sleep.' And they lay down and slept while
we sat up. At five o'clock we heard the cock crow, so we
shook them and said, 'Now you can take us back to the
camp.' And they did, and on the way Helunia threw away
the key.

When we came to the camp we were told that we were
lucky that we hadn't been there because it had been
terrible: the ordinary Russian soldiers had come and were
drunk and tried their luck with the girls, chasing them
and jumping over the bunks. Recia told us that there were
screams and horrible scenes. The Russians gave us rifles
and said, 'Shoot the Germans', but we said, 'No, we're not
going to do what the Germans did.'

The next day we decided to leave the camp, the five of
us. Sticking together made us stronger. We had nothing
in our hands, only what we wore, the clothes they'd put
on us in Auschwitz. Open Russian lorries passed us, so we
hitched a lift to the next place, Freudenthal. I said that
the first thing we must do is look for a chemist shop and
get some charcoal, in case we get diarrhoea from food. We
found a barred chemist shop and managed to push our way
in and discovered some charcoal. Everywhere was deserted
– it was all like ghost towns. Then we found a flat open

in Freudenthal with a whole pantry full of food –
marvellous, pickled mushrooms, rice, jars of meat. So I
said, 'moderately and slowly.' But we were terrified at night
of the Russian soldiers: they were wild people – they hadn't
had women for God knows how long, and here were nice
young women. So again one of us had to keep watch
every few hours and, because there were no keys, we
pushed a cupboard against the door so that nobody could
come in. That was May 9.

The next day we hitchhiked a bit further east towards
Kraków. And at last we came to Bohumin, the border, not
far from where Jelinek came. We arrived at midday in this
Russian open lorry, and saw Russian officers in the square.
Suddenly Jelinek got up and started gesturing wildly – we
thought she'd gone crazy. But one of the very good-
looking young officers, a colonel, rushed over and
embraced her: it was her first cousin, a Czech. He had
friends there, and he put us up with a very nice Czech
family. We could cook there, and he gave us a sack of
flour because bread was scarce. He paid them to keep us
for three days so that we could recover a little bit, and
gave Jelinek 1000 złoty, which was like £2–3 today.

Meanwhile, some friends of Jelinek in the same town
gave her news of her husband, Dolek, and her older son
Jerzy. One day we went out, and when we came back she
was lying on the bed and crying terribly that Jerzy had
been taken away and killed and never came back. He was
fourteen.

Some women went into flats and took away suitcases full
of clothes, but I didn't want the clothes of the Germans.
The women said, 'But they're yours – they robbed you of
all this.' I said, 'I don't want it.' Nor did Hela. What did
I take? A small sack of sugar, nothing else. I also changed
from my black Auschwitz dress into the dress of a fifteen-
year-old girl – that was just right for my figure because I
was so thin.

We were so happy I can't tell you, and feeling already stronger, though Jelinek was still very sad. We reached Katowice and our eyes couldn't believe it – suddenly we see a patisserie with cakes, cream cakes. The others stood in front of that shop and didn't want to leave, and I said, 'Come on. We can't eat any cakes, we haven't got any money.' We were walking towards the railway station to find out if there was a train which could take us to Kraków. And Helunia and Jelinek said, 'Excuse us for a second – we'll be back soon.' They disappeared; Recia, Cesia, and I stayed behind. And suddenly they come from the patisserie with five cream cakes. They paid 500 złoty out of the 1000 we had for five cream cakes! They said, 'We couldn't resist, it was impossible – we had to go back.' And we ate the cakes: it was like heaven in mouth. But now we had to find some way to get to Kraków for only 500 złoty, which was nothing.

(At this point the recordings ended, and we only resumed again nineteen months later, by which time – extraordinarily – I seemed to have forgotten almost everything that my mother had told me the previous year. So we unwittingly covered a lot of the same ground again, until we finally began to move forward.)

At the station there was such chaos and we found out that there were no trains to Kraków. But suddenly there was a rumour that a goods train to Kraków was coming. The others went and talked to the guard to see if he'd let us travel in the guards' van for the 500 złoty. He did, but it took us a whole night to get to Kraków instead of an hour and a half. On the way we met some Jews and they asked, 'Where are you going?' and we said, 'We're going to Kraków.' They said, 'You're absolutely crazy – you're going back to Poland, to these anti-Semites? Why don't you go somewhere else?' We said, 'Where shall we go, to Germany?

We can't go to Germany.' They said, 'This is the Russian part now. Or go to the American part of Germany.' Many people went to Sweden – they were taken there by the Red Cross, they never went back to Poland, and they did very well. But we wanted to find family, our people – that's why we went back. I knew that my father wasn't alive, but I hoped that my brother and my husband were.

We arrived at Kraków station, and suddenly sat down and said, 'Where are we going from here? What are our plans, what shall we do?' We had no idea where to go, where to look for people. I had no suitcase, no money: all I had with me was the little sack of sugar. Now we started worrying about money: for a few years, in the camps, we'd had no worries about money! And there, at the station, we met a few Jews we knew who'd come to the station to look for people, to see if they could find anyone arriving on the train. That was 15 May, seven days after the war was over, so whoever survived went to the station to look for people. They kept saying, 'You were stupid to come back, but there's a Jewish office and they have a list of the people who are alive who've come here already.' So Helunia said, 'Cesia and I will go to this office, and the rest of you stay here and wait.' It took them a few hours to come back. Cesia found out that her sister Lusia, her sister-in-law Dziunia, and her nine-year-old son were still alive (he died three weeks after the war had ended, of meningitis, can you believe it?), and that Jelinek's sister-in-law survived and was in Kraków, and that they had a flat. So we went to them: they gave Jelinek one bed, and Helunia and me another bed, and Recia went with Cesia to Lusia.

Kraków looked beautiful – not one house was ruined, it wasn't bombed, nothing. But it felt very strange being back: one was walking in the streets like in a strange place because before the war Kraków had had 65,000 Jews out of a quarter of a million inhabitants. So when you went out, to town, you met people you knew all the time. But now you didn't meet anybody. Nobody.

And I was questioning why me and not the others, how did it happen that I survived?

I discovered that my mother-in-law's flat was occupied, but I went there and said that we were the owners, and that we haven't got where to go, so you must give us at least one room. And they did. But we didn't have where to sleep, there were no beds – we slept on the floor – the windows were shattered. Jelinek found out that Dolek had returned from hiding in Warsaw and was back in Zakopane in their villa, but also that he'd sent Jerzy out for cigarettes and a Pole denounced him and that's why the boy never came back. She could never forgive him for that, that he survived and the child didn't.

AK: Or that she survived and the child didn't.

NK: So she went back to Zakopane. In Kraków, the other people moved out of my flat. There was some of my in-laws' furniture still there, but we didn't have any chairs: when we found out that there were chairs somewhere in a different part of Kraków, each of us carried one chair back to the flat through the whole town!

I felt as though someone had knocked me over the head and I was numb. Later, when you start thinking that your nearest and your dearest were killed in such a terrible way, whole families, hundreds of people from one family – until now I can't . . . When I start thinking of what my poor father suffered before he died, and other members of my family, my brother . . . At least my mother died a natural death – very young, but she wasn't tortured. Can you imagine when you think of your father being pushed into a gas chamber or tortured: how can one get over it, I don't know. I felt depressed, first of all because I was lonely. Helunia met up with [the man who was to become] her husband back in Kraków, and went to Wrocław with him. I felt unhappy about being parted from her – being together with my sister, and not being alone, had helped me survive – but she was happy to find him. It would have been better for her not to find him, maybe she would have still been alive, because if she'd stayed with me she would have come over here to England, and been saved perhaps from this terrible illness [cancer] which she probably got through the terrible shock of coming back from shopping and finding him dead on the floor, thirty-eight years old from a heart-attack in 1947, less than a year after she married him.

In the camp we didn't need any money – yes, we had become institutionalised. In July, I went to Zakopane to work in an orphanage with children whose parents were killed during the war or were missing, and Recia followed. We looked after them. It was a very nice thing to be with the children, and with Recia, and with Jelinek and Dolek not far away – they looked after us and helped us. I felt better and better, I gained weight, and started practising because there was a piano. I thought, 'I'm going to practise the Tchaikovsky Piano Concerto (which I've never played before) because it needs a lot of strength and I must show them that they didn't defeat me, they didn't get me down – I am stronger than before.' In September or October the director of Polish Joint, an international Jewish organisation, came in while I was practising. He said, 'Tell me, what are you doing here?' I said, 'I'm helping out because I haven't got any money and I haven't got an instrument at home, and I don't know what to do with myself after the war.' So he said, 'Don't be stupid, with such playing go back to Kraków and I'll give you a grant of 2500 złoty so that you'll be able to live on it.' So in October I left and went back.

In the meantime Helunia had got into a bombed house in Wrocław and got some men to take out the Blüthner grand piano she found standing there and sent it to me to Kraków – I remember they dropped it when they brought it in. So I could practise. I got in touch with one of my old teachers, and he gave me a job at the music academy, which also paid about 2500 złoty so, together with the grant, I had enough to live modestly on. But a few months later, the poor man from Joint was killed in a plane crash so I never got any more money from them, but by then I'd already started giving piano lessons so I had enough.

Can you imagine, after not playing for nearly six years, I started practising in October 1945 and on 17 March 1946 I played the Tchaikovsky Piano Concerto with the Kraków Philharmonic Orchestra. That was my first public engagement after the war, in a big hall which seated 2000 people, and it was full. I'd gone for an audition with this orchestra and they engaged me straight away. I didn't have a dress, but I met a woman through Cesia and Lusia who lent me a most beautiful blue evening dress. And six weeks later on 3 May I played the Chopin Piano Concerto No.1, and both concerts were relayed by Polish Radio. Recia was still in Zakopane and listened on the wireless: a few months before I'd told her that I was a pianist and she didn't believe me, and suddenly now she heard me on the radio playing the Tchaikovsky Piano Concerto – she was thrilled.

My playing was completely different after the war: more strength, I played more like a man, and I wasn't at all nervous because I didn't care – later the nerves came back! And if you have emotional upheavals it changes your playing completely: I remember playing once as a seventeen-year-old girl with an orchestra and a nice, very musical German woman came up to me and said, 'You are an excellent pianist, such a gifted girl, but you must fall in love or go through some emotions – then you'll play well.' I remembered her words all my life.

119

When I came back from Zakopane I felt terribly lonely. I was stuck in three rooms on my own – the only family I had there was Lusia and Cesia, to whom I went every second night. I sat every night and cried, praying to God that my husband should come back – I still didn't know that he'd died, but in the middle of January 1946 I went to a clairvoyant who looked at my hand. I wasn't wearing any rings, because the Germans had taken them, and my hands were still a bit ruined from the war. And she said to me, 'You're an artist, and you'll go abroad and you'll make a career. You were married but don't think of your husband any more because he got killed by a bomb.' Two weeks later his cousin called on me and told me the same news. 'But,' she said, 'you'll shortly meet a very cultivated, kind person whom you'll marry and with whom you'll go abroad and you'll have two children.'

Lusia and Cesia saw how lonely I was. They said that a friend of theirs had a friend, Josef Karpf, who was going on a diplomatic mission to Canada and wanted to get married; they said they'd introduce me to him. I said, 'Don't be silly, are you going to be a matchmaker?' Finally I agreed and his brother wrote to him to come and meet me. He wrote back, 'I've been waiting for forty-six years so I shall wait another week – I can't come next week, I'll come in a fortnight.' I had a pair of shoes made (my first new pair after the war) and my first coat, brown with a red fox collar, a blue dress, and a hat with a feather. I thought the idea of being introduced to someone was so funny.

On February 2, Lusia's husband took me to meet him for tea: in the distance we saw Josef's brother and Josef in a coat with fur lapels and a green hat – very tall and slim, elegant and distinguished-looking. He was a Councillor in the Treasury in Warsaw. I was a bit embarrassed. We met them on the street and we went to a coffee house for an hour or two. I was talking, he was quiet, listening to me.

Then he said, could he accompany me home, about five minutes away. And before we said goodbye, he said, 'Could I invite you tonight to a dinner and dance?' So I said, 'Yes', and I met him in the evening again, it was a Saturday evening – he used to come by train to Kraków overnight on Friday, and take the overnight train back to Warsaw on Sunday. He chose the wine and I thought, 'This is a man of the world – I've never been out with such a man before!' He took me home, and wanted to kiss me, but I didn't want to. He wanted to meet me again the next day, and we did.

On Friday February 15, I played on the radio, and he sent me a beautiful basket of flowers thanking me for the wonderful broadcast – which he never heard because he was on the train! We met the next day, when he said, 'I'm ready – will you marry me?' I said, 'I'm not ready yet.' On my birthday, February 27, he sent me another fantastic basket of flowers; by then I was looking forward to meeting him again.

When I saw him, I told him that. Later he came to fetch me, and I played something for him. And then he asked me, 'Did you know Gisela Rieser?' I told him that she was my first teacher when I was four and a half (she'd seemed old to me then, but she must have been only in her early twenties). He said, 'She was my sister-in-law: she was married to my brother Milek.' Then I remembered that when she'd got married her surname was Karpf: I visited her and met her husband. I told him I'd gone to see them in their chemist shop on the other side of the Vistula, and he told me that they were both killed in Płaszów before I arrived there. She would have been so happy that I became her sister-in-law if she'd survived. Then he told me that he had my name in his safe: one day a matchmaker had come to them with my name saying that I was a rich young woman called Natalia Weissman and would he meet

me (and I hadn't even known about it). But he hadn't
wanted to.

He asked me, 'Can I stop calling you Pani Hubler (Mrs
Hubler, the formal mode of address) can I call you "ti"
(you, the informal mode)?' I said, 'You can say as you wish.'
And he took that as an agreement to marry him (which I
hadn't understood it to be). When we arrived at his
brother's, he said, 'You can congratulate us, we're
engaged.' It came as such a shock to me, I felt as though
I'd been hit over the head, I felt bewildered, but I didn't
protest.

The day before, when I'd got back from the music
academy, a friend came to see me. And when she saw the
card on the basket of flowers, she said, 'My goodness,
you've got more mazel than verstand [more luck than
judgement]. You don't know who Josef Karpf is and was:
before the war there wasn't a girl good enough for him,
he was so choosy, he's from such a wonderful family, he's
a man you don't find very often – kindness itself.' So I'd
started thinking about it.

We all went out to celebrate. But I was scared. I thought,
'I haven't looked after a man for so many years, and now
I'll have to start darning socks again, and cooking.' We'd
only spent five days together before we got engaged.
We decided not to wait: he said, 'We're not children
any more, you've been married before, and I'm
forty-six.' So we decided to get married in one month's
time.

I didn't feel well the next day and I had a temperature.
He came with a bottle of champagne and a huge box of
chocolates. Then he went out and bought me some
medicine and I felt very happy – I thought that I'd be
protected.

AK: The day before you'd thought that you'd have to look

after him, and then you thought maybe he'd look after you.

NK: Yes, yes. And he looked after me and protected me all his life.

(At this point, the original tapes ran out, so we resumed recording in October 1995.)

NK: I didn't have a penny. He gave me money for my dress for the wedding – a very nice grey suit and blouse, made by the best salon in Kraków after the war, and a picture hat – and some other outfits. We got married on 7 April 1946. The aunt of my first husband (whom I'd taken into my flat after the war because she had nowhere to live) arranged the whole reception in my flat – she cooked for days. All our friends and family came – there were about thirty or forty of us: we danced, and we drank, and we ate a lot, until late night. I was happy and elated, though I wasn't in love yet – that only came later, the longer I was with him – but I liked him. He was very gentle and soft-spoken. I felt that I am in heaven, that something like this could happen again. It was a very exciting time – my career had started up again with wonderful reviews, my life had totally changed: life after the war moved so quickly into completely different ways from before, that I pushed the war away – I started a new life.

The day after the wedding, we left for Zakopane. It was completely different from my first honeymoon there, which had been in winter, whereas this was already spring. I was very, very happy to be with such a man – I felt very comfortable with him, although I'd only known him for five days, within six weeks!

After the honeymoon I moved to Warsaw with him, to Praga (a suburb) where he had a small room on the fourth floor in the flat of a couple with children: there was no water during the day, only at night. Warsaw looked terrible, completely bombed, though Praga still had a few blocks of flats standing. We slept on a couch which was so narrow that when one of us turned the other had to turn too! It was impossible to sleep on it comfortably, but we knew that it was only temporary – we hoped to go abroad. But in that small room I had an upright piano. I invited his colleagues from the Treasury and prepared food and baked cakes in the kitchen of that lady: they'd ask for what they wanted to hear and I'd play for them. I also gave some recitals. I'd said to Josef, 'I want a child straight away' and then I got pregnant – I felt elated and he was thrilled.

Josef was sent to the Polish Embassy in London. I felt relieved to be leaving Poland: I felt uncomfortable there after the war. When we heard about the Kielce pogrom in 1946, we felt terrible anger, rage that out of three million Jews who were in Poland, only a small number came back, and that something like this could happen – and there were only about 100 or 150 Jews in Kielce at the time. I wanted to get away from there. If we hadn't come to England, we would probably have gone to Israel, like his brother later did. We decided that if he was sent abroad we wouldn't come back. I felt no sadness to leave Poland, only at the thought of leaving my sister, but I hoped that she would come and join us. All the Jews were beginning to leave: I was pregnant and I didn't want to have children in Poland, because of the anti-Semitism, because of what we'd been through there.

So we left for England.

4

The break-up with P only confirmed what, viscerally, I'd always supposed: that I wasn't allowed to have. One day in June I reached my lowest point. It was a Saturday, warm and bright. The world was busy: everyone seemed purposeful, or frisking with friends. I kept seeing patently imperfect people whom other people seemed to like and even tolerate being intimate with. I scanned the faces of couples in the street as if they might give off information about what kept them together.

I couldn't bear to be outside. It seemed unsafe and exposed: I felt like a character on an overlit stage trying to avoid the audience. I also needed privacy to claw at my neck. I retreated to my bedroom, and half pulled down the blind. The centre of life seemed to have migrated elsewhere. I slumped against the side of the bed, in a pool of misery.

The phone rang. It was someone who'd invited me to a party then taking place. She wanted to know if I was OK and offered to come and collect me. I didn't want to talk, and knew I couldn't sustain a convincing sunny politeness for more than half a minute. I told her I was all right and managed to get off the phone. I waited for night.

But while feeling so bereft and abandoned was terrible, in some curious way it also seemed fitting. I'd always envied my parents their suffering. This was so obviously shocking that I couldn't have admitted it, had I even been conscious of it. It didn't mean that I underestimated the horror of the war, or that I masochistically sought out pain, only that their terrible experiences seemed to diminish – even to taunt – anything bad which happened to us. In its drama, enormity, and significance, their war could never be matched. We would always be children in a playpen of misery.

But I also envied their suffering because it was so excluding and unshareable. It had originated before we were born, wasn't caused by us and, however much we tried, we would never be able to take it away. I wanted to force an entry into their closed world of grief. My whole life had been an act of solidarity – an attempt never to have more pleasure, fun, or success than they had had (while at the same time needing to be extravagantly happy and successful in order to keep them buoyant – no wonder I was confused). It was as if I'd been running in some perverse relay race and had gladly grasped the baton of unhappiness.

That was one reason why I'd felt comfort in discomfort, and had perched on the bed without back support, or felt guilt when leaving work at the end of the day. And why P had seemed so unavailable. It was also why I always (as my father put it) chose the path of most resistance. If good things came too easily I felt I didn't deserve them; I wanted to have to struggle, I was terrified of having. Maintaining myself at the edge of life was a way of making common cause with my mother – to have jumped in would have seemed like abandoning her. And the awful irony of it was that my mother herself was incomparably vibrant, and would have been appalled at this mandatory self-banishment.

Yet through the scratching and now the loss of P, it was as if I'd finally managed to prise off some particle of my mother's suffering and make it my own. I'd grafted on to myself a bit of her pain.

Now, as well as feeling like a victim, I'd also acquired

something to feel a victim about – I'd found an objective correlative (the best I could manage). After what seemed like only the briefest flirtation with having, I was back down among the have-nots, gazing enviously at other people's houses, their relationships and, most of all, their children. I felt as excluded as I had during adolescence, only this time I wasn't able to work it away – achievement no longer functioned as solace.

But, miserable though I was, wisps of insight were also appearing, and my own part in the split-up with P became apparent. One day, quite suddenly, I recognised that I'd always confused being intimate with another person and merging with them, having regarded any kind of separateness or difference as threatening. One dyad (with my parents) had been replaced by another (with P). We'd liquesced: two separate people had melted into one. (He, of course, had acquiesced. But that's another story, his.)

My skin meanwhile temporarily improved, then worsened again; my relationship with my parents remained combustible. I often hated my mother for all sorts of reasons which had nothing to do with the Holocaust and then, when I still didn't feel allowed to hate her properly, I hated her all the more.

But out of all the confusion came a new friendship, with an American woman herself emerging from a difficult period. Unprecedentedly, I allowed her sight of my distress, and it was liberating. And slowly, as it does after a relationship ends, the centre returned to my life.

Quite independently of this, so did P. He resumed contact and we tentatively began to meet. Through these encounters I became conscious, possibly for the first time, of my overwhelming urge to look after him. Sometimes I longed to shrink him to the size of a toy soldier, wrap him in cotton wool, and put him in my pocket for safe keeping; it was horribly redolent of my feelings for my parents. But alongside it, and warring with it, now came great flames of rage with which I regularly tried to singe him – my aptitude for anger had clearly increased – though he remained admirably uninflammable.

On one occasion we were heading for a pub in Maida Vale and having a row (unrelated to the break-up). When the argument was ostensibly over I still felt angry, but instead of hastily dowsing my anger as I normally would have, I decided to let it abate in its own time. We sat silently in the pub, with me in a state of shock at my own audacity, and regularly, anxiously, checking to see if the anger had subsided. Eventually it did, and we'd both survived it.

We were learning to fight, and felt proud (if slightly self-conscious) of our emerging ability to tolerate dissent and difference, our growing capacity each to stand our ground. We got close once more, but this time also separate.

My parents' reaction was less sanguine: P was *persona non grata* all over again. He was excluded from family gatherings and once, memorably, collecting me to drive us down to his mother's for a Christmas dinner straight after my family's Christmas lunch, he was forced to lurk in the penumbra at the end of my sister's drive like some Victorian psychopath.

At the same time I was becoming noticeably less permeable, more reluctant to play the chameleon. Increasingly, with friends, when a restaurant was being chosen or a novel discussed, I dared venture what I thought instead of taking on their preferences and values. And in 1985, at a sociology conference, I terrified myself with my outspokenness.

For several years this annual conference had coincided with Yom Kippur, so that I (and other Jews, including those as minimally observant as me) hadn't been able to attend. When, that year, it fell on a different date and I did go, I resolved to raise the issue. As the annual general meeting drew to a close, and 'any other business' was called, I raised my hand and wobbled into action. I argued that since it wouldn't be thought appropriate to hold the conference on

Christmas Day, steps should be taken to avoid it coinciding with the holiest day in the Jewish calendar.

The chairwoman seemed discomfited and tried to deflect me. The date of the conference for the next several years had already been fixed, she responded, but if I gave her a list of the dates of Yom Kippur in the more distant future they would see what they could do to avoid a clash, but could give no promises. Nor did they voice any expression of regret that potential conference participants had been excluded.

I persisted, some unaccountably bold part of me determined to have its say. I asked for a real commitment to end the clash and, as a sign of that commitment, I wanted them when fixing future conferences to look up the dates of Yom Kippur themselves (I could tell them where), just as they presumably routinely looked up the dates of Christian festivals or made a note of potentially clashing academic events.

By now, people were beginning to fidget uncomfortably, some craning their necks to see who was carrying on so. My intransigence amazed and half-appalled me: surely it was time to stop – I'd made my point. But evidently it was more than just a point that I wanted to make. After my decades of mutism, this speaking out produced its own risky but heady sense of momentum. It was a dizzying experience to hear myself calmly insist on acknowledgement.

Did I imagine it, or were those in that room whom I knew to be Jewish shrinking just a centimetre, their bodies braced as far as decently possible away from mine? Certainly, apart from one Jewish sociologist who spoke wholeheartedly in support, there now seemed only rows of unyielding heads. And yet, heart battering, I was undaunted, perhaps even fired, by their embarrassment, though the chair muttered some compromise and the meeting was disbanded.

For me the discussion continued in five successive conversations. A Jewish woman, clearly embarrassed by my performance, said she couldn't understand all the fuss – Yom

Kippur was nothing to her – and anyway the assembly's indifference would have been similar had the issue been a non-Jewish one. The specificity, the Jewishness, of the topic and my reaction to it both seemed to unnerve her.

A friend said she was sorry she hadn't endorsed my argument, and maybe the fact that she had a Jewish father made her feel more vulnerable than she'd realised. The chairwoman joined us and apologised, offering to introduce the changes I'd asked for, while another sociologist (his job being the analysis of societies and cultural beliefs) professed reservations: if Jews were thus conceded to, wouldn't every other religion want the same consideration? (Well, yes: and how many days might that potentially put out of commission – a dozen?)

And finally, a woman I knew slightly came up and thanked me for speaking out (probably the first time in my life that anyone had had occasion to do so). She said, in a trace of a German accent, 'We were always taught not to.' It was only years later, at a memorial meeting for her after her death, that I learned she was a refugee from Nazi Germany, and had come to Britain with the Kindertransport.

One factor which had probably helped embolden me was that, though I attended the conference each year, this year was the first time I'd also presented a paper. It was part of a chapter of a book I was writing, and constituted a kind of academic coming-out. My terror before I gave it transformed, when it was enthusiastically received, into a warming sense of legitimacy. Afterwards, conference participants seemed to treat me like an insider, and later I couldn't decide whether my action at the meeting reflected this new feeling of acceptance or was, on the contrary, an attempt to restore me to the more familiar role of outsider. Either way, I left the conference on a double high.

It was soon replaced by a disabling fear. In the aftermath of these small bursts of success and assertiveness I began to fantasise about having. Perhaps I would be allowed my book,

P, a house, and even a baby, too. The possibility of so much overwhelmed and quite incapacitated me; for weeks I could hardly get out of bed or stop scratching.

That summer, a French friend had come to stay. She was a charming woman whose recent doctoral thesis covered a similar area to my book: we'd shared material and swapped sources several times in the past. This time she mentioned a paper she was writing on a subject allied to that of her thesis but whose scope went beyond it. As it happened I'd researched this subject for my book, too. I had a file of my notes and thoughts on the subject, as well as material from different, sometimes unusual sources, though I was at least a year away from actually writing up those particular chapters. Immediately, in a reflex gesture, I found myself inviting her to peruse my bulging file and copy anything she liked.

The moment I'd made the offer I regretted it, and then felt terrible about my regret. After all, she was a generous woman and would herself, I imagined, have had no hesitation in making the same offer to me. Besides, we were writing in different countries for different readerships, and doubtless we'd interpret the same material in quite different ways. Thus at least I reasoned with myself, badgered myself, all night long, as I tried to expunge the anguish of having given away something which I'd accumulated with such delicious anticipation for my own use, before I myself had enjoyed the benefit of it.

It wasn't so much the fear that she would filch my ideas – after all, I'd freely offered her the file – that upset me. It was the fact that I'd felt compelled to share it in the first place: I was forcibly struck by my almost pathological inability to keep good things for myself alone.

As I wrestled with the situation into the small hours, the solution became ringingly clear. I could tell her that I'd changed my mind, and preferred not to lend her the file until I'd written my own chapters from the material. At first even contemplating such a declaration seemed beyond the pale, but soon it didn't seem such a terrible thing to say. On the one hand, it was unsisterly, mean, competitive. On the other hand, it was how I felt.

So when morning arrived, I told her. She appeared unfazed by this sudden reversal, while I felt elated. It also made me realise how consistently over the years I'd impoverished myself, and then seethed with self-pity at the resulting sparseness in my life; how I'd pass the parcel of good things or experiences that came my way as speedily as if it were a hand grenade, and then wonder why I felt bereft. But perhaps the parcel wasn't quite so incendiary after all, and I might now allow myself to retain it, unwrap it, even keep the prize inside. The idea seemed positively revolutionary.

It was beginning to inflect all my relationships, especially those with women. Over a decade or so I'd accumulated what amounted to a flock of needy women: they were bright, funny, and generous, but also hugely, undeniably needy. I'd felt flattered by their demands: our prolonged phone conversations and trading of confidences had made me feel like a supportive person and an insider. But this promiscuous intimacy had now begun to pall: increasingly I felt like an over-burdened social worker who had constantly to accommodate her clients. I chafed beneath the tyranny of obligatory sisterhood, while regularly having to fend off their rage and disappointment with me.

Gradually I discerned a pattern. I would start off friendships extravagantly, with an implicit promise of unlimited access to my time and sympathy. Then, when someone tried to avail herself of those resources – in abundance, just as I'd invited her to – I'd feel furious, as if she were cleaning me out or sucking me dry. I'd react either by giving grudgingly or, more commonly, by devising ways of not having to give at all. They, in turn, would then feel furious and cheated, as if I'd issued them with a promissory note which, when they tried to cash it, turned out to be worthless. They hated me for reclaiming what I should never have offered in the first place. I urgently needed limits.

Within a very short period of time in 1986, almost all my friendships changed. I sloughed off those which were beyond transformation; other friends drifted away, no doubt in terminal frustration at my repeated failure to deliver. And in other cases I renegotiated the terms of the friendship, so that they became more consonant with my own feelings. At least some of the time I relieved myself of the obligation to look after, and resolved not to offer an iota more than I was willing to give, even if this made me seem mean and withholding. I found I got better and better at this and, though I had fewer close friendships, they were less angry, more realistic, and rather more satisfying.

Things with my parents were changing too, softening on both sides. They'd always been hostile to the possibility that some part of my difficulties might be related to their experiences; having invested so much in the idea of their children as a new beginning, they couldn't bear to think that anything malign from the past had squeezed through. But one day I mentioned that a schoolfriend of my sister had recently described our childhood home as sad, and my mother nodded silently in assent. I checked to make sure that I'd understood her correctly; I had. I became positively jubilant at this fraction of acknowledgement.

Perhaps she'd sensed a reduction in my anger towards her and my father; certainly, I didn't seem to be attacking them quite so much any more. And my therapy was focusing less and less on my relationship with my parents, and more and more on my relationship with myself (which, alas, wasn't quite so gratifying). But P had remained banished from all family gatherings and my parents, though they knew we were back together again, never spoke of him. Then, one day, almost three years after P and I had broken up, my mother rang and declared, unprompted, that she was aware of how hard she and my father had made things for me

over my relationship with P, and she was sorry. I was flabber-
gasted, so overwhelmed by this unprecedented apology that
my first impulse was to protest that it was unnecessary
(though I managed to restrain myself and accept it instead).
On she went, in full reconciliatory bloom, saying that if I
believed P was right for me then they must accept him too,
and could we both come to tea the following week?

I hated myself for being so grateful but at the same time
wanted to reciprocate my parents' largesse (the result, I later
discovered, of several years' discreet but intense lobbying by
my sister, as well as my mother concertedly working on my
father – the domino effect of family pressure). So I went
out and bought the kind of fake fur coat – as thermal a
garment as I could find – which I knew for certain would
warm my parents quite as much as it would warm me.

The appointed day arrived: so did P and I, both of us a
little nervous, and with me wearing the said coat, which
drew many more exclamations from my parents than did
the presence of P. (Everyone seemed relieved to have the
coat to focus on and fuss over. In that single wearing it more
than recouped its cost.) P and I had role-played the event
in advance, allowing for every single scenario except one,
which duly occurred. From my parents, nothing, niente,
zilch, about the intervening three years. Instead they were
immaculately civil as only they knew how. It was a little
unnerving, Dorian Grayish, as if the passage of time had
been erased by an act of will. But relations had been re-
established, and life went on.

Somewhere in this period something else happened. Next
to these other events it was microscopic, a change between
my mother and me so infinitesimal that it would have been
imperceptible to anyone else. I got her to alter her embrace.
One day she hugged me, in her usual intense but abrupt
manner, but instead of allowing her to terminate it so unilat-
erally, I held on to try and make it more open-ended. She
yielded and laughed (as she did each subsequent time), and

in that sweet, slightly self-conscious giggle, I saw several things I hadn't met or noticed in her before: uncertainty, and some sort of recognition of my experience of our joint past. I basked in the warmth of this unlimited embrace, and felt tremendously grateful that both my parents had lived long enough to survive my onslaught – I couldn't imagine how I'd have coped with them dying during my years of attack. It would have confirmed all my fantasies about the murderous power of my rage.

Other, more visible, changes were also taking place. I stopped phoning home every day; I must have begun to trust that my parents could survive without me (and vice versa). I was becoming more able to desist from looking after strangers such as shop assistants and hairdressers. And quite suddenly, after five years, my skin began to heal. Since the scratching hadn't diminished and the healing was taking place all by itself, I had a sense that it was happening from the inside and some central conflict had been resolved. And within six weeks I no longer needed to scratch: my skin had healed altogether, leaving no scars.

But other things seemed unchangeable. Even while I dared believe that my parents' survival might not depend on my proximity, I became certain that my father (who was now eighty-six) would soon die. Until the age of eighty-five he'd been extraordinarily buoyant and robust, walking defiantly fast as if brandishing his energy. But at eighty-six, though he still strode determinedly without a stick, he began to feel weaker and found such signs of fragility intolerable – they angered him and ushered in a deep sense of despondency. The man who'd declared 'Depressed, what's depressed?' now found his own creeping fatigue a source of ineradicable despair. Whenever I saw him, I scanned him for signs of mortality.

In 1986, my sister and I celebrated our parents' fortieth wedding anniversary with a family trip to Paris. Their friends, fellow Polish Jewish Holocaust survivors who made up a small but substantial Parisian community, were holding a party for them. Such a gathering seemed like a triumphant snubbing of the war: there was handsome Tulek, who, abetted by my uncle Mundek, had been instrumental in introducing my parents to each other (and had survived the war by passing himself off as a Polish nobleman); Cesia, who had been with my mother in Płaszów and Auschwitz; her sister Lusia who had spent the war in hiding along with Lusia's sister-in-law Dziunia, also present; and the next generation. It was the first time we'd travelled abroad *en famille* for about sixteen years, and it seemed to me a little unreal, like being an adult wanting to be a child, or as though I were suspended between childhood and adulthood and couldn't go backwards or forwards. When we went out to an anniversary dinner in a restaurant in the Quartier Latin and the lights darkened and they brought out a cake, and my mother smiled thankfully for those four decades and my father disbelievingly (and now perhaps a tad indifferently), I wanted to seal up the moment to prevent it from ebbing away. And fearing that the strength of my father's resolve to stay in the world might be wavering, I also wanted to transfuse him with life. (My sister, by contrast, had what I thought was a breezy confidence in his survival.) For me, the happiness of the occasion was indelibly streaked with anxiety.

All the while there remained a nagging 'what if' quality to my actions: rarely uppermost in my mind, but generally simmering somewhere below was the unanswerable hypothetical question, 'What if I'd been in the war, would I have managed to survive?' In some unconscious sense my life was organised around this speculation, as if the more prodigious the energy I poured into my various activities, the safer I'd be. When I went shopping, I'd covertly search out the most perfect carton, I could never just take the first which presented itself. When I was working, I'd goad myself to excel – anything less was not enough.

But a degree of reflexivity now entered these activities. I became aware of how, in our family, every aspect of our lives was charged with importance: we had no place for trivia, no space for accident or improvisation. When I heard about people who'd left university and just roamed for a while, I felt jealous; I knew that for me this had never been an option – we were too purposeful, each moment of our lives endowed with intensity. To a great extent we hadn't been able to play.

Risk-taking of any kind seemed dangerous because it admitted the possibility of bad things happening, and I had no conception of bad passing by itself, or not lasting for ever. I waged an endless battle against the bad and, in my anxiety that the good might not suffice, I conscripted my every sinew and each experience.

In 1987 I went to interview a leading British psychoanalyst, Marion Milner, whose diary, written fifty years earlier, before she'd trained as an analyst, had just been republished. In it she described a kind of wide-focused gaze, a way of looking at one's surroundings without selection or judgement, an inclusive way of perceiving as opposed to that which organised perceptions around one's own pressing mental categories. I was immensely struck by this and knew exactly what she meant because, very occasionally, I'd experienced it too: the world outside – say, a vista in the park – suddenly just was, it no longer had to be rifled for its information, or for resources to ensure survival, or for endorsement, with everything else screened out. This fleeting experience would leave me calmer and more nourished, but above all it threw into relief just how little I was able to engage with the world outside my head, and how noisy was my own internal world. I remembered once rushing down a street in Oxford and suddenly looking up and seeing the tops of the buildings, and being shocked to discover that anything existed beyond the maelstrom of internal and external busyness, bursting thoughts, and eye-level life. Yet

I rarely permitted myself this broader view, for my energies were mostly given over to striving, ensuring that I had enough and was good enough.

What I did experience now, though, was a growing love for my mother: I'd always loved her, but it had sometimes been hard to detect the freely given love amongst that which had been requisitioned. This felt like a newer, more spontaneous feeling, and I liked it.

At about the same time P moved back in, and that too seemed different: I don't know if it was a particularly sunny February or whether some kind of *trompe-l'oeil* of the emotions was at work but the whole flat seemed to glow, and I felt entitled to him. We went on holiday to Yugoslavia and it was the first time I can remember ever being able to say unequivocally, unafraid that it was about to be taken away, that I was happy. That thought struck me as we walked at sunset along the seafront to a cavernous bar where they sold tumblers of brandy for forty pence, and struck me with renewed drunken force later as we wandered back again.

I was now nearing completion of my book and as we were enlarging our flat and surrounded by builders, I moved my computer to my parents' home and went there every day to work. Sometimes, when I finished late at night, I went into my father's room for a chat before I left. I found these poignant times; I wanted so much to sustain him, but there was nothing, usefully or actually, to be done. As he lay there I tried, as often before, to imagine him dead, to dare myself to withstand it. My fear always was that it would be insupportable and that I would want to go with him, as if a reverse, unsevered umbilical cord would drag me along behind. It was my own life force which was at issue, not his.

Leaving their house on these nights was hard – it felt as if I was abandoning them – but also a relief. I'd walk briskly through the dark streets, disengaging from their world and re-engaging with my own – ladders and plaster, paint and decisions, all with an insistent immediacy of their own.

One day I took my father to the Jewish Film Festival to see a documentary about pre-war Polish Jewish life. Its images of vanished communities filled me with regret and yearning. I was astonished at how like me those young, amused women looked: if the war hadn't happened, that's where and how I'd have been, and this fantasy of being on the inside, among similars, intrigued me. My father was always a great reminiscer and the film oiled his recollections, but his nostalgia about pre-war Poland was terribly unsentimental. Certainly, he told animated stories about friends, relatives and the estate where he grew up; his eyes watered when he talked about his father, or his adored namesake cousin murdered by the Nazis. But though he fiercely wanted us to know about his past, at the same time there was a kind of detachment in the way he described pre-war Poland, and the same went for my mother. Bizarrely, I felt as if I were more sentimental about their past than they were: I was horribly aware that their lives had been bisected, but whereas they always seemed to accept the bisection and fully inhabit the second half, I was in some way always trying to recover the former half, for which I felt an enormous sense of loss. (This embarrassed me a little – it seemed excessive and, given that I was British-born, inappropriate; my sister, I suspect, regarded it as a bit of an affectation. It was only later that I discovered how common such a sense of longing is among children of survivors and refugees.) Perhaps my parents couldn't afford the luxury of retrospection and had shaken off their pasts as an act of self-preservation; perhaps I wasn't able to or hadn't had to. Perhaps, also, they were so resilient and adaptable that they'd managed to put down satisfactory roots in their new world. Or perhaps I felt their loss for them.

In any case I'd begun to understand them a little more. Now, when one of our political arguments threatened, I wouldn't allow myself to be drawn but tried to deflect it instead. Yet still I found it hard to fathom how my parents' wartime experiences could have left them so unsympathetic to the oppressed and disenfranchised. They seemed to refuse a sympathetic identification with the powerless and expounded instead what seemed like a steely philosophy of self-sufficiency. Then one day I began to see it differently. They'd been deprived, humiliated, and brutalised; after, through extreme exertion, they'd clawed their way back and made for themselves an ample new life. The last thing that interested them now was other people's deprivation, they had no wish voluntarily to revisit the depths. For once, instead of condemning their position, I could appreciate (if not applaud) its logic. And when I tried out my explanation on my mother, she didn't deny it but instead nodded silently in assent.

Around this time another unprecedented thing happened: I started running. In some ways this was unremarkable – most indolent people with sedentary jobs were noticing their flab and the effects of age at the time. Like many people I'd been athletic in primary school and good at sport in my secondary years, but thereafter I didn't merely become a slob by default like the majority of school-leavers, I turned actively inert. Moving came to frighten me, it seemed so destabilising, while stasis supplied a security of sorts – if I could sit, I might just be able to be. In any case, you can't run while depressed (I couldn't, anyway: all those media exhortations to exercise in order to lift one's mood struck me as so much bunkum – you need to be relatively undepressed to have the energy to start running in the first place) and I was starting to see that a pall of depression, often in the form of anxiety, had hung over much of my life.

I also hadn't been able to move earlier because my body had been the site of war and my skin its front line. My posture during the scratching years was entirely collapsed:

140

I would hunch over, sheltering my solar plexus and trying to contract. I may not have been able to withdraw from the world but I did my best to make myself invisible. Standing up straight was unimaginable: the brief occasions I managed it, I fantasised that someone would come along and chop off my head. A straight back and proud bearing would have expressed a quite alien fearlessness.

Running, on the other hand, entailed a recognition that me didn't reside just in my head, to where it had long been exiled (with my neck a drawbridge, preventing the free passage of energy). Me was also below the neck, which hitherto I'd treated merely as an appendage, the servants' quarters of my intellect. Running, swimming, indeed exercise of any kind involved an alliance with the body rather than a war.

And so I began to exercise each day religiously, even if (as happened quite often) this entailed a midnight workout. Exercise introduced me to a whole new class of sensation: for some of the time I now felt part of the world and more open to it, exhaling freely without fearing that an essential internal organ would drop out.

It was part of a growing tendency to allow myself to have. I was able to finish my book and it was duly published; our flat conversion was completed, doubling our living and working space; we decided to try to have a baby. All the good things which had seemed so threatening and potentially overwhelming three years earlier had now happened or were on the cards. My relationship with my parents was also very different; there was no backlog of anger which might be kindled by each row. We still bickered and argued but each quarrel stood alone – it would flare but it would also subside without leaving me still seething.

Yet why bracket all this with the Holocaust? Perfectly common and far less sensational explanations can be adduced for almost every problem described here. Separating from one's parents is sometimes hard for most people, almost every spotty adolescent goes through a period of feeling alienated from her peers and unconnected with her body, and no halfway sensitive person can expect to get through life without often finding her social persona at odds with her emotions. You certainly don't need to be the child of survivors or even Jewish to have an ongoing sense of exclusion – any unresolved Oedipal complex will do the trick. And speculate as I may (and this damned persistent but unanswerable question has stalked me for decades), I've no way of knowing whether or how my parents would have been different had the Holocaust never happened.

Nevertheless, when I started researching some of the international psychoanalytic literature about the effects of the Second World War on what had come to be called the second generation, I discovered infinite refractions of my own struggles, recurring patterns of behaviour identified among children of survivors across several continents. On the one hand, the whole notion of blaming the Holocaust for one's psychological problems had the strong aroma of special pleading: it seemed suspiciously like an attempt to annexe the forces of history so as to dignify what would otherwise seem like ordinary, common-or-garden neurosis. Indeed, some people with whom I began to talk about it turned distinctly resentful, as if I were using my family background to legitimate psychic infractions while they were obliged to stick to the mental straight and narrow, *their* problems treated as mere personal pathology. (There's only so much psychic distress that the culture will permit before dishing out the labels.) On the other hand, imagine emerging from a massive social, cultural, and psychic trauma and soon after becoming a parent – how could your parenting not be affected in some way? The consequences on the next generation had necessarily lain dormant for a couple of decades, putting a deceptive distance between the events of then and now.

I recognised that many of the difficulties I'd experienced

and continued to experience were particular to me – my sister, for example, had a different configuration of problems – and there were as many different kinds of survivor families as survivors. There were also other traumatised families who had similar difficulties to us – the families of alcoholics or drug addicts, for instance. And some of it pertained not specifically to being the child of survivors but more generally to being Jewish in Britain (the writer Howard Jacobson has written only semi-humorously of a particularly Jewish form of neurosis resulting from a combination of high expectations and low esteem). You only have to look at the personal columns of the *Jewish Chronicle* to find unbounded idealisation of family, and separation issues writ large.

If survivor families shared many problems with non-survivor families, in us these were often peculiarly intense and in my own case made many common solutions unavailable. Certainly my fear of annihilation was quite unlike anything expressed by my peers and bore no relation to my actual experiences. Yet this too had begun to change, as I noticed when I stayed at an alternative health holiday centre on a Greek island which I was writing about for a woman's magazine. Suddenly catching sight of someone I wanted to talk to who was about to go out for the evening, I ran from the bar where I'd been sitting, realising in that instant that I was leaving my handbag open on the counter, and yet continuing to run. I didn't have to worry that my purse would be pinched – this was a place where doors were never locked and nothing ever got stolen – but it seemed a Herculean step to trust that me and something of mine could be parted and then reunited. We were.

Another unprecedented change was getting acquainted with an Austrian woman. P and I had argued often and hard over my hostility to Germans and Austrians. He'd insist, quite rationally, that the younger generation couldn't be held responsible for their parents' actions; I'd only be prepared to countenance those who'd actively renounced the behaviour of the previous generation – they needed to demonstrate their purity to my satisfaction. (On this my mother was much more liberal: she'd happily visited East Germany after the war on concert tours, though on holidays in Italy, if she saw a German of a certain age on a neighbouring table, she'd suddenly say nervously, 'I'm sure I know that man.') While my hostility to Germans was in the circumstances, I think, entirely understandable, there was also a whiff of milked victimhood and assumed saintliness in my attitude; I felt a certain licence to bully them back which I was reluctant to relinquish but which had become increasingly difficult to justify down the years.

I'd once met a young German woman – fittingly, at a self-defence class. She was friendly and, when she learned that I was Jewish, extra-friendly, seeking out my company and asking to visit. But our meeting ended badly, with me haranguing her – a twenty-year-old – about the Nazis and the war, leaving her feeling battered (she phoned a mutual friend for comfort) and me specious. Years later I chided myself about that encounter and the way that I'd bellowed at her, instead of communicating with her and using the occasion to find out what it was like to be a young German in the early 1980s. Even more years later I didn't feel quite so bad about the episode, recognising that this was where I had stood at the time, and that I also hadn't felt comfortable with the way she'd sought me out, making me feel as though I were a bit of a curiosity – the vanishing Jew. I couldn't have appreciated then how intriguing and mythological I must have seemed to a young German who had, on her own admission, never met a Jew before: perhaps she wanted to touch me to assure herself of my realness, and perhaps I seemed a potential object for some kind of symbolic expiation, to supply her with a ritual sense of abasement and punishment. I'd duly delivered.

By the time I met the Austrian woman in Greece, it

seemed dishonest to use German war-guilt as a cover for my own sadism. Between myself and the Austrian some connection was forged, even if for the most part I remained self-conscious and a touch paranoid in the presence of Germans and Austrians.

It was then also that I started learning the Alexander Technique, a method of altering posture and the carriage of the body which rests on the idea of 'allowing' rather than forcing. What, not cajole and insist, not drive and demand, just 'let' and assume all will be well? It was a totally foreign concept, one quite at odds with my naturally kinetic style.

Around that time this book was commissioned and, with P accompanying me, I went to Israel for the First International Conference of Children of Holocaust Survivors. The opening evening reception in the lavish Ramada Renaissance Hotel in Jerusalem was a curious affair. A large group of people milled about, sipping wine and asking not about each other's occupation but 'Where were your parents?' We swapped the names of concentration camps over the canapés. Curious, for once, to feel so ordinary; I wasn't sure that I liked it.

At Yad Vashem, the Holocaust Memorial in Jerusalem, I searched the bursting archive (the results of the Nazis' passion for documentation) for information about my disappeared relatives, primarily my maternal grandfather Isidor Weissman, and my uncle Natan. I found one Isidor Weissman on the microfiche, then another, and another – I hadn't realised it was such a common name – but none had the right birthplace or date. It was shocking to see them aggregated like this, so that they lost all their specificity and became a mass or category: the Jew.

I was also stunned to find my mother logged on the microfiche, along with dates of her wartime experiences – when she'd left and arrived at each camp. This documentary evidence provided another level of reality to her story.

At one point in the conference we all gathered together

at Yad Vashem for prayers for the victims of the Holocaust. I began to sob in a way which made me feel uncomfortable: I was crying so personally over something which hadn't happened to me. It seemed then as if I hadn't lived the central experience of my life – at its heart, at mine, was an absence.

I'd planned, along with everyone else, to visit the Wailing Wall to insert into a crack – as is the custom – a slip of paper on which I'd written my hopes. I was trying to get pregnant, but before I'd had a chance to visit the Wall I realised that I already was. I was the same age as my mother when she conceived me, and it was seven years since I'd started to grapple with all my difficulties. When I eventually told my mother, she said that perhaps I'd had to go through a war of my own before being able to have a child. I think I may have gasped.

JOSEF KARPF: My first impression of London wasn't very good: we were tired, and arrived at a small hotel. I spoke a little English, and Natalia even less. Eve was born, she was a delightful child. And we started slogging. I was a Councillor of the Polish Treasury attached to the Polish Embassy. I reported back regularly to Poland about the financial situation here. I stayed at the Embassy until 1950, and then I left because they recalled me to Poland and I didn't want to go: they knew that I wouldn't go. The man who served my recalling papers came and said, 'Listen, I've been carrying these papers recalling you for six months, but I knew that, having been in Russia, you won't go back to Poland!' There was also already a lot of anti-Semitism in Poland.

I resigned and sought political asylum. The English were most forthcoming, as though they were waiting for me!

They knew everything that had been going on in the Embassy and in Poland, more than I knew. I was interviewed by MI5: two people sat there, and I told them what I knew. They said, 'Of course you can have asylum, and if you want to apply for naturalisation, those three years which you spent at the Embassy will be counted as part of the five years you have to have lived here' – that was the only case where that happened to a diplomat.

I did apply for naturalisation two years later.

In January 1951, I went to Israel, to the Ministry of Foreign Affairs. I'd thought seriously of moving to Israel, but I didn't like what I saw, the whole tussle there. (We couldn't have gone there in 1947, it was impossible – people who went at that time to Israel had to try to smuggle themselves in.)

I was fifty, unemployed with two children, but the main thing was that I didn't have one real friend here. It was not pleasant, I can tell you. I was very much concerned what to do. After a year I went into business with a friend of Natalia's.

(And here my father's tapes end.)

NATALIA KARPF: In 1947 we came to England by train via Prague, where we met up with Jelinek on the station platform, and via Paris, where we saw Recia, Cesia, Lusia, and Dziunia, who were already living there. We travelled with thirteen suitcases, because we were told that there was rationing in England and they didn't even have dish-cloths, let alone pots and pans. So we brought suitcases full of pots and pans and dish-cloths and God knows what! But, of course, it wasn't that bad – food was rationed but not everything. Later, Josef's brother sent on a lot of our furniture from Poland – a big sofa, an enormous cupboard and sideboard, a table, Josef's desk, and the Blüthner grand piano which Hela had rescued from a bombed house. I still have the table.

I was overwhelmed by London when I first came – such a big city, and I didn't have many friends here, though I found two or three from Poland. We rented one room in Marylebone. My English was very poor, though Josef got me to read out articles in English from newspapers – he already spoke some English. Then we moved to a flat in Swiss Cottage, with a shared bathroom – we knew that there were quite a lot of Jewish refugees and émigrés living there already. Josef's aunt lived there, she'd moved here before the war.

I was anxious in my pregnancy because of the stillbirth I'd had before. I went to a Polish doctor who'd been recommended: when she heard that Josef worked at the Embassy, she told me that I'd have to go back to Poland to have the baby there because I wouldn't get into any hospital in London – you had to book here nine months in advance after the war to get a place in a hospital to have a baby. I was in despair. Then my friend talked to the doctor, and she changed completely, and booked me into an antenatal clinic and later a hospital.

I was sharing an ordinary women's ward with seven other women when my waters broke, and I was anxious to get out of there into the labour ward. But the sister was very anti-foreigner, and when I called her she told me that I was naughty (it was only four months after we'd arrived: I didn't even know what naughty meant, I asked the women after, and they told me) and she wouldn't let me, so I had to lie in a pool of water. I was very upset.

Eve was born – I just couldn't believe it, I was crying for joy, holding her in my arms. We called her after my mother, though I regret that I didn't call her Eva: I was persuaded by people that Eve was better, more English.

It was frightening at the beginning – I was very anxious for her survival, I was always frightened of losing the child. That fear lasted about a year or a year and a half. She was very lively, she used to call out 'Hello' to everyone from her pram when she was just one year old! Josef was so thrilled, he adored her. But when she started walking we were always frightened that she would fall or something would happen, and when I used to go shopping with her, I didn't leave the pram anywhere, I took it everywhere with me – people used to leave prams outside shops in those days, but I never did.

I started practising straight away, and a year later, in 1948, I already gave a recital in the Wigmore Hall. That was my first recital in England, though I'd already played in the Polish Embassy.

No Jewish organisation in England ever approached us to offer help, and we never heard of any such group giving help – only my few friends. Whenever we met Holocaust survivors in England we always talked about the war – somehow the conversation always came back to wartime, and it still does – about the camps, what happened there, what happened here. We can't forget it, from the end of the war until now we don't stop talking. We wanted other people to know, but some people didn't want to hear it and we didn't talk to English people about it. I went once to a reception at a friend's house for the violinist Mischa Elman, and there was a lady who saw the number on my arm, and she came to me and said, 'What have you put here – your telephone number?' When I said, 'Yes, it's the telephone number of Auschwitz', I thought that this woman would faint. She said, 'Oh my God, I'm so sorry, I've never seen such a tattoo before, and I never knew that something like that exists.' I don't think people here really knew about the camps – they just couldn't believe when they heard it. For many years people weren't interested at all – it's only recently, I think the last few years, that they started talking about the Holocaust and more and more has been written and published. But for many years it wasn't.

AK: So it was almost like a private thing between you and the other survivors?

NK: Absolutely.

AK: The world outside resumed, almost as if nothing had happened?

NK: Yes.

AK: Wasn't that difficult for you?

NK: It was very difficult. It was difficult with the language, it was difficult with no special help, and not much money, and not many friends. I had lost everything – all my family, all my belongings, everything I'd ever possessed . . .

AK: . . . your country of birth, your mother tongue. And you arrive in a strange place, and no one really wants to know?

NK: No – although Josef asked me all the time about my experiences, and was interested in everything: he so admired that my spirit hadn't been broken – he couldn't understand how one could suffer so much and survive it. He knew it would help me if I talked about it. And it did help me. He told me his stories, too.

AK: But you could go crazy in a situation like that.

NK: You could. Only I was so happy that I had a family, that I had a child, and I was so absorbed with that, and with beginning from scratch again my career. I'd started a big career before the war in Berlin, then my mother died and I had to go back to Poland. Then the war broke out, and after it ended I started my career again in Poland. And then I had to start a third time in a strange country, without any help, all on my own. It wasn't like nowadays, there are all these competitions: if you are talented, you go in for a competition and you win, you're made as an artist, and you can get sponsors. Forty-eight or forty-nine years ago it was very difficult.

AK: And the sadness and the grief, did some of that go into the music?

NK: Yes.

AK: Because your life was divided totally into two halves: what continuity was there between them?

NK: Only the music – nothing else. It was a completely new start in my life, as if I'd been reborn. All the rest completely disappeared. But in 1949 I went back to Poland, because Helunia wrote to me that she had exhumed Mania's remains from the Catholic cemetery in Warsaw (my poor sister went through a terrible time because she was present when Mania's body was exhumed) to bury in the Jewish cemetery in Kraków, which had been Mania's wish. Helunia didn't have any money but she had her late husband's motor cycle, which she sold to pay for it. So in July 1949 I went to Poland on my own for two or three weeks: we'd been blacklisted at the Embassy for being anti-Communist so I was frightened to go, but I'd promised Helunia that I'd come. At the stone-setting, there were just the two of us and a rabbi saying the prayers. It was very sad.

I wasn't happy being in Poland during that whole trip: I

only went because I wanted to be at the stone-setting and see Hela. I'd got her a visa to come to London but she didn't want to leave her late husband's dog. She mourned her husband, wearing a black veil, for two years, though he beat her up. He was a victim of the war: he was a doctor of economics and spoke six languages, but he couldn't get over his whole family vanishing and began to drink and get violent.

I gave two broadcast concerts while I was in Poland in 1949, and, with the money I earned from them, I took Helunia to the Grand Hotel at Sopot, by the sea, for a few days' holiday. When I left Poland, I knew that I was leaving it for the last time, and I felt relieved to arrive back in England: when Josef picked me up at London airport, I said to him, 'Kiss this earth, that you are here and not there.'

When I came back from Poland, I got pregnant straight away. I was thrilled to have two girls. When you were six weeks old you got eczema: you were scratching, you were itching, we had to put mittens on you for the night, and you screamed until three in the morning every night. It was horrible to see a child suffer and cry and not to be able to help. We ran from one doctor to another and no one could help me. It was very hard the first year: up to one year it was hell, but Josef was an angel – he looked after you mostly at that time. We were tense, and I was screaming at Eve and you sometimes. When you were one year old, it got better.

On 16 August 1950, Josef came home with a letter saying that at the end of the month he'd be transferred back to the Treasury in Warsaw, and they offered him a Grade 4 position, much higher than he had already (the President was Grade 1). He came home and showed it to me. I said, 'Darling, I'm not going back to Poland – I have two British-born children, and I'm not going back to the Communists. It will be hard for us because we haven't got any money' (we had £200 altogether). So he went back to the Embassy and said, 'I'm afraid I won't go back to Poland, I will ask for asylum.'

So he applied for political asylum, and he was interviewed by the Foreign Office: they treated us wonderfully, they gave us asylum. But he became unemployed, because wherever he applied for a position they told him that he was too old – he was fifty years old. We were very hard up and couldn't afford any help. Money was so tight that when I heard that something was a penny cheaper in a shop a mile away, I'd go pushing you in the pram and with Eve in a seat on top to get it cheaper. And when I wanted to go to the cinema, I had to go on my own and Josef on his own – we didn't have the money for babysitting. That was a very hard time, but we loved having two children, and I was very involved in my music. Whenever I was unhappy, I sat at the piano, and got carried away with a piece of music, and I forgot about any worries I had.

AK: So the music helped you out again.

NK: Yes. Josef couldn't find work for a year, and I only managed to play because he was at home and helped me. He got very depressed for a year, and then he decided to go to Israel to visit his cousins there, one of whom was in the Treasury in Israel and suggested to Josef that he should go and work in the Treasury in Israel. Josef was tempted but I wasn't, because it was very difficult in Israel, we would have had to start again, the third time after the war, and it was very difficult for artists then in Israel.

Also, I didn't want to be among so many Jews: I'd been only among Jews during the war in the camps, and there were so many unpleasant types there (it was difficult to survive, and mostly those who were pushy without any consideration for others survived) that I didn't want to live

153

any more only among Jews, I wanted to live among different races, different colours, different religions. Some time later, when I went to Israel, I thought perhaps it would have been better, I had so many friends afterwards there, and Josef's family – we would have had more family there, because here we were isolated a little bit, we felt a bit like strangers for many years, an outsider, and it wasn't a very pleasant feeling (I don't feel it now, because I've been longer here, in this country, than in any other country in my life) and it's such a big place, the distances were a bit disturbing here.

But in 1951, I passed an audition for the BBC, and made so many broadcasts for them over the years – over 100 broadcasts – and I played with almost all the BBC orchestras, concertos and recitals. I played in the Wigmore Hall, the Albert Hall, the Proms, later Queen Elizabeth Hall so many times, and in Switzerland and France. In the 1950s, I formed a chamber music trio, with two other Jewish women.

Josef got involved in a silk-screen printing business, though he was never happy in it. He was also involved in editing a Jewish newspaper, and borrowed some money from the bank to buy some properties. He hated being a landlord – he wanted to paint – but he had no choice.

In September 1954, I hadn't had a letter from Hela for a few weeks and I was very worried. Then suddenly I get a telegram from Israel – I was frightened, but then I opened it and couldn't believe it. It was from Hela and said, 'I am here.' In the 1950s, people weren't allowed out of Poland, but she'd been smuggled out through East Germany to Israel. She started performing there – singing, gave ballet lessons, writing poems. And suddenly, in spring 1955, she didn't feel well. She went to the doctor, and they told her that she had something wrong with her bowels. A friend phoned me to tell me that she was very sick, and had to have an operation in July. We didn't have any money at that time, we were very hard up still. I said to Josef, 'If I had some money, I'd fly over to Israel for the operation.' Josef didn't say anything but the next day he came and said, 'Here's your passport with a visa to Israel and an air ticket to Israel.' I said, 'How did you do it?' He'd gone to El Al and he asked them to let us pay for the flight in instalments.

So I flew over, and she was in Hadassah Hospital, and had a five-hour operation. The professor who operated on her fell in love with her: he came out of the operating theatre like a broken man. He said, 'She survived it for the time being, but we don't know what will be.' She was so strong-willed to survive – she didn't know she had cancer – that after two weeks she was walking around the whole hospital and cheering up people, performing to them, and even helping with the nursing. I stayed there for five weeks, and she eventually got a bit better.

I came back, and tried to bring her over here, but they didn't want to give her a visa. Because she'd gone to Israel, they didn't want to let her in – they didn't want to let people come from Israel even for a visit. They knew that she was a Holocaust survivor but that didn't change matters. A friend rang from Israel and told me that the professor had said that she had only three months to live. So I went to the Home Office and then they agreed to give her a three-month visa. She flew over via Paris in February 1956, and I went to the airport to meet her. The flight came in and everybody came out, except her – I was in despair. Suddenly, one of the immigration officers came out and said, 'Is there a Natalia Karpf here?' I said, 'Yes.' He said, 'Would you come through with me, your sister has arrived.' And he took me over there, and she didn't speak English, only a few words, and he asked me, in her presence, 'How long has she got?' I said to him very quietly, 'Three months.' So they gave her a visa, either for three months or a bit longer, and later, when she was dead, they wrote to say that her visa had expired and why hadn't she reported to the Home Office. So I wrote to them, 'She doesn't need your visa any more because she is buried here.'

It was such a tragedy for me, such a loss, a terrible loss – and she was so young, and so beautiful. I was more anxious after my sister died, because that was the end of my family – on my side of the family, everyone gone. I had nobody, only my husband and my two daughters. I was always anxious that I might lose you both when you were small. I protected you as much as I could. One feels so helpless not to be able to do anything against this losing people – terrible. I was devastated for a long time. But having children helped – I had to do everything which needed to be done, shopping and cooking and everyday life, and I had engagements, and that helped. But it was very hard.

AK: When we were little, there must have been a lot of sadness in the house.

NK: There was. But there was also a lot of happiness. One day, in the late 1950s, a well-known Polish pianist came to visit me. She was going to Dresden to play with the Dresden Philharmonic Orchestra, and I asked her who the conductor was. She said Professor Heinz Bongartz. I said, 'No! That's the conductor who conducted my concert with the Berlin Philharmonic Orchestra in 1929, and with whom I later had a few other concerts in Germany. Give him my regards.' I knew he wasn't a Nazi. So she told him that I was alive and living here – he'd looked for me everywhere, searching in Poland after the war after I'd left and couldn't find me. He wrote me a letter, saying, 'What the Germans did to you I can't make good. But you know me, you know who I am, please do come and play the Tchaikovsky Concerto with me.'

I didn't know what to do, I was struggling because I didn't want to go to Germany, and especially to East Germany. But I wanted to go to my mother's grave, which was in East Berlin, because I was the only survivor of her three children. Also, we didn't know if it was safe politically for me to go, so Josef went to the Foreign Office to ask them. They said, 'Yes, she should go: what the politicians spoil, the artists repair.' So I decided to go.

I had to travel by train because it was foggy, and they were waiting for me at the station with flowers. It didn't feel very comfortable being in Germany, only I knew that I had these friends, the Bongartzes, there. The first concert was sold out, and the same programme was repeated the day after. The reviews said, 'She came, played, and conquered.' That concert tour was a great success, I got so many engagements from it, and each time I returned everything was sold out a few days before, people were begging me for tickets. I used to take all the flowers I received after all the concerts to my mother's grave. I ended up making, I think, nine tours to Germany. But I missed my children so much and my husband's voice, which was like music to me, that I used to phone every day or every second day, and I counted the days to get home.

AK: Did you not look around at your concerts, and think one of the audience might be Grunow, or one of the others . . .?

NK: . . . whenever I met an older German. I met a couple in Flims, Switzerland, about fifteen years ago, and he was grey-haired, and when I heard them speaking German in the hotel, I said, 'Whenever I see a German man of your age, I always wonder whether you didn't kill my father.' He said, 'Oh, I was lucky that I didn't go to the Front and I didn't go anywhere; I had to work in the factory because

I was an engineer.' You have to believe him or not. They were a nice couple.

But I didn't blame the young generation – although some of them are still Nazis, but most of them questioned their parents and grandparents and I didn't blame them.

When I look at the photo of my father, I think what did he suffer before they finished him – burnt him or gassed him or God knows what . . . How can one go on living when one knows what these people suffered? That comes back to me more and more.

I didn't tell you both about the war when you were very small, because I didn't want to upset you: when children hear of killing or shooting they are frightened. I told you when you were five or six. Some of my friends didn't tell their children because they thought that they protect them. But I didn't want my children to be protected in this way, I wanted them to know the truth. And it helped me, and it helped you, I suppose, in a way. What do you think?

AK: I have mixed feelings, I think.

NK: Should I have not told you?

AK: No. But whether you tell or you don't tell, there's no good way of doing it.

NK: Yes.

AK: I think if you don't tell children, they pick up on the fact that there's this thing which hasn't been told, and it's terrible to think there's something very important that's being withheld from you. At the same time, children take responsibility for things: on some level, I think that I felt that I was responsible for the war, that my badness somehow caused it . . .

NK: Either in 1948 or 1949 I'd got Jelinek an invitation to come to London as an au-pair. She got a pension from the Germans, as we all did. In the mid-1950s, she moved into a flat round the corner from us, I saw a lot of her, and it was very nice to have her so near. Recia moved to England in 1952, and the three of us met up a lot. When Hela came, the four of us were together again, and we kept in touch with Cesia in Paris.

Jelinek always hoped that one of her children was still alive and would come back. I never knew what went wrong between us: she died in 1983, and a few years earlier she felt Josef had given her bad advice, and she suddenly refused to talk to us. It was very painful for me, because we went through the war together, and after the war – everywhere we were together. I suffered so much when she died without any reconciliation, I thought I'd go mad – why, why was she like this? And why didn't I force her to change her mind? But I was afraid that it wouldn't be good for her health if I went there and talked to her: so many times I passed her flat with my grandson and I thought I'll go in there and say, 'Why don't you want to see us?' but I was frightened. I push away from me the thought that she's dead because I can't get over it, it hurts me so much. She was so stubborn. Her state of mind was such that she slept on a little cushion inside which she had her little son's braces and some other things. And she always fasted on 14 May, the anniversary of the Selektion [of the children, including her ten-year-old son, Wojtuc, at Płaszów].

AK: Maybe the fact that you'd had a grandson was too much for her to bear.

NK: I think so.

AK: Because I remember pleading with her to talk to you, and she wouldn't.

159

NK: I had many dreams that the Germans take my children away – and I didn't have any children until after the war, but I saw so many terrible scenes involving children and shooting children that I couldn't forget it, it was haunting me. And one dream that I still have – and Josef had the same dream – that we go somewhere by train, we come out, and we don't know the way to go: we can't find the street, we can't find the house, we can't find anything – everything is strange and we can't find the way out.

The only way I could have started up again after the war was through my husband. He was so protective of me and so gentle and wonderful. I remember when you went to Oxford, that was for me such a sad day. We took you to Oxford and when we came back I went into your room and I was crying as if someone had died. And Josef was so sweet, he said, 'Come. Let's not stay in tonight, I'll take you out for dinner.'

It's difficult to grasp such cruelty and humiliation that happened during the war – that it was possible. Sometimes I'm not surprised that they say it couldn't have happened, it's impossible, it's not true, because it's difficult to understand how it could have been. But it is true. And it happened.

AK: And it's important that people should know about it.

NK: Absolutely. Everybody, every human being, because it's happening again. When we came out of the camps, we thought, 'Now, we'll never need any passports, there will never be any more wars', we were sure of it. What a disappointment, that so many Holocausts happen again in the world, like Rwanda and Yugoslavia – it's horrifying. I can't stand seeing the pictures from Bosnia, it enrages me. When I see the ethnic cleansing and how the refugees cry and leave and go with the bundles – exactly the same as the Jews were during the war. I see the same pictures again, and I can't believe that it repeats itself.

Part Two

5

I was touched but also always a little embarrassed by the gratitude which my parents felt for Britain as the country which took them in (albeit after the event, as it were). But their enthusiasm for England, both when they first arrived and later, didn't appear to be reciprocated: they were granted entry (as part of the diplomatic service), and even early naturalisation, but otherwise the host country seems to have extended them little hospitality, either in the form of help with settling down or other gestures of welcome.

More surprisingly, perhaps, neither did the indigenous Jewish community. As Jews newly delivered from wartime Poland and the camps, my parents might reasonably have expected from British Jews some kind of recognition of their experience or simply practical help. But like other Holocaust survivors who came to Britain, they seem to have been greeted instead with a kind of collective indifference. Though there were individual acts of generosity, and child survivors (who comprised the majority of Jewish post-Holocaust immigrants to England and the only ones to arrive in a group) did receive organised help, adult survivors met with few communal attempts to ease their transition or material hardship, and no one to mediate between them and the alien new culture. Left largely to their own devices, they were obliged to establish themselves individually, leaving some with an enduring sense of bitterness. Most wounding of all was the disinclination of the citizens of the new country, its Jews included, to hear about, let alone invite discussion of, their experience in the camps.

One survivor recalls that, 'People simply didn't understand what we'd been through . . . We lived among Jewish people, indeed our landlady and her daughter were observant Jews, and they all knew that we had come out of the camps, and yet not one of them lifted a finger to help us.'[1] Another survivor recalled that her uncle, with whom she came to stay in Birmingham in 1946, vetoed all references to the camps. Though she was keen to make up for her lost years of schooling (from thirteen to eighteen), she couldn't get a grant or any help with rehabilitation. 'What I find it particularly hard to forgive is that there was no programme even within the Jewish community.'[2]

A survivor from Oskar Schindler's list didn't talk about his experiences for twenty years because he felt no one was interested, and only told his second wife when Steven Spielberg's film came out.[3] An Auschwitz survivor recalls, 'They say that some survivors didn't want to talk but I wanted to talk, but I think my words fell on deaf ears and we had to bury all the trauma and fear . . . because people really didn't want to know, or they came up and said, "You know we didn't have it so good either – we had bombs here."'[4] Primo Levi has argued that survivors' need to relate their story and have it heard became, both before and after liberation, irresistible and inexorable: Levi himself had a recurring dream of telling friends and family about his camp experiences but finding them completely indifferent – 'they speak confusedly of other things among themselves, as if I was not there'.[5] This dream 'of speaking and not being listened to, of finding liberty and remaining alone'[6] was felt to be a wound almost as grievous as the original camp experiences, a second abandonment by the world after the first which had taken place during the war.

Why was British Jewry apparently so insensitive to their European cousins? Why was the British state also so uninterested? And why has it taken so long for the Holocaust to arrive on to the British public agenda? The reasons lie in the past, in the history and status of Anglo-Jewry, and dominant Christian beliefs about Jews.

The three chapters which make up Part Two try to place my family's experience in its historical context. In this chapter, I look back at how British Jews came to find themselves in such a relatively weak position at the outbreak of the war. Drawing on exciting recent historical work by young Anglo-Jewish historians like Tony Kushner and David Cesarani, I explore some of the shocking attitudes of the British Establishment to Jews, and the Jewish community's reaction to them, up to and during the Second World War. The next chapter deals with the post-war period and charts the changing attitudes to the Holocaust and to survivors both in Britain and abroad up to the present, focusing especially on the long international silence on the subject. Chapter 7 traces the emergence of professional interest in and concern with the psychological effects of the Holocaust on both survivors and their families, and examines critically its major themes and biases. Part Three returns to my personal story.

Though the first Jewish communities were established in England in the early Middle Ages, relations between Christians and Jews were scarcely harmonious: at the time of the Third Crusade, 200 besieged Jews committed suicide in York in 1190 rather than face forcible conversion or death, and England pioneered mass expulsion of Jews in 1290. In 1656, under Cromwell's republic, Jews were readmitted (contingent on them not being 'a charge on the parish' or the state), but by the end of the eighteenth century there were only 25,000 Jews living in England.[7] The major waves of immigration began only in the late–nineteenth century, in response to persecution in Eastern Europe.

Until the mid–nineteenth century all public offices were closed to practising Jews. They were excluded from Parliament and all those professions – like the Bar, medicine, and schoolteaching – that required members to take the oath of abjuration, which ended with the words 'upon the true faith of a Christian'. They weren't allowed to study at Oxford and Cambridge Universities either.[8] Beginning in 1847, Baron Lionel de Rothschild was elected three times to the House of Commons by the City of London, but each time was unable to take his seat because he wouldn't swear the Christian oath. In 1858 the law was finally changed, and Rothschild became the first practising Jew to be a Member of Parliament (sixty-seven years after the Jews had achieved emancipation in France).

Yet anti-Semitism remained rife in nineteenth-century England. Even a champion of the rights of Jews such as Whig MP Macaulay felt uneasy if actually exposed to their company: he wrote to his sister that after attending a ball thrown by a Jewish family he was unable to sleep – 'the sound of fiddles was in mine ears, and gaudy dresses, and black hair, and Jewish noses were fluctuating up and down before mine eyes'.[9] It was commonly assumed that Jews could not be patriots; they were also thought to be simultaneously 'exclusive' and 'parasitical'. As the *Manchester City News* put it in 1889, '[the Jew] herds together with his kind, learns little about the country where he has fixed his home, and takes no interest in its affairs', while a decade later the same publication was declaring of Eastern European Jewish immigrants that, 'They like dirt, a variety of smells, phenomenally large families, and overcrowding ... It is not nice to have them as neigbours.'[10]

Matthew Arnold was a leading campaigner against the admission of Jews into Parliament, considering them a 'petty, unsuccessful, unamiable people', and insisting that

'England is the land of Englishmen, not Jews'.[11] Trollope satirised what he deemed the hideous accents and greed of the Jewish parvenu, a theme G.K. Chesterton was to pursue. By the 1930s H.G. Wells was describing Jews as a 'perpetual irritant to statesmen, a breach in the collective solidarity everywhere'.[12] Wells later went further, suggesting that Nazism was 'essentially Jewish in spirit and origin': he responded to Jan Karski's eye-witness account of Bełzec death camp in November 1942 by wondering why 'in every country where Jews reside, sooner or later anti-Semitism emerges'.[13] But perhaps the most famous 'literary anti-Semitism' was penned by T.S. Eliot in his poems 'Gerontion':

My house is a decayed house,
And the Jew squats on the window-sill[14]

and 'Burbank with a Baedeker: Bleistein with a Cigar':

The rats are underneath the piles.
The Jew is underneath the lot.[15]

Again and again Christian commentators made a distinction between the assimilated Jew (good) and the unassimilated one (bad). As George Bernard Shaw put it in 1938, 'The observing circumcised Jew from the Ghetto may still present a problem to Gentile States; but an absorbed Jew presents no problem at all.'[16] Wells even argued that 'the systematic attempt to exterminate' the Jew was the inevitable result of Jews' refusal to assimilate.[17]

The assimilated or acculturated Jew – for which German Jews were the template – was explicitly contrasted with the Yiddish-speaking 'ghetto' Jew from Eastern Europe, the Ostjude or Galician Jew, who was widely perceived as uneducated, uncouth, even 'half-wild'[18] not just by Christians, but by the indigenous Jewish community itself, many members of which concurred with the view that the failure to assimilate was the cause of anti-Semitism. Yiddish was denigrated as degraded German or patois; not just in Britain but throughout Western Europe, you could read off the fears and anxieties of the assimilating Western Jew in the popular stereotype of the Eastern European Jew: 'They served as a huge refuse bin of human characteristics into which all that . . . filled [the Western Jew] with shame was dumped.'[19] (Indeed it's been suggested that the longstanding contempt of Jewish communities in Western European countries like Holland towards their fellow Jews in Eastern European countries like Poland was a significant factor in preventing them from recognising, in Eastern Jews' experience in the 1930s, a harbinger of their own fate.[20]) Assimilation, it was believed, went hand in hand with progress and Enlightenment; anti-Semitism was a relic of the irrational and the primitive.

Socialists, too, subscribed to the assimilation thesis. Following Marx, they believed that Judaism was a manifestation of capitalist society: the universalism of Communism would render Jewish particularism redundant, and progressive movements would free modern society from nationalist and sectionalist interests. Assimilation would occur naturally when Jews and other minorities acquired freedom and equality under socialism. (Poor Trotsky was therefore dreadfully shocked to encounter anti-Semitic innuendo from Stalin.[21])

On the other hand, there was also a strand of Western European thought which treated Jewish assimilation itself as sinister: when the Jew was no longer distinctive and immediately identifiable, his or her presence and influence could be imagined as infinite. As Alain Finkielkraut, sensitive to this diabolical irony, put it: 'Genocide was not imposed on the Jews *in spite of* their effort to assimilate, but *in response* to this very attempt. The more they hid their Jewishness, the more terrifying they became to others . . . Assimilation thus became a strange kind of trial in which the defendants completely misunderstood the indictment their judges had prepared. Assimilated Jews thought they were being charged with excessively Jewish behaviour, when it was their will to integration that was really the crime.'[22] Which led Finkielkraut to his necessarily bitter coda: 'The Nazi way of death, as we know, drew no distinctions between different kinds of Jews.'[23]

But in nineteenth-century Britain, the Jewish community expressed no qualms about jettisoning some of their traditional collective identity. They saw emancipation – the dismantling of their civic disabilities – as something lying in the gift of the British, part of a contract to which Jews on their side should contribute gratitude and loyalty. In return for civic equality from the (Gentile) state, they'd abandon all claims to nationality, and exist instead solely as a religious community.[24] 'This emancipation "contract" negated political action: it prevented the community from asserting its influence on any issue involving the Gentile world.'[25] On the contrary, whenever possible, in exchange for the tolerance promised by liberalism, Jews publicly proclaimed their patriotism.

Anglo-Jewry's communal organisations were dominated by an élite composed of a small group of wealthy families – the Rothschilds, the Mocattas, the Montefiores – 'West End Jews' who for the most part looked, sounded, and acted like members of the English aristocracy. The institutions they established, like the Jewish Board of Guardians, the Jewish Ladies' Visiting Association, the Jews' School and the Jewish Lads' Brigade, modelled themselves on English institutions (down to their top hats). Foreign-born Jews, so flagrantly distinct in appearance, speech, and culture, so self-evidently Jewish and therefore alien, threatened this 'emancipation contract', and therefore were targeted by British-Jewish institutions intent on rapidly anglicising them. Anglo-Jewry aimed to 'iron out the ghetto bend', to convert the 'slouching children of the ghetto' into upstanding Englishmen and women. A leader in the *Jewish Chronicle* in 1881 declared that 'one of the most pressing problems of the future' was 'how best to facilitate the transformation of Polish into English Jews ... We may not be able to make them rich; but we may hope to render them English in feeling and in conduct.'[26] Writing on another occasion in 1881 about foreign immigrants, it thundered, 'They come mostly from Poland; they, as it were, bring Poland with them, and they retain Poland while they stop here. This is most undesirable: it is more than a misfortune, it is a calamity. We cannot afford to "let them slide". Our outside world is not capable of making minute discrimination between Jew and Jew and forms its opinion of Jews in general as much, if not more, from them than from the Anglicised portion of the community. We are then responsible for them.'[27]

So Jewish immigrants' acceptance was contingent upon their conforming to the precepts of the Gentile bourgeoisie; 'the abandonment of a "foreign" culture was the price of entry into English society.'[28] Anglo-Jewish institutions did all they could to foster an interest in respectable British working-class pastimes – billiards and table-tennis, debating and brass bands.[29] The Jewish Lads' Brigade attempted to instil the British values of team spirit and playing the game.[30] The Jewish Board of Guardians' distinction between the deserving and undeserving poor may have been contrary to traditional Jewish charitable practice but was quite in keeping with the English Poor Law.[31]

The disapproval of Yiddish made some children feel ashamed of their Yiddish-speaking relatives. In one Manchester School in 1907 when four-fifths of its pupils were Jewish, Christmas decorations were put up.[32] The grandees of the Jewish Working Men's Club sat on a platform beneath a banner with a picture of the Queen[33] (and even today synagogue services routinely include prayers for the health of the royal family and the government). There was no commitment to preserve and respect the old culture, let alone encourage it or even allow it to metamorphose in its own time. On the contrary, an alternative new culture – English, middle-class, and public school – was to be substituted, imposed in its place.[34] The old came soaked in superstition – it was thought pre-modern and almost oriental; the new represented a higher stage of civilisation. The old was pallid, lacking in stamina, and brought about segregation; the new was muscular, energetic, and facilitated integration. It required vigilance and prodigious energy to avoid the influx of the old from polluting the new.

The poet Israel Zangwill satirised the pressures to assimilate:

> My brothers, sisters, newly here,
> Listen to my wise oration,
> You can live without the fear
> Of hatred and repatriation
> All you have to do, I bid
> Is stop acting like a yid
>
> Ei, ei, ei is so demeaning,
> English voices sing so sweet;
> Ei, ei, ei, is so unseeming,
> Oi, oi, oi, an ugly bleat.
> Pom, pom, pom is rude and crazy,
> Try instead Tra La or Daisy.[35]

Some have argued that nineteenth- and twentieth-century Anglo-Jewry was acculturated – not quite so thorough a process – rather than assimilated.[36] Others have claimed that immigrant groups didn't simply yield to social pressures but were subjected to conflicting notions of anglicisation and modernity, and resisted the ideologies and pressures from those institutions they found uncongenial.[37] Whichever is true, the fact is that the Anglo-Jewish élite almost always reacted to anti-Semitism by conciliatory, private initiatives rather than through mobilising public protest. So when confronted, in 1881 and 1882, with the plight of Jews seeking to escape from the Russian pogroms, Anglo-Jewry was more concerned with not offending English public opinion than bringing practical help to Russian Jews in a crisis. Just as they would be again later, in the 1930s and '40s, communal leaders in the 1880s were reluctant to speak out loudly and press the Jewish cause, angling instead to get Christian clergymen to speak on their behalf.[38]

Indeed, by 1888, the main Jewish welfare organisation, the Jewish Board of Guardians, was priding itself on having arranged the repatriation of thousands of Jewish families – 'who, having wandered here, prove themselves to be useless or helpless'[39] – back to the Eastern Europe from which they'd fled. There was greater friction with the state following the Aliens Act of 1905 (aimed at restricting Jewish immigration, and under which immigrants had to prove that they'd be able to support themselves and their dependents 'decently'), but, in 1914, in the wake of government measures to register enemy aliens, the Board of Deputies refused to intervene on behalf of the thousands of Galician Jews thus labelled and interned.[40]

By the 1930s, Anglo-Jewry had no history of successfully impressing the British state with its interests, needs, and preoccupations. On the contrary, its sense of vulnerability and apologetic stance were by now well-established and these, together with its fear of anti-Semitism, determined its response to the rise of Hitler, the Second World War and its aftermath, and helped to ensure that the United Kingdom's conduct towards Jews before, during, and after the war was for the most part shameful – far from the idealised mythology of the British at war which has prevailed for so long.

Right until 31 October 1941 when the Nazis finally closed the door on Jewish emigration from German-held territory, there were still opportunities to escape open to European Jews who could find a country to take them in. But British immigration policy was restrictive, and the British government continued to see the situation of the Jews as an immigration problem rather than a moral or humanitarian one: they were immigrants first and only secondly refugees. Indeed, Britain in 1933 had no refugee policy or right of asylum: such matters were subsumed under the rubric of 'alien immigration'.[41]

Most pre-war Jewish immigration was concentrated in the nine months between the anti-Jewish riots of Kristallnacht (the night of broken glass), on 9 November 1938, and the outbreak of war in September 1939: 40,000 Jewish refugees were allowed into Britain in this period, compared with 11,000 in the previous five years. They were admitted mostly on a strictly temporary basis, with the proviso that they'd eventually re-emigrate, and they were only allowed to stay if they didn't represent a threat to British jobs. The reasoning behind this policy was anxiety not only about increasing British unemployment, but also about adding to the Jewish population in Britain lest this might foster anti-Semitism – a recurring official argument, based on the notion that anti-Semitism was partly created by Jews (and not just suffered by them) and therefore could be controlled by restricting their numbers.[42]

Anglo-Jewish communal bodies, themselves permanently frightened of anti-Semitism, also had no wish to see Britain's Jewish population expand hugely. The Jewish refugee organisations were still governed by the leadership which had so chafed against the distinctiveness of Eastern European Jewish immigrants in 1880–1914, and now they acquiesced with Home Office criteria in selecting refugees 'whose "desirability" seemed greater the less they resembled the Eastern European Jewish immigrants of a generation earlier'.[43] They preferred young, able-bodied refugees, and those less overtly Jewish – either because of inter-marriage or because they'd become secularised – to those who were distinctively, uncompromisingly Jewish, the 'kaftaned Jews of Poland' who didn't realise the need to 'discard their distinctive attire, although they cannot shed their Jewish features'.[44] The orthodox Rabbi Solomon Schonfeld, rescuer of orthodox Jews, was a rare dissenter from this view.

The Anglo-Jewish community of course also felt concern

over what was happening in Europe. In 1933 they petitioned the government to admit German refugees but, assuming that humanitarian grounds wouldn't prove sufficiently persuasive, needing also to conform with the continuing aliens legislation requiring proof of self-sufficiency, and having then no inkling of the large numbers who would eventually arrive, they guaranteed that the Jewish community would see to it that no refugee would become a charge on public funds – the Jewish community, in the form of the Jewish Refugees Committee and later the Central British Fund for German Jewry (CBF), would shoulder the burden. This policy, it's been suggested, was double-edged, enabling state immigration policy to be more liberal in admitting Jews than it might otherwise have been, but at the same time strictly controlling the numbers admitted.[45] What's more, the guarantee ended up placing a desperate strain on the voluntary bodies which administered it, but it was a logical consequence of the emancipation contract, and its preoccupation with not making demands on the state.[46]

There was one remaining way in for refugees who couldn't support themselves: they could still get permits if they were willing to take posts which the British considered disagreeable – principally, given the 'servant problem', domestic service. These jobs had the added advantage of including board and lodging, and 20,000 (predominantly female) refugees came as domestic labour. The motive of some of those employing refugees was altruistic, to enable them to get a visa; others saw it as an opportunity to get cheap domestic help.[47] But the CBF's guarantee only extended to German Jews: visas were still required by Polish, Hungarian, and stateless Jews, and it was British policy to refuse visas to Polish and Hungarian Jews suspected of being refugees.[48]

With the likelihood of a new exodus of Austrian Jews after the Anschluss (the annexation of Austria on 13 March 1938), the government decided to reintroduce visas for German and Austrian refugees. As a Home Office memorandum put it, 'The real point is to prevent potential refugees from getting here at all.'[49] Later in 1938, after Kristallnacht, the British government liberalised its admissions policy: Jews from certain occupations would be welcomed, though for others whose professional bodies were hostile and powerful (most notably the Medical Practitioners' Union and the British Medical Association[50]), strict limits remained. Nevertheless, the large number of people wanting to get out, and the bureaucratic procedures needed to process them, put an enormous strain on the Jewish refugee bodies congregated in Woburn House and later Bloomsbury House in London – generating endless queues, countless forms, and a chronic financial cash crisis (which was only eased to any extent by the government's decision, after the outbreak of war, to contribute half the cost of the maintenance of destitute refugees). A young German woman, Alice Strauss, who'd secured a domestic position in Hendon, tried early in 1939 to get a short stay visa for her parents; their file was 390 letters thick.[51]

One notable success of the British Jewish refugee organisations in 1938–9 was the Refugee Children's Movement (RCM), which secured government cooperation resulting in the removal of the visa or passport requirement for child refugees. In what has been called a unique scheme of rescue,[52] the subsequent Kindertransporte saved 10,000 children up to the age of sixteen, ninety per cent of them Jewish, in the ten months before the outbreak of war: they came in groups of 100 to 600, escorted by train from Berlin or Vienna, and by boat from the Hook of Holland to Harwich. They were classified as 'Guaranteed' (those for whom individual friends or relations undertook to provide maintenance) and 'Non-Guaranteed' (for whom the RCM itself or local committees gave the undertaking).[53] Once in Britain, they were placed in private homes, not necessarily Jewish ones.

After the war broke out, the Home Office refused to

countenance further significant immigration (partly on the grounds that refugees might be enemy agents) and all pre-war visas granted to refugees were treated as invalid. In December 1939 it was decided that Jews still in Germany couldn't be admitted to Britain as refugees because if any were given permission 'we are bound to receive a flood of applications'.[54] Once again the likely increase of anti-Semitism was cited as the reason even though, in a national poll asking whether the British government should assist any refugees who could get out, seventy-eight per cent said that they should.[55] Yet prejudice persisted. The actress Joyce Grenfell decided against having 'a foreigner ... There's something a bit un-cosy about a non-Aryan refugee in one's kitchen.'[56] In any case, as a Foreign Office official noted in 1943, 'from our point of view, fortunately, the German government appear to be intending to persist to the last in their refusal to allow Jews to leave Germany'.[57]

After the refugees had arrived in Britain, their problems didn't end: once again a heavy pressure to assimilate was exerted. The Board of Deputies, which saw itself chiefly as representing Anglo-Jewry rather than the incomers and was anxious to preserve harmony between Jews and non-Jews in Britain, appointed a Public Relations Officer to monitor and improve refugees' public behaviour in London. She would accost those speaking German too loudly in the street and remonstrate with café-owners displaying German language newspapers. She even organised the setting-up of Jewish vigilante committees for the surveillance of refugees who'd settled in regional communities.[58]

In June 1939, the Board of Deputies, together with the German-Jewish Aid Committee, issued a booklet entitled 'Helpful Information and Guidance for Every Refugee'. It urged each refugee to start learning English and its correct pronunciation immediately, and to refrain from speaking German or reading German newspapers in public, or from speaking in a loud voice altogether. (So much so that the son of one German refugee, when he finally visited Germany in the 1980s, was astonished to find a whole population talking loudly, he'd so accustomed himself to the injunction that German must be spoken softly, if at all.) Among the list of prohibitions it included, 'Do not criticise any government regulation or the way things are done over here ... Do not join any political organisation or take part in any political activities.'[59] And reproducing the prevailing stereotypes about Jews (and indeed the English), the booklet advised refugees that 'the Englishman attaches very great importance to modesty, understatement in speech rather than overstatement, and quietness of dress and manner. He values good manners far more than he values the evidence of wealth.'[60] One refugee remembers that he 'had to become more English than the English, play cricket, drink in pubs. I always felt I was acting a part'.[61] (And now I understand why my friend who'd come over on the Kindertransport was so struck by my intransigence over Yom Kippur at the academic conference.)

The refugees weren't exactly embraced by the Anglo-Jewish community. The publisher George Weidenfeld recounts in his memoirs how, when he arrived in London from Nazi Vienna, he found himself scrutinised by Jews who brandished their friendships with the Kensington and Mayfair gentry. 'Don't waste your time on him, he's an *Emigrant*,' a banker's wife whispered dismissively into her daughter's ear when she asked about him.[62] A historian of the period found that none of the refugees 'rose into the hierarchy of British Jewry's institutions despite the high intellectual calibre, professional stature, creativity and vigour of many of them. Indeed they were discouraged from pursuing political activity of any sort. As a result ... the most informed body within the community played no part in the Anglo-Jewish response to the events of Europe.'[63]

The refugee organisations, fearing once again that the concentration of refugees in one place would provoke anti-

Semitism, had a policy of trying to disperse them around the country, as if this might somehow 'dilute them, and mean there was only so much Jewishness per acre'.[64] Nevertheless, there was an eruption of hostility to Jewish refugees in North-West London where local refugees were accused of being foreign agents, and five months after the end of the war a Hampstead petition to clear the district of 'aliens' attracted 2000 signatures.[65]

Those who'd secured posts as domestics experienced frustrations of their own: the former employers of servants now became servants themselves, and had to grapple not only with an arcane new cultural code but also with the vagaries of British cookers and fires. Rarely did their new employers appreciate the enormity in their change of circumstance. What's more, many of the families employing them were second-generation descendants of the Jews who'd come from Eastern Europe: only now the situation was reversed, with the former Ostjude as resident, and the German Jew in the position of vulnerable newcomer.[66]

As regards the children, Anglo-Jewry didn't put its mouth where its money was: the *Jewish Chronicle* reported that 'when the (10,000 Kindertransporte) children were brought over in 1938 the Jewish community, which had shown such great generosity when it was a question of donating money for the refugee organisation, showed themselves very reluctant to take Jewish refugee children into their homes'.[67] Many of the Christian families where the children were sent had never previously encountered a Jew and had no knowledge of Judaism. While some families were kind and thoughtful, others marched their Jewish children each Sunday to the local church. Some Jewish child refugees were adopted and had then to become Christian.[68] And there are dispiriting recollections of being greeted by committee-ladies expecting gratitude, and hostels insensitive to the new arrivals' psychological and spiritual needs, let alone the urgency of teaching them English.[69]

Soon an added complication set in – evacuation. For those so recently prised away from their families, this second separation was particularly hard. One ten-year-old recalls his feelings as the train left London: 'Once again I was utterly alone, not really knowing anyone and this time not being able to converse in a language that I knew.'[70] A sixteen-year-old watched the families parting from their children at the station and observed, 'No one gave us a send-off.'[71] She remembers arriving with her cousin in the Home Counties, where they were unsuccessfully hawked round the local houses.'Who, after all, would be prepared to take two foreigners into their home – from Germany, the enemy, of all places! Many doors were shut in our faces without ceremony.'[72] Many Jewish children were billeted in areas where hitherto there had never been Jews: to one East Anglian, the Jews evacuated to her village were 'as completely Oriental and foreign to our northern green as so many exotic black parrots',[73] while in countless areas Jews were asked about their horns.[74] Yet the authorities could, and sometimes did, refuse permission to transfer a Jewish child from the Christian billet to which it had been first assigned,[75] though the Jewish community also set up 'evacuee hostels' where children could live in a Jewish environment while attending local schools.

The older refugee children emerged from evacuation only to face, along with the adults, another trial – internment. From May 1940 there was such hostility to refugee aliens that even the *Jewish Chronicle* supported the principle of internment, as did whole sections of Anglo-Jewish society. Aliens had already been divided by tribunals into three categories: C – undoubtedly loyal, B – needing to be kept under supervision, and A – whose loyalty was suspect; only Category A had been interned. But in mid–1940 a policy of mass internment was initiated: over 20,000 people, some one-third of the refugees from Nazism, were interned in Britain,[76] in makeshift and overcrowded centres, mostly on the Isle of Man, largely on the grounds that they might be fifth columnists. Remarkably, the state suspected them of allegiance to Nazi Germany, and often mixed together pro-Nazi and Jewish refugees in the same camp: some camp governors had difficulty 'grasping the difference between German Jews and Nazis', while others felt that the ones they 'could trust were real Germans and not German Jews'.[77]

Some internees suffered psychological after-effects, in particular those who'd been inmates in German concentration camps in the 1930s.[78] One Jewish child refugee couldn't help thinking that 'if Britain should lose the war, Hitler would find us very neatly rounded up in one place'.[79] Another recalls that 'in Berlin I had a very long walk to and from school each day and frequently I was jeered and spat at when the German people realised I was Jewish. Now [in Douglas, in the Isle of Man], as we passed crowds of people, on either side we were jeered and spat at not because we were Jewish but because we were German.'[80] (Again and again, refugees who had led assimilated lives in Germany until the arrival of Nazism relate how strange it felt once more, this time in Britain, to be defined as Jews from the outside.) According to a leading historian of the period, 'the internment of aliens . . . was no aberration – it was an episode that witnessed the disintegration of liberal sympathy to the refugees and the success of forces that had been hostile to the exiles of Nazism since their arrival in Britain. It was not so much "May Madness" as a sign of the power of British intolerance when freed from its usual restraints.'[81]

It seems to us today perverse that anti-Semitism in Britain could have survived the Second World War, let alone increased during that period. Yet wartime surveys by Mass-Observation found a large proportion of the population believing Jews to be 'un-British', and over fifty-five per cent feeling some hostility to Jews, mostly in private. One British Jew, a boy in 1939, remembers that anti-Semitism was rife: 'I heard British people say, "The sooner Hitler gets here and clears them out, the better." ' Generally, public expression of anti-Semitism was more muted: as a Scottish novelist reported, she and her friends discussed it amongst themselves 'so that one can get it off one's chest and not say [it] in public',[82] while others testified to ambivalent feelings about Hitler's treatment of the Jews, with one liberal novelist admitting in 1943 to 'a tendency to think serve them right before one can catch oneself up'.[83] Many people shared the contradictory views of Harold Nicolson, who declared that 'Although I loathe anti-Semitism I do dislike Jews'.[84] A.J.P. Taylor remarked that many people were 'annoyed at having to repudiate [because of Nazi persecution of the Jews] the anti-Semitism which they had secretly cherished'.[85] In response to another survey, also in 1943, on how anti-Semitism could be defeated, the unanimous response was 'that it was up to the Jews themselves to combat [it]'.[86] Once again, Jews were held responsible for anti-Semitism: indeed, during the Second World War the connection between Nazism/Fascism and anti-Semitism, it's been suggested, 'was not widely grasped in Britain'.[87]

Certainly literature, the arts, and the media were full of unsympathetic and stereotypical images of Jews in general and refugees in particular. In 1940, Orwell declared 'for the time being we have heard enough about the concentration camps and the persecution of the Jews'.[88] Sympathy for European Jews coexisted quite happily with antipathy to British ones. Indeed, historian Tony Kushner, author of an exhaustive study of anti-Semitism in Britain during the Second World War, concluded that 'the most remarkable aspect of the Jewish image in the war is the lack of change that took place, despite the background of Jewish persecution in Europe'.[89]

In 1943, twelve per cent of the population thought that there were more than three million Jews in Britain, and forty-two per cent overestimated the real figure of 400,000.[90] The two most enduring stereotypes of Jews concerned money and power. A child refugee recalled encountering an 'endemic anti-Semitism . . . It was never something open or violent . . . However there was often a slight reference to money – either about one's vast quantities of it or of a certain tightness in wanting to spend it.'[91] Kushner has identified two kinds of anti-Semitism prevalent during the war – 'rich Jew anti-Semitism' and 'poor Jew anti-Semitism', the first directed at the supposedly opulent 'Golders Green' Jew, and the second against the poor oriental 'Whitechapel' Jew. (Sometimes they coalesced, as in Dorothy Sayers's widely acclaimed series of BBC radio plays, *The Man Born to Be King*, based on the life of Jesus, in which Matthew is described as 'as vulgar a little commercial Jew as ever walked Whitechapel'.[92]) The first stereotype tapped into age-old images of Jews as usurers, and drew on veteran conspiracy theories about international Jewish financiers seeking world domination, as embodied in the 1903 fake Russian document *The Protocols of the Elders of Zion*, whose fantasies about a secret Jewish world government began to circulate in Britain once again during the war. The preoccupation with Jews and finance capital was encouraged by Britain's Communists, and was amplified when Jews were scapegoated for the existence of the black-market. It was matched by the notion of Jews as bolsheviks: Marx and Rothschild coexisted as bogeys in the demonology surrounding Jews, furnishing a justification for hatred by both the Left and the Right.[93] The conception of Jews as an omnipotent world power flourished quite untarnished by news of the systematic extermination of European Jewry.[94]

Jews in Britain, still clinging to the emancipation contract, simply didn't possess the tools to make sense of all this and challenge it. They continued to adhere to the notion that anti-Semitism, if it occurred, was somehow earned,[95] and tried to disprove anti-Semitic stereotypes both through their own model behaviour and through argument, as if it might be rationally disposed of (as liberalism had always promised).[96]

They were also quite unequal to the task of exerting political pressure on the government to take whatever limited opportunities were possible to save European Jews, since political action *qua* Jews was precisely what they'd relinquished in return for civic rights and might, they feared, be taken both as criticism of the British government and ingratitude, thereby generating domestic anti-Semitism: 'Frightened for its own safety and of appearing disloyal, the Board of Deputies was trapped in its special relationship with the government and thus made impotent regarding European Jewry.'[97] There was no lack of knowledge about extermination of the Jews: from 1942 onwards both the Jewish and British national press carried abundant reports of mass slaughter, and on 11 December 1942 the *Jewish Chronicle* appeared with a black-bordered front page bearing the headline 'Two Million Jews Slaughtered; Most Terrible Massacre of All Time: Appalling Horrors of Nazi Mass Murders'.[98] At the same time there was an understandable inability to comprehend and process such information, to make sense of such an unprecedented occurrence: it's all too easy to impute, retrospectively, post-Holocaust knowledge to those in the midst of unfolding events which were a complete rupture in the continuity of the Jewish experience of discrimination and oppression. (As the third president of Israel later put it, 'We thought Nazism meant that Dr Cohen could not be a physician and Dr Levy could not be a lawyer.'[99]) It's hard to remember that they didn't know the ending.

What they did know was enough not only to cause them to fear for their own safety but also to induce a feeling of overwhelming powerlessness, paralysis, and despair.[100] Anglo-Jewish communal institutions during this period were riven by personality conflicts and heated debates about Zionism. As the *Jewish Chronicle* reported in a September 1943 editorial on Anglo-Jewry's reaction to the war: 'they have stood bewildered, stunned, unable to grasp the situation as events have unfolded themselves. And not merely bewildered but divided! . . . Jewish feelings tend to find an outlet in domestic faction and quarrels which can only still further confuse their minds and confound their counsels.'[101] As the paper hinted, one can't help but see such disputes as a distraction from the unbearable. Though some British Jews felt fury at the apparent indifference of their peers – in 1944 Chief Rabbi Joseph Hertz declared that 'Anglo-Jewry does not know what is going on, and the few who do, do not seem to care much'[102] – most assuaged their consciences by raising money for relief for Jewish refugees. Meanwhile, the extermination of European Jewry often appeared as the final item on the Board of Deputies' plenary session agenda, if at all.[103]

The historically determined sense of vulnerability among Anglo-Jewry meant that they couldn't counter the central tenet of Allied policy – that the only way to save the Jews was by winning the war: 'nothing could be done to interfere with that objective – including, ironically, the rescue of the Jews'.[104] At no point did British Jewry unite in a campaign to attempt to persuade the government that striking directly at the Nazis' extermination programme could play a central role in trying to achieve their military objectives, or was equally important. Indeed, 'Anglo-Jewry mounted no effective or popular campaign to pressurise the government in any way' because of its 'phobia about anti-Semitism – a neurosis which at times verged on self-hatred'.[105] Jewish MPs were reluctant to speak out in the House of Commons on behalf of European Jewry: once again they considered non-Jews the most appropriate protesters against the extermination of the Jews, and contrived to persuade non-Jewish MPs to petition on their behalf. So it was largely left to sympathetic non-Jewish campaigners like the tireless Eleanor Rathbone MP publicly to plead the Jewish cause.

When British Jews did speak out, in order to show that Jews were loyal patriots and not only concerned with the fate of their own kind, they stressed Nazi racism as a whole, rather than drawing attention to the specifically anti-Jewish nature of the Nazi programme, as if Jews were somehow less deserving of being saved than Gentiles or humanity in general.[106]

Above all, whenever non-Jews spoke for them, or were prepared to grant them a hearing, Anglo-Jewry responded with ritual displays of gratitude and obsequiousness, so much so that even when non-Jewish leaders reacted with inaction, they were thanked merely for having listened. After Churchill refused to send a message of support or even a Minister to represent the government at a Board of Deputies' meeting on the Nazi extermination of the Jews at the Albert Hall in October 1942, the President of the Anglo-Jewish Association wrote to him 'to thank you for the consideration which has been given to the matter and I hope you will forgive me for having troubled you'.[107] And in December 1942, after meeting a delegation from the Council of Christians and Jews, Eden's Under-Secretary Richard Law noted that 'in spite of the fact that the deputation expressed great appreciation of my alleged sympathetic attitude, I don't think that I gave anything away'.[108]

Yet it's too easy to judge British Jewry with hindsight, without taking into account their full circumstances: by the start of the war, the cost of supporting an unanticipated swell of refugees had squeezed them financially as never before. And as Tony Kushner remarks, 'British Jewry during the conflict was a frightened community preoccupied with its own defence and the pressures to keep Jewish traditions alive in unfavourable circumstances . . . [it] had neither the moral energy, vision and self-confidence to confront the horrors facing the Jews of Europe.'[109]

It's less easy to exonerate the British government for its reaction to the extermination of European Jews. The only Jewish member of the Cabinet, Leslie Hore-Belisha, Secretary of State for War, was dismissed in January 1940: his Jewishness may not have been the cause of his dismissal, but neither was it unconnected.[110] The government, obsessed with avoiding anti-Semitism rather than considering ways of challenging it, pandered again and again to anti-alien sentiment; it didn't appreciate that Jews aren't the source of anti-Semitism – non-Jews are. Yet any discussion of anti-Semitism was banned from BBC Radio's prestigious *Brains' Trust* programme.[111] And as Eden said, at a gathering of the Allies in Washington in 1941, 'Let me murmur in your ear: I prefer Arabs to Jews.'[112]

The collected sayings of civil servants and Foreign Office officials, on the few occasions when they were lobbied by Jewish groups, make sorry reading. The government was unwilling to feature Jewish persecution in its anti-German propaganda: 'Horror,' insisted a 1941 Ministry of Information memo, 'must be used very sparingly and must deal always with treatment of indisputably innocent people. Not with violently political opponents. And not with Jews.'[113] When, at the beginning of the war, the government contemplated releasing a White Paper on conditions in German concentration camps, the Permanent Under-Secretary at the Foreign Office objected because 'hair-raising reports about Jewish concentration camps' came from Jews themselves 'who were entirely unreliable witnesses'.[114]

The Colonial Office official responsible for immigration never missed an opportunity to articulate his own similar sentiments regarding Jews. In April 1940 he declared that 'as a general rule Jews are inclined to magnify their persecution'.[115] 'What is disturbing,' he wrote again in December 1942, 'is the apparent readiness of the new Colonial Secretary to take Jewish Agency "sob-stuff" at its face value.' Reading eye-witness accounts of German brutality, he commented, 'Familiar stuff. The Jews have spoilt their case by laying it on too thick for years past.'[116] And, explaining why he wouldn't help European Jewry, he said simply, 'Why should the Jews be spared distress and humiliation when they have earned it?'[117]

His wasn't a lone voice. One Foreign Office official remarked in 1944 on the 'Jewish tendency to superlative', while another in the same year regretted the wasting of Foreign Office time 'with these wailing Jews'.[118] When, early in the war, the clergyman James Parkes wrote a report for the Foreign Office about the situation of European Jewry and referred to the murder of 50,000 Jews, the Foreign Office crossed out one of his noughts. Later on, when his second version referred to half a million, the same happened, and it occurred yet again towards the end of the war when he estimated that five million Jews had been murdered.[119]

The government didn't want to raise public expectations that it would be intervening to help European Jews since it had no intention of instituting such a policy: according to Tony Kushner, on only one occasion, at the end of 1942, 'did the British government acknowledge the plight of European Jewry',[120] and 'government officials were more concerned with the post-war removal of [Jewish] refugees in Britain than with efforts to help the victims of Nazism in Europe'.[121]

The Allies never really took on board the destruction of Polish Jewry, as opposed to that of German Jews. Polish Jews were seemingly forever associated in British minds with turn-of-the-century Eastern European pogroms, leaving the experience of Eastern European Jewry (until recently) largely ignored and unspoken for.[122] When, in June 1942, information about the fate of Polish Jewry was smuggled out of the Warsaw ghetto, reached London, and was broadcast over the BBC, the ghetto underground group was jubilant, assuming that the British government would be moved, there would be massive retaliatory attacks, and the remnants of Polish Jewry would be saved. But nothing happened.[123]

Also in 1942, Jan Karski arrived in London as a secret

envoy to the Polish government in exile and to the Allied governments, to report on the situation in Poland (having seen with his own eyes the Warsaw ghetto and Bełzec concentration camp) and to relay demands from the Jewish underground, including the plea that Allied governments should publicly announce that the protection of the Jews would be part of the overall Allied strategy. He met with Eden and three other members of the War Cabinet who declared that the Jewish leaders' demands couldn't be met, and reasserted that 'the main task of the Allies was winning the war, and therefore anything not strictly of a military character was regarded as a side issue'.[124] Yet after the war and the liberation of the concentration camps, the Allied victory was represented as a triumph over the Nazi policy of genocide against the Jews, and was retrospectively imputed as part of their motivation all along.[125]

Many of the problems which pro-Jewish lobbyists met in trying to persuade the government to take action to help European Jewry arose out of the tendency of British officials to disbelieve any but their own sources. So not only were Jews inherently untrustworthy, but so were the Soviets: their liberation of Majdanek (in July 1944) and Auschwitz (in January 1945) received scant attention in the British media compared with that given to Belsen, liberated (in April 1945) by British troops. (And the 1947 Auschwitz trial was virtually ignored by Western media.[126]) There was also a great degree of official and public cynicism about 'atrocity stories' in general, because many of those current in the First World War were later found to have been exaggerated. The problem, as one commentator has pointed out, was 'that acts which had been faked for propaganda purposes in World War I were real in World War II'.[127] As a result, the stories coming out of Eastern Europe appeared mythological, and government and other institutions were soon unable to distinguish severe brutality from propaganda. The Ministry of Information argued that, in order to make the

Nazi project 'credible' to the British people, it shouldn't be represented as 'too extreme'.[128]

For its part, the BBC, having been founded at least in part to prevent the recurrence of First World War 'atrocity' propaganda,[129] wasn't well-suited to report on the occurrence of real, unprecedented and systematic atrocities.[130] It also adhered to a pragmatic worldview where people were essentially decent: the epic horrors of the Holocaust lay beyond its frame of reference. On the one hand, the BBC treated the *Jewish Chronicle* as a reliable source, taking up many of its front-page lead articles as news stories. On the other hand, there was an emphasis on deportation rather than murder and a refusal to engage with the reality of Jews dispatched to extermination camps. The Corporation wasn't free of anti-Semitism either: as a memo about *Children's Hour* put it in 1943, 'In our experience if Jewish broadcasters are given an inch they come back clamouring for an ell.'[131] And the BBC responded to complaints that the Rumanian, Hungarian, and Polish Services were impaired by Jewish accents not by dismissing them but by appointing an 'assessor' in the Polish Service to detect 'traces of the Jewish accent and manner'.[132]

Jews weren't allowed to speak for themselves: a 1943 proposal by the BBC Talks Department on 'the subject of the Jew', given by 'a Jew unconnected with the world of business, explaining that he has no particular brief for the Jews but is unashamed of being one' was rejected. As the Assistant Director of Talks wrote, 'We agreed to drop the suggestion of a talk by a Jew, but would still like to submit the proposal for a talk on race hatreds of which the German attitude to the Jews might be an example, to be undertaken from a fairly lofty standpoint', perhaps by Julian Huxley.[133]

Indeed, the BBC categorically refused to accept 'pro-Semite' programmes arguing, in a *reductio ad absurdum* of balance, that it would thereby be obliged to give equal space to anti-Semites. On this issue as on most others, the BBC of the time followed the government's political lead.[134]

Given all this, perhaps it's not too surprising that public awareness of and knowledge about the extermination of European Jewry declined between 1943 and the end of the war.[135]

6

According to the popular mythology of the Second World War, the newsreels filmed at the liberation of Belsen devastated the British public and caused an enormous outflow of sympathy for European Jewry. At a stroke (it's assumed) they also raised public consciousness and put the Holocaust on the map. The evidence, however, gainsays this comforting image. Incredibly, a Mass-Observation report of 1946 found some Britons expressing support for the gassing of Jews, with many people still blaming Jews for the existence of anti-Semitism.[1] At the same time, renewed antagonism to Germany after its defeat once again produced hostility towards German-Jewish refugees,[2] while the violent exploits of the Jewish underground in Palestine also helped foster British antipathy towards Jews in general, giving rise to anti-Jewish riots in almost every major British city in 1947. All of this apparently combined to obliterate the memory of the still very recent Jewish experience in Europe: in 1947, Mass-Observation was already suggesting that 'people are no longer moved by the thought of Jewish suffering in concentration camps'.[3]

Even more striking was the refusal to acknowledge that Nazi policy was directed specifically against the Jews. Common to almost every nation, this attitude dates back to the war, has lasted until recently, and constitutes perhaps the deepest wound to survivors and refugees. The 1943 Bermuda Conference on the Jewish refugee crisis decided that, because of 'signs of increasing anti-Semitic feeling' in Britain, its public statements would 'avoid implying that refugees were necessarily Jewish' and would refer to them instead 'by nationality rather than race'.[4] When, in 1944, the Chief Rabbi asked the British government to declare all Jews in enemy territory protected persons, the reply came back: 'It is not the policy of HMG to regard Jews as belonging to a separate category. It is felt that discrimination of this kind savours too strongly of Nazi attitudes to Jews.'[5] Again and again, the British government – in the abiding spirit of the emancipation contract – refused to recognise any Jewish 'nationality'.[6] Indeed, Kushner alleges that on only one occasion during the war, in December 1942, had British or American official and semi-official statements stressed the sufferings of Jews in particular under the Nazi regime.[7]

Broadcasting pursued the same policy. The BBC, together with the Ministry of Information, decided that the best way of dealing with anti-Semitism was simply not to mention Jews.[8] A 299-page volume of great speeches and first-hand accounts about the development of the Second World War as described over the BBC includes only four references to Jews: astonishingly in Ed Murrow's broadcast about the liberation of Buchenwald there were none,[9] nor any in Leonard Cottrell's 1946 radio documentary on Nazi concentration camp life as seen and experienced by a prisoner, 'The Man from Belsen'.[10]

According to Ben Helfgott, a child survivor and chair of the Yad Vashem Committee of the Board of Deputies, Richard Dimbleby's historic BBC radio report on the liberation of Belsen (reshown with the addition of pictures on the BBC in 1965, and again in 1995 to mark the fiftieth anniversary of the end of the war) 'made a lot of people angry: over footage of the liberation of Belsen, he mentioned Jews only once. In spite of the fact that there were Jews in Belsen, he didn't refer to it. And to show (in 1965) survivors of the Holocaust, they filmed an elderly Polish survivor in a Sue Ryder home – the Jews didn't exist.'[11] Yet more Jews – 40,000 – were liberated from Belsen than from any other concentration camp.[12] When the Dimbleby broadcast was rescreened in 1995, it ended (without apparent irony) with a prayer over an image of a cross.

This wasn't an exclusively British phenomenon. Kushner notes the same trend in American coverage of the liberation of Belsen – 'the word "Jew" is conspicuous by its absence'.[13] The 1945 trial of Marshal Pétain, leader of the Vichy government, scarcely mentioned his role in the Holocaust and the fact that he sent 75,000 French Jews to their death in concentration camps. 'The trial didn't dwell on the deportations of the Jews,' Nazi-hunter Serge Klarsfeld has remarked, 'because, at the time, there was very little interest in that particular category of victim.'[14] Post-war France didn't discriminate between members of the Resistance and Communists who'd been sent to labour camps like Buchenwald, and Jews sent to Auschwitz to be exterminated[15] – both were subsumed under the term 'deportees', a word which focused on their departure and eviction rather than their arrival and subsequent fate. (Even today, many French people and Britons are unable to differentiate between labour and death camps: Belsen, a labour camp, still seems to have equal resonance for the British with Auschwitz, an extermination camp.)

Poland, for its part, has posthumously 'polonised' the Polish Jews massacred in the Holocaust:[16] when, in 1979, the Pope reinterpreted a memorial at Auschwitz commemorating the 'Six Million' as meaning that 'six million Poles lost their lives during the Second World War', he was according Jews the status of Poles and membership of the Polish family, something conspicuously denied them when they were alive.[17] The establishment of a Carmelite monastery at Auschwitz and the shrine to the martyred Roman Catholic Father Kolbe, pre-war author of virulently anti-Semitic writings, are all part of the same refusal to acknowledge Jewish particularity,[18] one which continues today in Britain. In 1990, the British journalist Jill Tweedie, in an outburst against Jews in the *Guardian*, recalled walking 'up the Avenue of the Righteous Gentile in Jerusalem while my guide pointed out the plaques on either side in memory of Gentiles who'd helped JEWS in the war. Oh, please. Those plaques marked human beings, not simply Gentiles, who'd had the courage . . . to risk their lives for other human beings, not simply JEWS.'[19]

At least after the war, when the truth about the experiences of European Jewry had become incontestable, one might have imagined that the British government would have taken practical steps to help its surviving remnants. But in fact Britain's post-war record on Jewish immigration is far shabbier than its pre-war one. Once again, children were the chief benefactors. At the suggestion of Leonard Montefiore, the Central British Fund (CBF) World Jewish Relief set up the Committee for the Care of Children from the Concentration Camps (CCCC),[20] which got Home Office permission to adopt 1000 Jewish orphaned child camp survivors under the age of sixteen. No government money was involved.[21] In the event only 732 eligible children could be found; they were taken to a reception camp in Windermere and eventually housed in twenty-eight hostels around the country, the youngest – mostly survivors of Theresienstadt and Auschwitz – in Lingfield House. As they were driven into Windermere at nightfall 'townspeople had come out with torches and stood on the streets shouting their welcome to the children' (and inadvertently terrifying them).[22] The CCCC gave them food, clothing, and pocket money: it sent them to school and generally took care of them. Many of the child and teenage survivors who arrived in 1945–46 became a cohesive group: those who eventually fetched up in North London formed a mutual support youth club called the Primrose Club, and later went on to found the 45 Aid Society, now an international network.[23]

The policy on adult survivors, however, was much less welcoming. The best which the British could come up with was the Distressed Relatives Scheme, which introduced a procedure which was 'ingeniously elaborate'[24] and which 'set restrictions so tightly that in practice it turned out to be nearly unworkable'.[25] A British subject with permanent residence in Britain could apply for permission to bring over family members who'd suffered at the hands of the Nazis, providing that their only remaining family lived in Britain. If permission was granted, the ticket had to be bought in England, the exit permit and visa had to be obtained from a special office, and transport had to be by sea from Hamburg to Tilbury.[26] The whole process was designed to ensure that the numbers who qualified 'would be in 100s rather than 1000s'.[27] The constraints proved effective: just over 1200 Jews entered Britain under the scheme (compared with the 100,000 post-war Jewish refugees admitted to the United States).[28]

British post-war immigration policy in fact specifically proscribed Jews (and non-white immigrants). In 1947, the British Control Commission in Germany and Austria was told that 'ex-enemy nationals, Jews and Volksdeutsche are to be excluded from the field of recruitment but the possibility of considering some Volksdeutsche at a later date will be further examined'. The British Commission in Vienna responded with a request 'to recruit displaced persons (excluding Jews of any nationality)'. Jews weren't considered assimilable, and Cabinet minutes of 1945 argued that 'the admission of a further batch of refugees, many of whom would be Jews, might provoke strong reactions from certain sections of public opinion. There was a real risk of a wave of anti-Semitic feeling in this country.'[29] Once again, anticipation of other people's anti-Semitism was used to justify anti-Semitic policies. In May 1945, a group of Conservative MPs lobbied the Home Secretary to announce when those Jewish refugees who'd been admitted before the war would be repatriated.[30]

Britain's record on admitting Jewish Holocaust survivors is especially shocking when compared with its post-war immigration policy regarding other nationalities, including Nazi war criminals. In 1946, Britain was experiencing a severe labour shortage: a government committee identified a 'manpower gap' which might reach 600,000. It was decided that foreign labour, especially that of Baltic origin, could supply the shortfall. Consequently, members of the frontline Latvian Waffen-SS, who'd voluntarily helped the Einsatzgruppen (mobile killing squads), along with the entire Ukrainian membership of the Galician Division of the Waffen-SS, were among those given priority under labour recruitment schemes, with the barest screening out of war criminals.

David Cesarani, chronicler of the process, argues that the Foreign Office was either complicit or extremely gullible, concluding that the former was most likely, and that in some cases the Foreign Office operated a cover-up. Britain, suggests Cesarani, was a haven for collaborators and war criminals, some of whom joined a veterans' association which openly celebrated its war service in the Waffen-SS. Two hundred thousand refugees, Displaced Persons, and immigrant workers were admitted to Britain between 1945 and 1950. Just over 1200 were Jews, whilst by 1949 almost 10,000 were Latvians,[31] with the incipient Cold War providing the ideological justification. Many Holocaust survivors remain angry about the British government's contrasting rules regarding the entry of Balts and Jews.[32]

My parents, after their arrival in Britain in 1947, received no help whatsoever from either the government or the Jewish community. My mother recalls, 'I was a complete stranger – I didn't know where to turn. I just had a few

friends already here, otherwise we were completely alone.'
Adult Holocaust survivors, in contrast to the children admitted into Britain, came as individuals and not in a transport.
Being dispersed, they'd not only have been harder to locate,
but were also assumed to be the responsibility of the families
who'd sponsored them.[33] The circumstances of my parents'
entry, because of my father's posting with the Polish Embassy
in London, were even more particular. Yet my parents met
regularly with other Polish Holocaust survivors in London,
so it wouldn't have been inordinately hard for a Jewish
agency intent on giving relief to survivors to find them.
Along with many other children of camp survivors, I have
felt bitter about their failure to do so, and have only recently
come to understand the reasons for and deep historical
roots of Anglo-Jewry's inaction.

If British Jews had felt paralysed and shocked during the
war, they must have felt even more so afterwards on seeing
searing images of Jewish suffering and knowing how little
pressure they'd attempted to exert from a position of relative safety. One can imagine their sense of guilt and discomfort in the presence of survivors, walking reminders of
what they were doubtless trying to forget. Survivors thus
became begetters of embarrassment who, in a ghastly inversion of expectation and a shocking continuity of the *univers
concentrationnaire*, had to be careful not to upset those who
hadn't been through the experience: survivors had been
transformed from actual sufferers of distress into potential
creators of it.

Kushner confirms that few British Jews became involved
in distributing relief and rescue for survivors, that groups
like the CCCC were disappointed by British Jewry's response
to appeals for money and clothes, and that survivors who
came to Britain were obliged to repress their camp experiences.[34] Again and again, the stereotype of the survivor who
didn't want to talk about his or her experiences was (and
still is) invoked as a justification for the silence greeting

Holocaust survivors in Britain. Although this was true of some, it certainly wasn't true of all survivors: my parents talked freely and were eager to do so. In the absence of others to talk to (apart from fellow sufferers), they spoke to their children.

The result, for us, was a complete disjuncture between the world outside the home (one where, I discovered from a school geography lesson, no one in my class had even heard of Poland, let alone had the merest knowledge of where it was or what had happened there) and the world within, between a private cosmos informed by the Holocaust and concentration camps and a public one from which they'd been almost entirely evacuated. We had to breach this chasm each day, in a tiny simulacrum of the task my parents faced in having to find a way to bridge their pre- and post-war lives.

But if Anglo-Jewry and the British government couldn't provide any support, what about the substantial psychoanalytic community in England, which contained so many Jews in its ranks? Although the concept of Post-Traumatic Stress Disorder is a relatively modern one, which only emerged properly in the wake of the Vietnam War, it wouldn't have required a great feat of the imagination to realise that Holocaust survivors had mental and spiritual as well as physical needs. Of course, psychoanalysis in the immediate post-war period was still (relatively speaking) in its infancy, and certainly couldn't have been expected to organise mass provision for the survivors of such an unprecedented collective trauma, however attractive such a retrospective fantasy might be. And most survivors set great store by independence and self-reliance, seeing their strength as the means by which they'd survived the war, and were unwilling to focus on weakness, vulnerability, and fear, or voluntarily to experience dependence and defencelessness. My parents, for example, never thought of asking for psychological help and never saw themselves as psychologically damaged.

What's more, if such help (as opposed to material assistance) had been offered, they would have rejected it. And this has remained their position until today. But it also took a long time before psychoanalysis took on board the Holocaust: many of those survivors and children of survivors who were analysed in the 1950s, '60s, and even '70s, report that their own or their parents' Holocaust experiences scarcely figured in the analysis: analysts hadn't yet begun to understand the issues.[35]

In the 1940s and early '50s, the concept of trauma was still associated more with children than with adults,[36] and the sort of issues exercising the immediate post-war psychologists (with a couple of notable exceptions) were what life had been like for children living under the Nazi system,[37] the emotional problems of displaced children,[38] and the readjustment of children in the post-war world.[39] Anna Freud also observed some child survivors in a special Sussex home, charting both their aggression and sense of community, and trying to relate their present behaviour to their past camp experience.[40]

Regarding adults, the preoccupations of British and American psychologists during and soon after the Second World War were remarkably similar to those after the First World War when the concept of 'shell-shock' became current. This time 'war neuroses' among civilians and the armed forces were discussed, along with the effects of psychological warfare on the general population, 'war weariness', and 'neurotic behaviour after liberation'.[41] There was international debate about the difficulties facing military women readjusting to civilian life, about group psychotherapy for 'neurotic soldiers' and about combat neuroses,[42] and an account of treatment of 'psychoneurosis' in the British army.[43] But on adult concentration camp survivors – nothing. Shell-shock extended only to combatants: the victims of war weren't assumed to have also suffered from it. In the absence of this understanding, no appropriate, culturally sensitive help could be offered to Holocaust survivors in those early days – a lack some of their children still rue.

Some analysts have suggested that 'psychoanalysis wasn't the first thing these people needed – they needed physical and social rehabilitation, to settle down and learn the language ... They needed settling-in, and psychological intervention wasn't appropriate at the beginning. After a while, psychological problems became apparent and by then they spoke English ... Even the children – the first two years they needed food, care, love, etc.'[44]

There was another factor in operation. As the distinguished training analyst Pearl King points out, 'Quite a lot of the analysts were already refugees from the continent, so it was very difficult for them. Analysing survivors wasn't a high profile thing because people hardly dared think about it.'[45] King asserts that the idea of adult trauma was current at the time 'but refugee analysts were traumatised themselves by having had to leave their homes, their countries, friends, and language – we in the British [Psychoanalytical] Society were landed with a whole lot of traumatised people as analysts.'[46]

European psychoanalysis had been deeply affected by Nazism. In 1933, shortly after Hitler came to power, Freud's books were burnt in a great bonfire in Berlin, the Jewish President of the Berlin Psychoanalytical Institute and Society, and all Jewish members of the Berlin Institute and the German Society for Psychotherapy (now under Nazi control) resigned, and the first of the German-Jewish analysts arrived in Britain.

In 1934, most of the remaining Jewish analysts fled from Germany into exile, to either New York or London. Fifteen who didn't were eventually tortured and killed in concentration camps (including Karl Landauer who, along with some of his colleagues, incredibly managed to provide some psychotherapy inside Bergen-Belsen).[47] German-Jewish analysts had a strong sense of having been abandoned by their Gentile colleagues, who had stood by for the most part in silence during the liquidation of psychoanalysis (as it had existed hitherto) in Germany. (This taboo issue wasn't aired until the Congress of the International Psychoanalytical Association in Hamburg in 1985, the first IPA congress to take place in Germany since the war.[48])

In Austria, the Anschluss brought about the rapid dissolution of the Vienna Psychoanalytic Society and the exclusion of all non-Aryan members from the body which replaced it. Freud was reluctantly persuaded by colleagues and friends to leave Vienna for London, where he arrived in May 1938 with Anna (who earlier had been detained for a day in Vienna by the Gestapo).[49] Of the sixty-nine members of the Vienna Psychoanalytical Society, there were only three remaining in Vienna in 1945.[50]

By 1938, one-third of the analysts in the British Society were from the continent. But they didn't receive a warm welcome from British analysts, who were worried that there wouldn't be sufficient work to go round, and they felt disoriented by having to sit in meetings in rows rather than gathered round a table as in Vienna. Regarded as enemy aliens, they also weren't allowed to travel out of London.[51]

Melanie Klein, resident in London since 1926, had experienced violent anti-Semitism in Hungary in 1919 and in 1938 became anxious about the possibility of a Nazi invasion.[52] The arrival of Anna Freud in London initiated the bitter feud between the two women and their followers which was to last for decades and divided British psychoanalysis. Pearl King suggests interestingly that 'the battle between Melanie Klein and Anna Freud was perhaps a diversion from the depression of what had happened, of having had to leave their homeland. There was rather a taboo about talking about it. Those people gradually started thinking about what had happened to their relatives – for a lot of the time they hoped they'd got away.'[53] So it's scarcely surprising that those psychoanalysts resident in Britain whom one would have thought ideally placed to empathise with the trauma of Holocaust survivors were, in the event, actually particularly ill-suited to the task on account of their own trauma. Moreover, like every other refugee, they were mustering their energies to establish themselves in Britain and to come to terms with the destruction wrought on Europe.

The now considerable literature about Holocaust survivors, as well as the testimonies of survivors and refugees, stress the critical importance they attribute to being heard, with testimony and survival being seen as integral. As one commentator put it, 'A survivor's writing after the Holocaust is proof that he has defeated the "final solution"; it is indisputable evidence that he exists, a notion that no survivor ever takes for granted.'[54]

Yet, in post-war Britain, silence took up residence instead. Isaac Deutscher was able to write, quite accurately, in 1958, that 'It is an indubitable fact that the Nazi massacre of six million Jews has not made any deep impression on the nations of Europe.'[55] It was as if the annihilation of European Jewry had itself been incinerated, leaving no trace (itself another part of the Nazi project: Himmler acknowledged the Nazi intention to leave behind no witnesses or record – 'this is an unwritten and never to be written page of glory in our history'[56]). As one psychoanalyst has suggested, 'The absence of an empathetic listener, or more radically, the absence of an addressable other, an other who can hear the anguish of one's memories and thus affirm and recognise their realness, annihilates the story.'[57] The collective silence seemed to furnish the final proof, if any were needed, that the Jews lay outside what Europeans saw as their 'universe of obligation'.[58]

The word 'Holocaust' didn't actually come into usage until between 1957 and 1959, and then only in limited circles.[59] The European Jewish war experience was almost entirely absent from British books about the war published in the late 1940s and 1950s: what little emerged was based on the Nuremberg Trial evidence which was almost exclusively made up of German documents and concerned with rooting out the perpetrators' perspective: 'The voice of the survivors was not heard,'[60] while the victims were conceived of solely in aggregate – reduced to an abstract notion, they became the matter over which the Nazi-protagonist exercised his demonic power. As Kushner succinctly put it, 'The British weren't at Auschwitz, either in person or spiritually,' and the obsession with the mythology of British wartime heroism, both in Europe and on the home front, left no space for the Jewish experience.[61]

As a result, until the early 1960s, the Holocaust was represented almost entirely by *The Diary of Anne Frank* (published in English in 1952) and Lord Russell's *The Scourge of the Swastika*, an almost pornographic account of concentration camp sadism.[62] A British journalist who was a schoolboy in the 1950s recalls how the Second World War dominated playground games, furnishing ready-made baddies (the Germans) and goodies (British military types), yet he can't remember a single word about Jewish suffering in the concentration camps,[63] and Tony Kushner, who was a schoolboy in Manchester in the 1960s and '70s, recalls that the Holocaust was barely referred to either at school or in Jewish activities.[64] Indeed, it's been pointed out that paradoxically, public consciousness of the Holocaust is more extensive today than it was ten years after it ended.[65] My own recollection of references to the Holocaust (outside my home) at school, university, work, or socially, right up until the late 1970s, was that they emanated almost invariably from me.

On the rare occasions during those years when survivors were the subject of public interest, it was purely on account of their wartime experiences, as if their lives only began with the rise of Nazism and had ended with its defeat. In the absence of any context it was thus impossible to appreciate the enormity of the rupture which the war had wrought on their lives: they came purely to embody victimhood, to stand for the objects of evil, and were thereby denuded of culture and agency. The Jews, as constructed by the British until well into the 1970s, were virtually a product of the Nazi imagination and lacking in any independent existence. So the survivors were obliged to fall back on their own resources and landsmen.

The 1961 Eichmann Trial is generally heralded as an international turning-point in consciousness about the Holocaust. The regular media reports from the heavily protected Jerusalem courthouse reminded the world of the extermination of the Jews, and introduced – in Hannah Arendt's memorable phrase about 'the banality of evil' – alternative ways of thinking about it. But, though survivors' testimony played an important role in the trial, there was an enduring fascination with Nazi evil, as evidenced in Robert Shaw's play about Eichmann *The Man in the Glass Booth* (1967) and American films like *The Pawnbroker* (1964), and Kushner suggests that the trial made less of an impact in Britain than in America.[66]

For my family, the 1964 Dering Trial (of a Polish doctor accused of carrying out hideous operations on Jewish prisoners in Auschwitz) was much more significant: a friend of my parents was a witness, and we followed her testimony daily in the newspapers. At last it appeared that a smattering of what had been contained in the home had spilled out. It was an odd feeling, as if some family secret had now been shared, and this critical experience of my parents was now receiving a smidgeon of public acknowledgement. But for the most part the Holocaust remained our private affair: we'd be taken to events like the twenty-fifth anniversary of the Warsaw Ghetto Uprising and find it packed with other people like us (part of the closed world of Holocaust survivors in Britain), but such events seemed not to obtrude at all on the wider culture.

Jeremy Isaacs's 1975 unsparing television film 'Genocide'

in the ITV *World at War* series is credited with beginning the process of introducing the Holocaust into British public consciousness, although the accompanying book indexes Auschwitz only once, Jews not at all, and lists the extermination camps incorrectly (including Belsen, but omitting Chełmno and Bełzec).[67] But it was the 1978 American TV series *Holocaust* which, though widely derided for its soapiness, properly initiated international public debate. Nevertheless the Holocaust was still seen as primarily a European experience unconnected with Britain, whose own survivor community remained effectively invisible. Holocaust survivors rarely figured in British television documentaries about the war: the speakers were almost always survivors living in America, Israel, or France. One day in the early 1980s when I was in the middle of taping the interviews with my mother, I went to the BBC to take part in an edition of *Woman's Hour* (on a quite different subject). When the presenter asked me (in pre-recording hospitality small-talk) what I'd just been doing and I told her, she expressed amazement that a Holocaust survivor should be living in England in the 1980s, as though such a person – if not extinct – would necessarily reside abroad.

Perhaps the most telling proof of the long absence of the Jewish experience of the Holocaust from British public life is the continuing lack of any major, well-known monument. Tony Kushner charts the struggle to erect one, which culminated in 1983 in a 'small and unobtrusive' memorial garden in London's Hyde Park.[68] In James Young's important recent study of Holocaust memorials around the world, there isn't a single entry for Britain, though he notes the existence of acclaimed memorials in Miami, Atlanta, Baltimore, Toledo, Philadelphia, and even New Haven.[69]

Britain in 1995 has no Holocaust Museum (the only major country in Europe without one[70]), and the campaign to establish one has only just been joined; the country's first centre dedicated to the Holocaust is an entirely private initiative.[71] London has had a Holocaust Survivors' Centre only since 1993. An opinion poll on what the British know about the Holocaust, conducted by Gallup in 1994, found that only thirty-three per cent of respondents knew what the term meant. An Institute of Jewish Affairs report commented, without apparent irony, that this (along with only slightly higher percentages in answer to most of the other questions) demonstrated an impressive degree of knowledge about the Holocaust.[72]

It was only with the arrival of Steven Spielberg's film *Schindler's List* in 1994 and the 1995 commemorations of the liberation of Auschwitz that the Jewish experience of the Holocaust seemed finally to have arrived on the British public agenda (see Chapter 10), although other important less-fêted initiatives had prepared the ground. Originally omitted from the proposed new National Curriculum (only the British experience in the 1930s was at first included, with the Holocaust merely an 'optional unit'), the Holocaust was finally instated after a vocal public campaign, and this has already led to the production of some fine indigenous educational material on the subject.[73] In July 1995, an international conference on teaching the Holocaust was held at the Spiro Institute in London, and over 900 copies of the Institute's teachers' GCSE and A' Level pack on the Holocaust have been sent to schools across Britain. Holocaust Studies have also begun to appear in higher education, and are no longer seen as the preserve of Jewish students.[74] Yet the Holocaust is not offered as part of London University's BA degree in history, and there is no Chair in Holocaust Studies at any British university.[75]

Survivors living in Britain were at last given a voice in Anton Gill's book on survivors' lives.[76] And now, finally, at the eleventh hour, other Holocaust survivors (and their children) are being sought out and interviewed for the British Library National Sound Archive's National Life Story Collection, while the British Library's recent four audiocassette resource pack describes the war through the first-hand accounts of survivors living in Britain.[77] Survivors and refugees are in demand at talks and schools, and lead tours round the Anne Frank in the World exhibition (which 62,200 people visited in Britain in 1994 alone[78]), while the *Library of Holocaust Testimonies* published by Vallentine Mitchell has launched the publication of a stream of survivors' memoirs. Ben Helfgott, heartened by the interest touched off by the fiftieth anniversary of the liberation of Auschwitz, notes that 'Now they've suddenly discovered the Holocaust and it's not too late.'[79]

But Britain wasn't unique in its treatment of survivors. Though far more Eastern European Holocaust survivors entered the United States than Britain, often living near each other in the same neighbourhood so that they constituted a real community (some American children of survivors grew up thinking that everyone's parents had survived the Holocaust), nevertheless survivors there echo the complaints voiced by those who came to Britain – almost to the phrase. American Jews, they say, didn't want to hear about the camps, bringing up supposedly parallel deprivations of their own instead. One survivor remembers, 'I heard many remarks like, "We didn't have much to eat during the Depression either." I don't have to tell you how that made me feel', while another declared, 'American Jews? They're pampered. They tell me that during World War II they didn't have their tickets for gasoline.'[80]

Primo Levi's American publisher recalls that the Holocaust was never spoken about in his home or in school in the 1950s and '60s: he first heard the term in Israel in the early 1970s, and notes that Levi only reached a wide audience in the United States in the 1980s, after America had become saturated with images of Jewish suffering through the television series *Holocaust* and the like.[81] In 1969, there were only two courses on the Holocaust taught at American universities; by 1979 there were 200, and in the 1980s 2000.[82]

In France, too – reeling, no doubt, from the Vichy Regime's collaborationist policy – there was almost total silence about the Jewish experience until Marcel Ophuls's landmark 1971 documentary *The Sorrow and the Pity* (*Le Chagrin et la Pitié*) forced a re-evaluation of Vichy, challenged the Gaullist mythology of noble wartime France struggling to liberate itself, and drew attention to French anti-Semitism. Yet even the definitive 1985 film *Shoah*, directed by Claude Lanzmann, a French Jew, remained silent on the wartime fate of Jews from France: though one of the film's dominant languages is French, Lanzmann nowhere brings in French witnesses to talk about the events on his doorstep.[83]

Poland's silence lasted even longer, until the publication, in 1987, of 'The Poor Poles Look at the Ghetto', an article by Jan Blonski, which touched off an extensive, heated debate about the Polish response to the extermination of the Jews, and provoked 200 letters and articles. In 1939, Poland had had the second largest Jewish community in the world after the United States – it was the cradle of European Jewish culture. Blonski charged the Poles with at best indifference to their fate, an indictment echoed by one Polish Jew who wrote that, 'The Poles did not mourn their Jews. After 700 years of common life on Polish soil, the Poles did not shed even one tear over the Jews turned into ashes. For their surviving brothers and sisters the greatest pain was just that silence. The Church and the nation were silent. They decided to forget. To pretend that there were never Jews in Poland . . . There were no flowers in the small towns and settlements, no services in the churches. People moved into empty houses. The cemeteries were covered with grass. It was decided to forget.'[84]

Even in Israel, where one might have expected Holocaust survivors to have been embraced by a society anxious to hear about their experiences, the reality was much more equivocal. The Holocaust was viewed as a Jewish defeat.[85] In the early 1950s, the Ministry of Education had published a pamphlet on the Holocaust entitled 'Like Sheep to Slaughter'.[86] Survivors said they felt either as if they were blamed for having stayed alive or, as another who settled in a kibbutz found, 'Everyone was nice to her, but they did not want to hear what had happened to her. Instead they spoke of what had happened to them. How the Arabs had attacked the kibbutz. A shell had landed near the chicken coop, they told her over and over again ... Those people who knew her story always asked her why she and her husband had not done anything against the Nazis early on ... The country wanted heroes. The Brands could only offer a story of survival.'[87]

Israel constructed its national identity in opposition to the Holocaust and the prevailing image of the Diaspora Jew: its citizens were to be heroic and muscular as opposed to fearful and studious; proud and nationalistic rather than religious; virile, in contrast to the stereotype of passive, impotent, stooping Holocaust victims and survivors. Action was prized, introspection scorned.[88] There was even a special term, 'Galuthit', to connote a meek and frightened attitude, caused by centuries of living as an unfree, often persecuted minority.[89] Jewish jokes proliferated: at one point young Israelis referred to survivors as 'sabon' (soap), an allusion to the belief that the Nazis made soap out of dead Jews.[90] In Israel, Holocaust survivors were known simply as refugees.[91] If they experienced problems on kibbutzim, it was their own fault.[92]

The Eichmann Trial proved a landmark in Israeli attitudes towards the Holocaust and its survivors and was deliberately designed to be educational.[93] The prosecution set out to persuade Israeli youth to identify with the Holocaust's victims and not to show arrogance towards its survivors.[94] To this end, it brought more than 100 Holocaust witnesses to give testimony before the court. The trial got massive daily publicity in the press, with live coverage on radio news bulletins transmitted in public buses. Schools cancelled some lessons to allow pupils to listen; people queued for hours to get into the courtroom.[95] A study of Israeli young people's reactions to the trial found, in answer to the question 'How did Jews behave in the Holocaust?' fifteen per cent answering 'heroically', almost twenty-four per cent judging with 'Galuthit' behaviour, and fifty-one per cent responding 'understandably'.[96] The Eichmann trial proved both cathartic and uniting for Israel, and for survivors it legitimated the disclosure of their past: many discussed their camp experiences with their children for the first time.[97]

Yet when, over fifteen years later, in 1978, an American psychotherapist attempted to set up an awareness group for children of Holocaust survivors in the Hebrew University, Jerusalem (reckoning around one half of the university's 10,000 students to be members of the second generation) she received only twelve enquiries, and of the eight eventual participants only one was an Israeli.[98] And in 1995, 'Polish' was still used as a pejorative term by young Israelis, as in 'long boring Seders with Polish aunts and other nudniky relatives'.[99]

In Germany, it wasn't until 1967 and the publication of Alexander and Margarete Mitscherlich's landmark book, *The Inability to Mourn*, that the country's blocking-out of its recent history was really addressed. In a key work of psychohistory the Mitscherlichs argued that Germany's relationship with the Second World War was characterised by evasion, collective denial, and 'a total lack of any sense that an effort should be made – from kindergarten to the university – to incorporate the disasters of the past into the stock of experience of German young people ... Germans still have no emotional perception of the *real* people whom they were ready to sacrifice to their dream of being a master race: as people, these have remained part of the de-realised reality.'[100] Instead, Germany threw itself into the massive job of reconstruction with unrestrained fervour: the 'German economic miracle' was a manic defence used successfully to obliterate the past, greatly aided by the Cold War, which sanctioned the cessation of the denazification process in 1948.

As a consequence, until the late 1960s, the Final Solution was scarcely mentioned in German schools: German pupils learned little about anti-Semitism and almost nothing about Judaism and Jewish life.[101] A Jewish teenager living in Germany recalls that even in 1970, when a visiting Israeli journalist asked her class what they knew about Hitler, they answered that he was a dictator who'd been very good for the German economy because he'd built the Autobahn and put an end to unemployment; they didn't mention the Holocaust.[102]

The screening of *Holocaust* on German television in 1979 both made the term current in Germany and enabled 'millions of post-war Germans to shed tears, for the first time, for the people next door'.[103] But though hundreds of thousands of Germans gathered movingly in 1992 for a vigil against violent attacks on immigrants, the mid- and late-1980s' 'Historikerstreit' (historians' debate) relativised Nazi crimes (yes, they were evil, but no more so than those of the Allies and the Bolsheviks), providing ideological support for those many young Germans who conceive of themselves as victims of those intent on reminding them of the Holocaust. On the one hand, in an unprecedented 'impulse to memorialise their own crimes',[104] Germans have built countless monuments and memorials to the Holocaust, agonising over what form these should take so that they won't simply become inert, reified parts of the landscape but living reminders of its past. On the other hand, in a 1990 survey, sixty-five per cent of West Germans agreed that, 'It is time to put the memory of the Holocaust behind us.'[105]

The approaching millennium has seen a growing international preoccupation with the politics of the representation of the Holocaust,[106] and how the Second World War is remembered: one recent book on the Shoah lists nine others with 'memory' in the title.[107] Yet the position of Holocaust survivors and their children in Britain today is shaped more by contemporary anti-Semitism. For a long time it was widely believed that the Holocaust had seen off European anti-Semitism, and that such' racist views were untenable after the consequences of racial discrimination had become known. Yet such optimism proved unfounded, and in Britain – as elsewhere in Europe – anti-Semitism has become an increasingly evident feature of everyday life. Despite the prevailing view that only 'golf-club' anti-Semitism[108] – a mild kind of discrimination – persists in Britain and that Jews have been replaced as targets of racism by newer immigrants,[109] many commentators have remarked on the resilience of anti-Semitism in British culture and society:[110] a recent report, *A very light sleeper* (based on Conor Cruise O'Brien's comment that 'anti-Semitism is a very light sleeper') suggests that 'social anti-Semitism', as expressed in casual remarks, references, and 'jokes', continues to be current in many circles, notes the anti-Semitic undertone still felt in media reporting of financial scandals, and records an eighty-five per cent increase between 1984 and 1992 in reported anti-Semitic incidents such as physical attacks, graffiti, and the desecration of cemeteries.[111] In 1994, the Board of Deputies also recorded incidents of extreme violence (defined as potentially life threatening) for the first time since 1991,[112] and all Jewish buildings are today policed by security guards with walkie-talkies.

Yet Anglo-Jewish institutions assume that Jews aren't first in line for racist attacks (and sometimes seem almost relieved that Asian and Afro-Caribbean communities now occupy that position), rather than realising that anti-black activists like the rightwing Combat 18 group are *also* anti-Semitic. Still abiding by the supposed terms of the emancipation contract, the Anglo-Jewish establishment persists in a softly-softly approach, playing down the seriousness of the attacks, and refusing publicity about anti-Semitic incidents, in the enduring belief that it will stir up further anti-Semitism, and in contrast to the much more active anti-racist initiatives taken by the Asian and Afro-Caribbean communities.[113]

British anti-Semitism is particularly pernicious because for so much of the time it's covert and based on the suppression of difference. Particularly enraging are public figures' references to 'Christian values', as if Christians had a monopoly on charitable qualities. (When, in the 1980s, the government debated war crimes legislation, peers spoke of alien pressures and Jews seeking vengeance while *The Times* thundered, 'Britain is a Christian country. Its laws enshrine principles of justice tempered with mercy, not vengeance.'[114]) P's mother often expressed exasperation with people harping on about difference – why couldn't we all concentrate on our shared humanity? Yet this apparently liberal position in fact forces obeisance to the dominant values – theirs. And while the dominant culture appears neutral and its Christian hegemony is virtually invisible, minority groups are chastised for insisting on difference, for Othering themselves. As a historian has written, 'When we find these discussions concerned with the nature of the Jews' difference we need to ask the question "different from what?"'[115]

(A Jewish New Yorker I know, on first meeting her New Zealand non-Jewish parents-in-law, was asked if she was going to bring up the children as Jews 'with all those strange customs'. 'They're not strange to me,' she replied.)

A British-Jewish woman observes that even in her early forties 'I wouldn't have dreamt of speaking to my colleagues about my Judaism. I was in my mid-forties before I could speak with confidence about it.'[116] Another, who, in disgust, abandoned Britain for the United States, contrasts the American Jews who revel in their Jewishness with English

Jews who 'retreat, as though living in a constant state of repressed anxiety about it. In that sense, they are being very English – trapped in passivity, unwilling to react, rock the boat, make a fuss. After all, it's only been 400 years since they were allowed back into England.'[117]

An Anglo-Jewish film-maker confirms her view, recalling the codes he'd internalised, growing up in Britain after the war: 'Don't be too Jewish in public.' Anglo-Jewry, he asserts, is still a frightened community. Researching a television series on British Jews, he was shocked by how little archive film about Jews in Britain he was able to unearth, reflecting both the reticence of British Jews, their relative invisibility, and the uninterest of the British media.[118] Poet Sue Hubbard talked of learning 'to stitch on/that elastic tennis-club smile/to cover the slow dawning/that I was a Jew'.[119]

Britain isn't comfortable with a strong sense of ethnic identity: there are no accepted hyphenated equivalents to African-American or Irish-American.[120] One of the most powerful indicators of Jews' enduring unease in Britain lies in the issue of names. British Jews were always under pressure to anglicise their names – turn-of-the-century immigrants were encouraged to swap their Yiddish- or Jewish-sounding names for English ones as soon as possible[121] (though Anna Freud, soon after the war, noted that name-changes which occur to facilitate assimilation cause adults as well as children to wonder who they are[122]). Yet at the same time people like G.K. Chesterton seized on Jews' anglicised names as evidence of an attempt to conceal their Jewishness.[123] Rosemary Friedman, an Anglo-Jewish novelist who didn't change her name, remarks that 'I am aware that the declaration of my name to a non-Jew is greeted with a frisson, signalling the fact that the "Jew" is encountered before any attempt is made to reach the person.'[124]

My own name is routinely misspelled, mispronounced, and even joked about by people who assume I won't mind and even expect me to participate. Though I used try to ease their discomfort by doing it myself first, now I remain militantly, stonily silent, while my interlocutor tries to quip his or her way out of having to learn to spell or pronounce an unfamiliar name.

In fact the British inability to spell or pronounce any name beyond Smith or Jones is part of its general blindness towards other cultures, the linguistic equivalent of 'they all look the same'. For years, two Asian women, Urvashi and Shampa, have been called by their English colleagues Eyewash and Shampoo – affectionate monikers perhaps, but reflecting a deep-seated conviction that their real names are too hard, too Other. When another Asian woman, Khanoma, began working in a nursery, her English colleagues called her a different name each day, even sometimes 'Chanukah' (presumably on the basis that anything ethnic would do).

It isn't only complex names which get manhandled. In a vivid BBC Radio 5 portrait of growing up in England, Chinese writer and actress Pui Fan Lee described how her teachers mispronounced her name for her entire school career – five years. 'It's hard,' she noted drily, 'to remember one syllable.' It's thought acceptable instead to reduce foreign-sounding names to their nearest phonetic equivalent, so people often address me as Anne Clarke, rather than asking how my name's spelled or pronounced (I'd be only too happy to oblige). My mother, bowing to *force majeure*, dropped the final 'f' from her professional name and reluctantly named me Anne instead of Anna. I, on the other hand, have insisted on bequeathing my children my apparently intractable surname, along with foreign-sounding first names.

One can't help but envy American Jews for the centrality they occupy in North American culture. Partly it's a question of numbers: with so many Jews living and working in New York, the *New York Times* announces on its front page when it's Yom Kippur, and the city suspends its normal parking regulations for the day. (In London, making my behatted way to synagogue, I run into one of my daughter's bright, charming nursery staff. 'You look smart,' she says. 'I'm going to synagogue, it's Yom Kippur,' I reply. 'What's that?' she asks.) In November, Bloomingdales has three equal displays: Christmas, Thanksgiving, and Chanukah; the London bookshops I ring can come up with just one children's book about Chanukah.

But it isn't only numbers – their millions to our hundreds of thousands – it's also confidence. American non-Jews blithely use Yiddish words like 'shlepp' and 'nosh' (long assimilated into the language, but only just beginning to be understood over here). American-Jewish comedians have had a key influence on American humour. And while the burghers of Peoria may never have met a Jew and their bookshops may be as bereft of Chanukah books as London's, why are we comparing London with Peoria? I'll bet anyway that even some Peorians have seen Woody Allen films and can quip Yiddishly.

British Jews have visibly gained in confidence over the past decade. London has an annual Jewish Film Festival; in the 1980s the Jewish mother was accorded the ultimate accolade – a starring role in the British Telecom television ads; and a growing band of Anglo-Jewish comedians are attracting media attention.

One summer evening in 1994 my American girlfriend and I go to an evening of Anglo-Jewish humour in the Queen Elizabeth Hall in London, only to be greeted by a humour almost exclusively about lifestyle, and recurring jokes about synagogue and liturgy, Volvos and the awfulness of kosher wine. But almost nothing about living in a non-Jewish culture and being marginalised: you'd never have guessed that Britain wasn't coterminous with Golders Green, its boundaries marked by the white cliffs of Edgware. There was no angst (Jewish humour without angst?), no history, only a joint celebration of habit and an almost psychotic sense of denial, as if daring to speak publicly about Jews were inherently inconoclastic. Is this what Englishness does to Jewishness?

All this goes some way to explaining why it's taken British children of refugees and survivors so long to identify themselves, meet together, and organise the groups and conferences which have been prevalent for so long in the United States, Canada, and Israel. The first British conference for members of the second generation wasn't held until the summer of 1994. Holocaust survivors and refugees who came to Britain have had to raise their children in a culture at best indifferent to Jews.

The unchanging nature of British anti-Semitism was revealed in October 1994 in an article in the *Spectator* magazine about Jews in Hollywood, a reunion of every veteran anti-Semitic stereotype: Jews are both clubbish and infiltrating, they're driven, money-grabbing and wield disproportionate power. They're damned if they try to assimilate and aim for 'social respectability': indicted of Jewishness by their very attempts to blend in, their exaggerated insider behaviour only reinforces their outside status (so Louis Mayer is ridiculed for trying to get himself photographed shaking hands with the Prince of Wales, and other Hollywood Jews are derided for going fox-hunting). And they're equally damned if they don't try to assimilate (these 'white-socked' super-moguls, wearing chunky Stars of David and openly Zionist 'couldn't care less' attitudes).[125] The article was accepted for publication by Dominic Lawson, the magazine's Jewish editor, again following the accepted tradition of British Jews going out of their way to prove their impartiality and loyalty by giving space to anti-Semitic babblings. Those nineteenth-century Jewish immigrants to Britain must be shaking their heads in wry recognition in their graves.

7

The first I heard of research into the effects of the Holocaust on the second generation came during a lunch in Mayfair with the American writer of books for teenagers, Judy Blume. Interviewing her for a British magazine, I was soon telling her almost as much about my teenagehood as learning about hers. Did I know, she asked me, about the book on children of Holocaust survivors which had recently been published in the United States, and about the self-help groups for the second generation now running there?

Her question astounded me. It was 1979, and by now the categorisation of people into either deprived or advantaged – it was definitely a case of either/or – seemed to have been long since settled: the idea that I belonged to a group which might warrant being helped, rather than being purely privileged and morally obliged to help others, had frankly never even grazed my mind. I was intrigued, and she promised to send me the book which, a couple of weeks later, she duly did, along with a newspaper cutting about the growth in self-help groups for American children of survivors.

The book was Helen Epstein's pioneering *Children of the Holocaust*[1] and, though I didn't read it then, only skimming the first couple of chapters, I cherished it. Unlike many children of Holocaust survivors, when apprised of the psychological literature, I didn't feel stigmatised: on the contrary, I was relieved and even elated that my years of problems weren't necessarily the result of personal pathology but might have a shared and external source.

Thereafter, I became an indefatigable collector of the literature on the subject. Others amassed art deco tea-sets or kitsch souvenirs; I collected material about the psychological effects of the Holocaust. I still never read any of it: I probably wasn't ready until I went into therapy two years later and then my therapist discouraged me from pursuing any intellectual or head-bound approach to my problems, and it was anyway obvious that I needed to explore my own particular constellation of issues rather than apply the agenda of researchers. I continued to resist the seductive contents of the mounting pile of journals, papers and books even while I began to write my own account, since here again I wanted my own voice to emerge relatively uncontaminated by other people's experience, though many interchanges with other children of survivors at conferences and seminars over the years had given me some familiarity with current thinking. When, with this book nearing completion, I finally worked my way through the library of material I'd accumulated, I found myself initially reacting with a severe case of 'medical student syndrome', convinced that I suffered from every single symptom and disability mentioned, and then some.

The research on the second generation grew directly out of that on the first generation, the Holocaust survivors themselves, and even that was a long time coming. One prescient psychiatrist, Paul Friedman, observed as early as 1948 that, 'It seems altogether incredible today that when the first plans for the rehabilitation of Europe's surviving Jews were outlined, the psychiatric aspect of the problem was overlooked entirely. Everyone engaged in directing the relief work thought entirely in terms of material assistance . . . We accepted the theory that the very fact of survival was evidence of physical and psychological superiority – without looking too closely at the implications of this statement, which dishonoured millions of martyred dead.'[2] But thereafter there was only silence, until 1961.

Actually, there is one published account of the psychological impact of concentration camps which predates even Friedman, written by the psychoanalyst Bruno Bettelheim. Bettelheim was imprisoned in Dachau and Buchenwald for a year in 1938–39, and he deliberated on the broader aspects of the experience in an article published in a psychological journal in 1943. Expanding on his conclusions in a book *The Informed Heart*,[3] he argued that concentration camp inmates became shiftless, quarrelsome, and self-pitying. Their treatment by the SS induced a regression into childhood, and in their attitude towards their peers inmates also began to emulate the aggression of the Gestapo, exhibiting an identification with the enemy.

In Bettelheim's formulation we see the beginnings of the stereotyping of concentration camp survivors (and later their children) which was to develop so virulently in subsequent years, and which has drawn an equally robust response from critics. Bettelheim's perspective, they argued, was completely ahistorical, entirely erasing survivors' prewar experiences.[4] What's more, as a Freudian, Bettelheim couldn't deal with life-threatening physical and mental deprivation without recourse to a theory of regression: his explanations were rooted in the prisoners' unconscious, rather than in the unyielding physical and psychic reality they faced.[5] So, for example, Bettelheim saw 'anal regression' where other commentators acknowledged the strict control of inmates' access to latrines.[6] Bettelheim interpreted prisoners' behaviour through the prism of normal drives and impulses, when there was nothing normal to be found in the *univers concentrationnaire*.[7] Anyway, having been liberated in 1939, Bettelheim didn't live through the camps at their most brutal.[8]

In 1961, William Niederland identified the components of what was soon being called 'concentration camp syndrome'. They included a pervasive depressive mood with feelings of helplessness and insecurity, lack of initiative and interest, so that the sufferer resembles a 'living corpse'; a severe and persevering guilt complex; all manner of psychosomatic and hypochondriacal symptoms; anxiety and agitation leading to insomnia and sometimes paranoia.[9]

Although it's easy today to find fault with Niederland's crude typology, one becomes more charitable if the historical context in which it was developed is taken into account. Niederland and Krystal were examining concentration camp survivors who were making claims for compensation from the German government under 1952 Wiedergutmachung (making good again) legislation. Hence the more malign the after-effects they could identify, the greater the pension which the survivor would receive from the Germans. Those psychiatrists and doctors nominated by the German government often tried to minimise the effects of survivors' wartime experiences, arguing that their problems were based on pre-existing conditions and not what had happened to them in the camps. Many survivors felt that they were being retraumatised and revictimised both by the insensitivity of the German government and the way it regarded claimants' testimonies as inherently suspect[10] (as well as by being labelled as mentally impaired). So Niederland and Krystal were trying not to scapegoat survivors, but only – under hostile conditions – to establish the enormity of their suffering.

(My mother was examined by a German-Jewish doctor, not a German one, and both my parents' claims were based on physical suffering not on psychological damage, so they found the process relatively untraumatic – they used to quip that their annual check-up was to confirm that they were still alive. Certainly, they regarded the pension which each of them received from the German government as their right, and crucial in helping them re-establish themselves after the war.)

The focus of the psychiatric community fell on the survivors because the perpetrators were apparently betraying few after-effects: there were no signs of anxiety and guilt among ex-Nazis, nor reports of them presenting for psychiatric or psychological help.[11]

Although the concept of Post-Traumatic Stress Disorder wasn't accepted as a legitimate diagnostic category until 1980, all the early commentators noted the existence of what they called a 'latency' period in survivors – a post-war symptom-free interval which, according to some analysts, was merely the time which it took for survivors to give up a sustaining sense of denial.[12] Robert Jay Lifton, who compared survivors of Hiroshima with those of the Nazi persecution, argued that both groups exhibited what he called a 'psychic closing off' – a chronic defence which amounted to a symbolic psychic death, an extreme identification with the dead.[13]

It wasn't long before a crude stereotyping of Holocaust survivors gained hold: survivors ruminated obsessively about past traumatic events and displayed existential despair – an aura of apathy, gloom, and emptiness pervaded their families.[14] Unable to work and even to talk, they couldn't enjoy concerts, films, other people's company, or even sex.[15] At its most extreme, these typifications depicted survivors with the garish strokes of a Hollywood movie: one minute they'd be going about their business quite normally, the next some minor event – a knock at the door, a smoking chimney – would cause a major regression to their concentration camp experience, to which they'd react with barely controlled terror and hysteria. Although this might be true for those who were severely affected, the stereotypers made no distinctions: as one put it 'none escaped without serious personality damage'.[16] I certainly didn't recognise my almost preternaturally vibrant and positive parents in these portraits of despairing lassitude.

Yet even as these clumsy generalisations about Holocaust survivors were gaining currency, a backlash began, and researchers started to introduce serious qualifications in their hypotheses about the effects of the camps. They acknowledged that survivors' pre-camp personalities and experience influenced their reaction to the trauma,[17] and argued that the sensitive analyst wouldn't focus exclusively on a survivor's pre-Holocaust childhood experience nor on the Holocaust trauma, but needed to address both.[18] This was part of the growing recognition of individual differences between Holocaust survivors, who were no longer being conceptualised as a homogenous mass but a diverse group, coming from different European countries, speaking different languages, and differing too in their religious (orthodox or assimilated), cultural, and political beliefs, as well as educational and economic backgrounds.[19]

It was as if the incarcerated were finally beginning to emerge from beneath gross Nazi caricature, and a new set of questions could now be asked: How long had an individual spent in a concentration camp? Were they alone, or with friends and relatives? In a camp, a ghetto, in hiding, or all three?[20] Researchers became more sensitive to the differences between camps and between different people's experience within the same camp,[21] to the pre-war family constellation, the number of surviving members of a person's family of origin,[22] and the personal resources of the survivor (whether in hardship they were more prone to discover unanticipated strength or despair).[23]

They began to appreciate the importance of having survived in a group or at least as one of a pair (something my mother could have told them from the first) and the value of 'social bonding' both in the camps, and after.[24] For researchers had also begun to widen their gaze from an exclusive focus on the concentration camp experience, not just to the survivors' pre-war world but also to their post-war lives. The whole experience of immigration now became visible, and the professionals began to speculate that some of the difficulties which Holocaust survivors and their families encountered were due not only to their wartime trauma but to the subsequent and also traumatic experience of losing their homeland and mother tongue – studies began to compare the families of survivors with those of other immigrants,[25] and Holocaust survivors with survivors of other 'man-made' trauma.[26]

Attention was also focused on the age and stage in the life-cycle at which a person lived through the Holocaust. Child survivors had different experiences from adults – their trauma appeared less connected with the loss of homeland and more with the early separation from parents,[27] which could seriously arrest their psychological development. Married adults who lost a pre-war spouse and children had different experiences again. Young unmarried adults seemed the least affected; however, those who were in their twenties and thirties on their release and who married and had children soon after liberation didn't have the space or time to come to terms with their massive losses, often with serious consequences for their parenting.[28]

Mourning was seen as a problem for many survivors. Krystal and Niederland argued that not only did survivors have no opportunity to mourn their losses during the Holocaust, but that after the war their guilt at having survived prevented them from completing the work of mourning. For these early theorists, guilt at surviving was the prime example of survivors' psychopathology, and they claimed to have detected it in ninety-two per cent of 149 cases.[29] Indeed, the concept of survivor guilt became so prevalent that therapists often suggested to survivors that 'You must feel guilty for having survived when all around you died', as if guilt could be assumed and the survivor had indeed committed a crime.[30]

Certainly, some survivors did forcefully express a sense of guilt and shame at having lived: as Primo Levi put it, 'The "saved" of the Lager were not the best, those predestined to do good . . . The worst survived – that is, the fittest; the best all died.'[31] The task of mourning in such circumstances is, however, far more complex than the crude early formulation allowed. For example, many survivors felt, as an Israeli analyst put it, that 'if one mourns *too* well, one betrays the dead'.[32] Even under average conditions, another commentator stressed, mourning isn't necessarily ever complete – certainly not in the case of a parent for a child.[33] Other analysts claimed that the Freudian concept of mourning, as developed in everyday life, was inapplicable to the extreme situation of the Shoah: 'As we have learned from victims who lived through the perverse, psychotic horrors of Nazi persecution, such a process of mourning, of coming to terms *completely* with the abhorrent past, is absolutely impossible.'[34] As one survivor succinctly put it, 'It's too many to mourn.'[35]

Perhaps the most telling comment on the concept of survivor guilt came from Dr Jack Terry who argued that, 'The American psychiatrists who interviewed these survivors were usually German-speakers who had themselves escaped (in the nick of time) from being incarcerated in concentration camps, and who had left members of their families, relatives, or friends behind. It therefore stands to reason that it would be these individuals who were most likely to suffer from so-called survivor guilt and not the ones who had paid so dearly for their survival during their years in concentration camps.'[36]

At the same time, a counter-trend soon began to assert itself: instead of focusing exclusively on survivors' pathology, researchers began to acknowledge their exceptional strengths. In contrast to the stereotype of the walking corpse, some survivors' zest for life, drive, determination, and courage now came to be remarked upon.[37] When the child survivors who'd been taken to Windermere after the war were interviewed as adults, they demonstrated a 'stubborn durability' and affirmation of life. 'The outcome seems surprisingly positive for a few, and it is certainly not as bleak as the psychological, particularly the psychoanalytic, literature would have us believe . . . For, despite the persistence of problems and the ashes of the past, what we note in the Lingfield lives are endurance, resilience, and great individual adaptability.'[38] Generally, the focus shifted on to the 'unexpected resilience' of survivors and their families (which, it was suggested, had been previously ignored lest it should be taken as a recommendation of persecution for the development of positive qualities).[39] In 1992, the *New York Times* even carried an article headed 'Holocaust Survivors Had Skills To Prosper', which stressed survivors' initiative and tenacity, their successful careers and greater-than-average incomes, along with the unusual stability of their marriages, though it also acknowledged that social and economic success might well mask continuing internal turmoil.[40] Researchers elsewhere warned that over-emphasising the positive traits of some survivors could make others feel inadequate, as if they were to blame if they hadn't learned 'positive lessons' from the tragedy.[41]

What was missing (for over twenty years after the end of the war) from this orgy of research into Holocaust survivors was any reference to their children. For decades, analysts didn't connect the parents' Holocaust experience with the children's lives. Although many survivors and their children were analysed at Anna Freud's Hampstead Clinic, for instance, their records can't be found because the very specialised index didn't include the item 'survivor', let alone 'survivor's child'.[42] It wasn't until 1966 that a lone Canadian psychiatrist, Vivian Rakoff, noticed that he was seeing more adolescents whose parents were Holocaust survivors than he would have expected, and wrote an article giving three case-studies.[43] Krystal's important 1968 volume, *Massive Psychic Trauma*, suggested in passing that children of survivors were exploding with the aggression which their parents had suppressed, and argued that increasing numbers of the children were depressed and suffered from a symbiotic relationship with their mothers which hindered their separation. Social pathology, it claimed, was being transmitted to the next generation.[44]

Yet when, in 1970, American analyst Judith Kestenberg sent a questionnaire to her colleagues in many different countries to find out how many had treated children of survivors, she encountered surprise among many of them to whom it had never occurred to link patients' problems with their parents' persecutions during the Holocaust.[45] In 1973, the literature on the subject was still very small,[46] but as the decade developed there was a positive rush of studies and clinical reports on the so-called second generation[47] who seemed to be seeking professional help in alarming numbers.[48] Nevertheless, when in 1976, Helen Epstein tried to interest the *New York Times* in publishing an article on children of survivors, she was told that there was no indication that such a group even existed.[49]

It wasn't long, however, before children of Holocaust survivors were graced with a syndrome all of their own, and a torrent of academic papers to herald its arrival. They drew attention to disturbances in the parent-child relationship, suggesting that the offspring of people who'd experienced overwhelming physical and mental trauma might themselves manifest some of their parents' trauma.[50] Later commentators went further, arguing that 'the children of survivors show symptoms that would be expected if they actually lived through the Holocaust'.[51] The Holocaust, it was claimed, had become the unconscious organising principle for the second generation, shaping both their internal reality and interpersonal relationships.[52] Some even went so far as to assert that 'it is not possible for a child to grow up, without becoming scarred, in a world where the Holocaust is the dominant psychic reality. With few exceptions, the mental health of children of survivors is in jeopardy.'[53]

So what exactly is the second generation syndrome? It's a matter not only of 'transmitted presences, contents, and conflictual psychic matter ... but also ... [of] transmitted absences, vacuums, denials, gaps, and intergenerational psychic holes'.[54] Survivor parents, it was argued, tend to overinvest in their children and overprotect them: one child of survivors recalled, 'We were continually fed, burped, stroked, tweaked, and fondled until we were well into our thirties.'[55] The parents and children often develop extreme symbiotic ties;[56] the parents don't encourage the child's autonomy,[57] and experience the normal process of separation and individuation in their offspring as a threat and an acute narcissistic injury to the family[58] – after such overwhelming losses, all separation to them seems like loss.[59] To the child, separation also evokes fears of annihilation, and they feel considerable guilt at wanting to be different from their parents.[60] They find their parents' constant vigilance overcontrolling, interfering, and demanding, but reluctantly yield to it because they often experience their parents' anxieties as their own.[61] What's more, the studies appeared to show that children of survivors left their parents' homes later than other young adults, and after they'd left remained in close contact with their parents.[62]

Other clinicians observed a reversal of roles, a parenting of the parents, with the child comforting the adult rather than the other way round,[63] and the parents' needs becoming more important than the children's.[64] (It's no coincidence that one researcher found that sixty per cent of the children of survivors in his study sought work in the helping professions, such as social work, medicine, psychology, etc.[65]) Again and again the professionals mentioned the parents' high expectations for their children: the Holocaust survivor parent might exclaim, 'For this I survived the Nazis? For this I survived the camps?', inducing wholesale guilt in their children.[66] The survivor parents, it was also suggested, could not tolerate the merest unhappiness in their offspring: 'If they were to see me unhappy or unhealthy, they would feel punished and I didn't want to punish them.'[67]

The reports often detected in the second generation an extreme identification with the lives of the first. In a process labelled 'transposition', survivors' children were described as living simultaneously in the present and past, transposing themselves to their parents' past, and attempting to compensate for their parents' losses.[68] Sometimes they tested their body endurance, and their ability to survive being in hiding;[69] in extreme cases they alternately prepared for the Holocaust and attempted to see whether they could be freed.[70] In institutional settings, they reacted as if their very survival were at stake,[71] while in other situations they behaved as if every decision was a matter of life and death.[72] Illness was omnipresent: 'Every time my throat hurt, my mother was sure that I had cancer.'[73] Another child of survivors recalled that 'Everything was life and death. They were always waiting for the worst to happen.'[74]

An Israeli psychotherapist claimed that in most survivors' families one child is designated as a 'memorial candle' for the relatives who died in the Holocaust, and 'is given the burden of participating in his parents' emotional world to a much greater extent than any of his brothers or sisters', thus freeing the siblings from some of the trauma.[75] The child is often named after a dead relative or sibling, and regards him or herself as a substitute for a dead predecessor, having to live up to the lost relative's idealised memory. The American cartoonist Art Spiegelman referred to the blurred photograph of his 'ghost-brother', killed, aged five or six, before Spiegelman was born, which hung in his parents' bedroom: 'The photo never threw tantrums or got in any kind of trouble . . . It was an ideal kid, and *I* was a pain in the ass. I couldn't compete. They didn't talk about Richieu, but that photo was a kind of reproach. *He'd* have become a doctor, and married a wealthy Jewish girl ... The creep ... It's *spooky* having sibling rivalry with a snapshot.'[76]

A common theme in the literature is children of Holocaust survivors' difficulty in expressing anger towards their parents. The parents had to suppress their own rage during the Holocaust and were afforded few opportunities after to vent it; the children later experienced their own normal aggressive instincts as overwhelming: 'My rage is so big it will consume everyone. Almost like a Holocaust.'[77] Some researchers maintained that the parents, fearing their own rage, unconsciously encouraged the children in their aggressive behaviour, so that the children expressed the repressed aggression of the parents.[78] The parents, for obvious historical reasons, put a high premium on being 'right' and in control,[79] and ambivalence was not well tolerated.[80]

Yet more problems were identified. Children of survivors were judged unusually anxious, especially if they caused displeasure to their mothers.[81] Their 'tension tolerance' was impaired in infancy because their war-stressed parents couldn't function as a 'protective shield'.[82] They also often had difficulties developing a positive sense of Jewish identity because they associated being Jewish with being killed,[83] and because the parents, while wanting the children to settle comfortably into the Gentile society they inhabited, also desired them to remember the culture and families which they had lost.[84] Children of Holocaust survivors, it seems, were frequently high-achievers, following the pattern of their parents for whom 'activity and frequently over-activity is an important adaptive defence mechanism ... when concentration camp inmates couldn't go on working, this would usually mean selection for the gas chambers or other forms of death'.[85]

The literature frequently reports feeding problems in the families of Holocaust survivors, with parents who had survived starvation worrying about feeding their children as if it were a matter of life and death,[86] and many examples of the later development of eating disorders among daughters of survivors.[87] At the same time, children of Holocaust survivors were found to feel 'special' and unique, displaying excessive narcissism[88] and lasting infantile omnipotence.[89]

One can't help feeling that Holocaust survivors must have been very busy all those years to have managed to visit so much neurosis on to their children within such a comparatively short time. How on earth did they do it? What was the means of transmission? Children and family, of course, were exceptionally important to survivors: they tried 'to undo the destruction magically by creating a family as soon as possible – often under the most unfavourable conditions of the D.P. [Displaced Persons] camps'.[90] They taught their children that family was all you could trust – friends might turn out to betray you in the end[91] – thus creating a controlled, closed system.[92] Yet, within the family, the parents were often preoccupied, busy with the task of mourning, and hence responded to their children's normal robust behaviour as an interference or an extra burden on their already taxed resources,[93] displaying both an inaccessibility[94] and 'an acute lack of empathy' for their children's problems and emotional needs, especially as compared with their own.[95] So the children often struggled to win the mother's interest by identifying with her, 'which has led to the frequent complaint by second generation members that they are unable to experience themselves as alive or separate beings in their own right'.[96]

It's hard to imagine how Holocaust survivor parents could read some of the accounts of their parenting styles without feeling terribly persecuted. Berated for the inconsistent way they applied discipline – according to one mental health professional, they set limits either too rigidly or not at all[97] – indicted equally for wishing to spare their children from going through what they did,[98] and for viewing their children as narcissistic extensions of themselves[99] (and which parent doesn't to some extent view his or her children

233

thus?), it sometimes seems as if Holocaust survivor parents have been judged against some ideal of parenting rather than the norm, or even what might have been expected in the circumstances. What tended to get omitted from the descriptions of their failings was the often superabundant love they lavished on their children, which can't be entirely dismissed as toxic or narcissistic.

There were some attempts to distinguish differences between survivor parents: Danieli, for example, famously identified four types – 'victim' families, 'fighter' families, 'numb' families, and families of 'those who made it',[100] – though, frankly, all seemed equally pathological. Danieli also typified many survivor unions as 'marriages of despair',[101] though other researchers acknowledged the moderating influence of a nurturing, supportive spouse,[102] who was emotionally more available to the children.[103]

All in all, though an enormous amount of what I read in the literature on children of Holocaust survivors resonated very loudly and sometimes made me feel as if my own family had been eavesdropped on, I was also left feeling more than a little uncomfortable. This was partly because, for all the lip-service paid to survivors' strengths, many of the idiosyncratic skills they brought to their parenting went unacknowledged. My parents' more punitive tendencies, for example, were frequently leavened by their terrific sense of humour, and the extreme resourcefulness which they brought to bear on settling into a foreign country after such extreme trauma is awe-inspiring. My discomfort, like that of many of other people's, also derived from the profoundly pathologising and stigmatising tendencies of the less sensitive work in the field. What are we to make, for example, of the chapter called 'Hysterical Features among Children of Survivors' (even allowing for the fact that 'hysterical' in psychoanalysis is a technical word), especially since it appears in a book choking with myriad, undreamt-of ways in which survivor parents can (and have) messed up their kids?[104] Or of Dina

Wardi's *Memorial Candles*, which not only relates every single less-than-perfect condition in the children's lives to their parents' Holocaust experience, but also goes on to offer a crudely schematic vision of group therapy as a panacea?[105] It doesn't help all that much either to argue that the 'survivor's child syndrome' (implying pathology) should actually be called a 'complex' or 'constellation',[106] connoting a group of related feelings and fantasies which needn't necessarily be pathological.[107]

Much of the literature has also been found wanting methodologically. According to one critic, some of it amounts to no more than unsupported anecdotal findings and speculation, based on the assumption that there *must* have been damage to the second generation.[108] Others arraign many of the studies for their too small samples, and the fact that the subjects were clinical patients – in other words, people who had already sought psychotherapeutic help of some kind – which therefore generated findings which were in no way applicable to the entire second generation.[109] There are also many individual variables in the way in which the second generation has been raised, and a large number of them aren't susceptible to measurement.[110] The literature is bulging with generalisations and a readiness to attribute neurosis and psychosis; as one researcher aptly put it, 'We must respect and understand that what we sometimes consider psychiatrically "suspect" are the means whereby human beings cope with trauma and overcome its effects.'[111]

The many different studies on the second generation have, moreover, produced wildly inconsistent results. Many research projects and clinical reports by analysts, for example, show no distinctive psychopathology in children of survivors,[112] in contrast with the plentiful research already cited which found them to have significant problems. Interestingly, problems in the second generation have been found irrespective of whether the children were told what had happened to their parents or not, and it's been argued both that frank talk about the Holocaust in the family produces more psychological disturbance in the children, as well as less.[113] Certainly, silence and family secrets can exert a powerful effect on the child, but so too can the constant relating of brutal experiences.[114] What's more, parent and child experience the amount and form of telling in different ways: there are stories of children who felt that their parents talked endlessly about the war, whose parents claim they never mentioned it because it distressed them. A look, as one commentator reports, can be eloquent;[115] a pair of analysts have catalogued eight different ways of both 'knowing and not knowing' about the Holocaust.[116]

Holocaust survivors' reluctance to seek therapeutic help, as well as their resistance to the idea of their children being treated, is well documented.[117] Some of this has been attributed to survivors' need to forget past humiliations (which expresses itself in an exaggerated intolerance for human weakness[118]) and also to a desire, because Eastern European survivors commonly perceive that mental health intervention is only for the insane,[119] not to be retraumatised by being labelled 'mental patient'.[120] (My own father referred to my therapist charmingly as 'the witch', and checked with me regularly to ascertain if I was still seeing her and why; he longed for my announcement that I'd finished, with its implicit return to normality.)

Survivors' resistance to psychotherapeutic intervention has also been regarded as a simple case of denial.[121] In 1991, I attended a meeting of British children of Holocaust survivors to discuss the possibility of setting up a national organisation. The talk was all of social and educational functions, and when I mentioned a group for members of the second generation which I'd been attending, there was an outbreak of extraordinary hostility. 'We don't want any of that psychological business, all that depressing stuff,' one man almost shouted, to near unanimous murmurs of assent. The degree of anger, upset (and fear?) was almost out of control, as evidenced by his subsequent apology. Later, as we broke for refreshments, one by one, participants came up to me to ask about the group and whether it was open to new members. It seemed as if the taboo against speaking about their grief which the parents had encountered had been passed on to their children; there was a shared denial of difficulty. The children were honouring their parents by keeping silent about their own problems, and still wanting to talk only about their parents' lives rather than their own, or both.

On the other hand, the hostility to the psychological which survivor families so often express cannot be wholly attributed to denial and resistance. Some analysts have remarked on the curious inversion which has taken place over the years, a blaming of the victim, complete with talk of survivors 'identifying with the aggressor'. It's almost as if, to some professionals in contact with survivor families, the victims have been elided with the perpetrators, especially in the absence of the latter as a clinically accessible subject group: survivors have had to stand for both aggressor *and* victim. Primo Levi was unequivocally clear on this issue: 'I do not know, and it does not much interest me to know, whether in my depths there lurks a murderer, but I do know that I was a guiltless victim and I was not a murderer. I know that the murderers existed, not only in Germany, and still exist, retired or on active duty, and that to confuse them with their victims is a moral disease or an aesthetic affectation or a sinister sign of complicity.'[122]

Indeed, psychoanalysis does not emerge unblemished from its relations with Holocaust survivors and their children, and not only because of its tendency to generalise and pathologise. There are countless examples of psychoanalysts simply ignoring material relating to a patient's, or a patient's parent's, Holocaust experience. One analyst learned of the Nazi persecution of his client's parents in the very first session, but never referred to it again in the whole analysis.[123] A friend of Rabbi Hugo Gryn was treated by psychiatrists for years as a psychotic, without any connection ever being made between his symptoms and his time in Auschwitz.[124] And there are other stories of patients completing analyses with the admonition to 'live in the present', their therapists regarding references to the Holocaust as a defence against present-day conflicts.[125]

Holocaust survivor and second generation patients, whether consciously or unconsciously, sense this reluctance on the part of many therapists to attend directly to such traumatic material, and it can reinforce the patient's own sense of denial.[126] In some instances, patients notice a therapist fidgeting or constantly interrupting and decide to spare them what they clearly cannot bear to hear.[127] This discomfort has been explained as an unconscious contempt for suffering;[128] others regard it as evidence of the analyst's omnipotent wish to rescue and repair lives ravaged by the Holocaust, and the resulting feeling of helplessness when faced with the fact that they can't.[129] One critic has gone so far as to suggest, of his own profession, that 'therapists have inherited a vocabulary and terminology not adequate to describe or treat either generation'.[130]

At the same time, there are some tremendously sensitive accounts of therapeutic work with Holocaust survivors and their children. I cried when I read Joan Freyberg's deeply moving account of a slow and tortuous analysis with a daughter of survivors which ends both with her hard-won autonomy and a sense of compassion for her parents.[131] Analysts like Freyberg and Robert Krell really listen to the material which their patients bring them, are able to tolerate the patient's grief, and prepared to admit their own limitations in transforming it. The respect they show the Holocaust survivor patient and their offspring is among the most healing things they have to offer.[132] I was lucky enough to have such an analyst myself.

One of the difficulties in generalising about the experience of Holocaust survivors and their children is the lack of unanimity even over definition. Should a refugee from Nazi Germany be bracketed with a Holocaust survivor? Some argue that there's greater kinship between the problems of Holocaust survivors and refugees than between those of Holocaust survivors and survivors of other man-made disasters. Others suggest that, without minimising the fate of refugees, their problems and those of their children have been part of human suffering throughout history, whereas Hitler's Final Solution was unprecedented, and living in a concentration camp or in hiding, being daily exposed to the dangers of death was an incomparable experience.[133] Groups providing services for survivors use different working definitions: one agency includes in its target group any Jew who emigrated from Germany after 1933,[134] while membership of the Holocaust Survivors' Centre in London is open to anyone who came to Britain after Kristallnacht in 1938. Similar psychological effects – survivor guilt, feelings of helplessness – have been detected in those who left Nazi occupied countries between 1935 and 1939 as in those who remained.[135] They shared the experience of losing their homeland and mother tongue, but living under total terror, it's been suggested, was particular to survivors.[136]

The issue is hedged about with powerful feelings. There is a strong belief that insisting upon the difference between refugees from Nazi persecution and their children, and survivors and their children, merely reproduces the hierarchy of suffering which has been so oppressive to the second generation: some people see it as the revenge of those who've felt themselves to be relatively low in the pecking-order of pain – 'I haven't suffered as much as my parents, but you haven't suffered as much as me.' One therapist noticed that he was often asked by those who'd left Nazi Europe in the late 1930s if they, too, fell under the rubric of survivor. He concluded that 'The question has a pleading quality, the questioner seeking grace ... The question reflects the need to identify with those who suffered, and the disquieting belief that they themselves did not suffer enough.'[137] Robert Jay Lifton has remarked upon the way that guilt moves in concentric circles from the dead themselves: 'The survivors feel guilty towards the dead; those who just missed going through the experience feel guilty towards the survivors; those who were even further away feel guilty towards this latter group.'[138]

The issue is complex. Certainly refugees and survivors shared both pre-war experiences (discrimination, the threat and often actual experience of violence) as well as post-war ones (the discovery of the death of parents, grandparents, etc). Both groups experienced the trauma of relocation and loss of homeland. On the other hand, one sometimes gets an unpleasant whiff of competition for victimhood. For although victims today are stigmatised, the condition also brings a degree of status and other secondary gains. Those who refer glibly to a 'culture of complaint' have overstated it, but there's undoubtedly something satisfying in joining the ranks of the unequivocally wronged, those with an irrefutably legitimate claim on our sympathy. In a special recent issue of a Canadian feminist magazine on Jewish women, one woman, whose father was a child during pogroms in Europe early in the century and saw his own father killed, argued that 'to all intents and purposes' he should be considered a Holocaust survivor and she the child of a Holocaust survivor.[139] But he wasn't one, and it's disturbing that she believes that only by claiming membership of this victimised group will his (and consequently her) sufferings acquire legitimacy. It would be dreadful if being a child of survivors became, in some perverse way, a desirable badge of victimhood. It seems to be difficult for us to maintain the distinctiveness of different historical experiences without ranking them in order of importance and grading their suffering, but my own view is that there were real similarities and real differences in the experiences of refugees and survivors and their children, and both need acknowledging. The Nazis saw the Jews as a homogenous group, defined only by ethnicity; it behoves us to be able to examine our differences.

A major change occurred in the late 1970s and early 1980s: children of Holocaust survivors began to get together and find their own voice. Helen Epstein's book was the first on the subject to be authored by a child of survivors and, although its conclusions didn't differ hugely from those of the clinicians who'd hitherto monopolised field, it was far less stigmatising. What Epstein crucially identified was the hitherto hidden nature of the feelings of the second generation – emotions she likened to 'an iron box', buried so deeply inside her that she wasn't even aware of what it contained. By speaking out on the subject, Epstein helped to excavate it and name its contents. Self-help groups had already sprung up in the United States (which has a population of a quarter of a million children of survivors[140]) alongside therapeutic groups led by second generation therapists like Eva Fogelman and Bella Savran. Campaigning organisations like the International Network of Children of Jewish Holocaust Survivors were also established, though these often took a determinedly anti-therapeutic line, seeing their role as helping the world never to forget their parents' experience, rather than focusing on their own. Soon, especially in Israel, films, plays, and novels began to appear. Orna Ben Dor-Niv's powerful 1988 documentary *Because of That War* focused on the two well-known rock musician sons of Holocaust survivors, Yehuda Poliker and Yaacov Gilead, and mixed the parents' testimony with the sons' descriptions of their childhoods. Yossi Hadar's *Biboff* dealt with a son of survivors traumatised by his parents' past, while David Grossman's *See Under Love*, while not the work of a second generation writer, nevertheless captured with remarkable accuracy the interior life of an only child of survivors who had powerful rescue fantasies about his parents.[141]

An interesting fact to emerge from Epstein's and others'

interviews with the second generation was the difficulty they had in remembering their parents' stories. In one group of about thirty children of Holocaust survivors, ninety per cent of them couldn't consistently retain the memory of their parents' Holocaust experiences. So my own problems in this regard weren't unique.

The agenda of researchers into the after-effects of the Holocaust is changing. Studies are focusing increasingly on the effect on the third generation, the grandchildren of survivors, both regarding the ways in which the second generation have either mimicked or consciously rejected the child-rearing styles of their parents, and the decisions they've made over how much to tell their children about the Holocaust and when.[142] One interesting recent study comprises interviews with three generations in the same family, and explores the consequences on the subsequent generations of the different ways in which survivors reconstruct and shape their stories.[143]

Yet the research still includes some glaring omissions. When, for instance, I was asked to speak about gay and lesbian children of survivors at a London conference on Nazi persecution of lesbians and gays in 1995, I couldn't find a single reference to the subject in all the copious literature, though at the very least the gay and lesbian second generation has experienced the 'How can I do this to them?' problem *vis-à-vis* their parents with particular intensity, and by all accounts has also been on the receiving end of an extra dose of 'For this I survived the camps?' The whole issue of the lack of grandchildren and its meaning in the families of Holocaust survivors with gay and lesbian children surely merits study.

Even more serious has been the tendency to ignore cultural differences in survivor communities. Though much has been written about the special situations faced by the second generation in Israel and Germany, until recently almost all the rest of the literature came from the United

States but was camouflaged as universal, as if American was the default identity of all other children of survivors. And yet the norms and conventions of the country in which they're reared have an enormous impact on the development of the second generation.

Israel obviously presented a unique situation for Holocaust survivors and their children. There it was possible to exchange an identity as a child of Holocaust survivors for one of an Israeli pioneer, and to recast the Holocaust redemptively, as a precursor of Israeli heroism,[144] though this also made it harder for many Israelis to understand that the second generation might still be experiencing the effects of the past.[145] In the early post-war days, Freudian psychiatrists discovered all manner of complexes in child survivors and exhibited remarkable lack of understanding: of one child it was said that he was 'overattached to his mother'. She'd been killed in the war.[146]

On the other hand, the existence of Yom Hashoah, Holocaust Remembrance Day, afforded the chance of collective mourning, and put less pressure on children of survivor parents to act as a living memorial to the dead, since the state had institutionalised that function.[147] And the position of the country surrounded by hostile neighbours enabled some survivor families to displace their accumulated aggression and rage on to their current enemies.[148]

For many of Israel's 300,000 Holocaust survivors, and between 500,000 and 700,000 members of the second generation, the country embodied rebirth, with the kibbutz often functioning successfully as a new family to replace the pre-war ones which had been lost, and supplying survivors and their children with a new community to substitute for the ravaged European ones. Kibbutzim also provided multiple mother figures to complement the preoccupied survivor mother.[149]

From Germany have come interviews with children of Nazis,[150] psychoanalytic literature about the effects of the

Holocaust both on children of Nazis, German analysts, and the population in general,[151] as well as accounts about and by children of survivors in contemporary Germany.[152] (Sometimes, controversially, material about the effects of the Holocaust on children of survivors and of Nazis is juxtaposed.[153]) But all too often Germany is the only European country dwelled on in the literature about the second generation in the Diaspora, which is otherwise almost exclusively American; it is only recently, for instance, that information is emerging about the different experiences of being a child of Holocaust survivors in, for example, Poland, where the Communist regime and enduring anti-Semitism prevented what little cultural continuity was possible after the destruction of Polish Jewry, and has thrown up profound questions of cultural identity for Polish members of the second generation.[154] Holland, with its massively depleted post-war Jewish population, also presents some problems and outstanding solutions of its own. These latter include finance from the Dutch government for mental health facilities for survivors and their families, a special programme of activities for the second generation, and even a professor at the Catholic University of Nijmegen specialising in the second and third (Jewish and non-Jewish) generation.[155]

And what of Britain? Here, consciousness about the refugee and survivor communities is a very recent phenomenon. After Anna Freud's work with child survivors came a prolonged silence until a two-day 'Survivor Syndrome Workshop' organised by the Group-Analytic Society in London in September 1979, a first attempt to feed into Britain some of the work being done around the world on survivors and their families. Even the published case-histories of British analyst Dinora Pines include as many foreign-born children of survivors as British ones.[156] Indeed, the first substantial British work on the second generation is only just beginning to emerge from the National Life Story Collection interviews with survivors and the second generation (children of Holocaust survivors living in England, born between 1943 and 1967).[157] Since the late 1980s there have been second generation groups, as well as specialist psychotherapy services (Link, Shalvata, The Raphael Centre) for survivors and their children and so far two national conferences, but these voices are only just beginning to make themselves, ourselves, heard. It's as if children of survivors' reluctance to speak in the first person, and treat their experience as legitimate in its own right and not simply with reference to their parents', has combined with the British demand for reticence and politeness, to inhibit (or at least delay) the emergence of a distinctly British second generation. Until very recently, the second generation of both survivors and refugees has followed in the footsteps of the first – deferential, mute, acutely sensitive to the British culture of embarrassment. Of course, the survivor community in Britain is relatively small and the refugee community large, so perhaps it's not surprising that the psychosocial effects of the Holocaust only really came into public view with Diane Samuels's recent *Kindertransport*, a play about the experience of a child refugee to Britain and her daughter.

Britain still hasn't managed properly to acknowledge and integrate the trauma of its refugee and survivor communities.

Part Three

8

It's hard to speak about Holocaust survivors in anything but a reverent tone or without turning their suffering into a sacrament. People expect of them abnormally high standards of behaviour, as if a dehumanising experience might somehow dignify and elevate, and along with the loss of their worldly goods they should also have lost all worldliness. I was always angered (as he must have been) by a common supposition about Primo Levi – that he'd somehow managed to sidestep most of the terrible after-effects of the Holocaust. Some even believed (or wanted to believe) that his experience had ennobled him. People seemed suprised to learn of his suicide.

What are not visible in survivors are their anaesthetised parts, their necessary autism. I came to feel that my sense, as a child and young adult, of not being a proper person was somehow connected with this, with a whole school of emotions being out of bounds, and felt grateful to P for divining the alive parts of me.

There's a particularly eloquent photograph of my mother, taken sometime in the 1950s, displayed alongside other family photos on a wall in our hall which P and I only half-jokingly call Ancestors' Corner (a place where I tried, a little self-consciously, to establish some kind of familial continuity,

249

using the few photographs available. But it feels a little spurious, as if these people haven't really got anything to do with me: they remain immured in their own era and culture, and stubbornly resist assimilation into mine). My mother is wearing a strapless satin ball-dress (one of many similar gowns she had for concerts) and holding out the skirt as if, even though she was in our living-room, she might be about to curtsy. While the gesture seems to say, 'Look at this!', it's quite undercut by her sad expression, which suggests instead 'But what of it?' That was a sentiment which couldn't easily be articulated in my parents' house.

At the First International Conference of Children of Holocaust Survivors in Jerusalem in 1988 I met other British children of survivors, the first I'd knowingly met who weren't children of my parents' friends. (Among my parents' friends Auschwitz tattoos weren't uncommon, so as a child I was surrounded by other members of the second generation – but we never thought of ourselves in those terms.)

We decided to form a group, and began meeting in London in 1989. My feelings about the group at the beginning were ambivalent – again, partly, I suppose, through discomfort at not being unique: in this milieu my mother's story was only one of a collection of similarly grisly tales. I also considered myself somewhat superior to those group members who were only just beginning to contemplate how their parents' wartime experiences had affected them, whereas I'd been thinking about the subject for several years now, in my therapy and outside it. If I wasn't special, I was at least advanced.

The group soon ran into problems. The chief one seemed to be that collectively we couldn't deal with loss – hardly surprising since we weren't very adept at dealing with it individually either. But it meant that when someone left the group we found it difficult to confront the implications of his or her departure, and instead immediately regrouped more tightly and exclusively.

For me, the group constantly generated problems of protection: here, as elsewhere, I was instinctively inclined to look after whoever might be criticised or under attack, which helped prevent confrontations from arising, and left no place for my own less-than-benign feelings. But I did eventually ignite, for among our members were some who were both children of survivors and themselves child survivors, and increasingly I felt their presence inhibited me from expressing intemperate feelings about survivors – it seemed a bit like being in a group with one's parents. So after a while I spoke out about this confusion and its effect on me.

Nevertheless, the group flourished and I began to identify with the other members. Despite our differences we shared many central issues, and a lot of rueful head-nodding as well as laughter went on. One thing we had in common was seeing ourselves as children of Holocaust survivors. Of course, this wasn't our total identity – we didn't define ourselves exclusively in relation to our parents' trauma – but each of us, by the very fact of our joining the group, had acknowledged a certain historical and psychological lineage, and this distinguished us from children of survivors who never thought of themselves in those terms.

In my group one day we talk about what weakness must have meant to our parents during the war, when strength was imperative and vulnerability may have been literally fatal. (Quite often survivors who are peerless in a crisis get angry in situations where others might feel frightened or sad.) We also talk about how we, for whom weakness would have had no such consequences, learned to view it with similar disdain and fear.

'Victim' today has become so stigmatised a concept, such a term of abuse – as if we can't brook the notion that people might ever find themselves in positions of helplessness and we'd rather blame the victims of crime, thereby obliging them to assert that they didn't acquiesce. But those who died in the Holocaust *were* victims: as Levi stressed, most

Holocaust victims were placed in positions of total powerless-ness. Despite the extraordinary tales of resourcefulness and courage (as well as luck and its lack) among both victims and survivors, we must rage against the heroising and idealis-ing of survivors which dehumanises them once again, and is a way of not having to confront the shared helplessness of all those who experienced the Holocaust. Victims chal-lenge our belief in the infinite power of volition, a belief peculiarly resilient in my family.

We must also resist over-emphasising the divide between those Holocaust survivors who spoke about their experi-ences and those who didn't, as if its articulation were a panacea. For us, the children of survivors whose parents did speak, their experiences became stories which were repeated again and again down the years – stories about their close shaves, survival (how, and theories about why), and those who never made it. Our parents bore witness; in the absence of any other interested parties, they bore witness to their children. They told us those stories because they needed to tell them and because they wanted people to know. And for us those stories – through their power, repetition, and the sheer vehemence of the telling – took on the power of myth and fable: you knew them by heart, able even to prompt and remind, you internalised them – they became yours. The parents left their stories to the safe keeping of their children.

Is it any surprise that some of us longed to appropriate their narratives for our own lives? I always felt that my life had been inflected around an event I'd never experienced. Once, watching a made-for-television movie about Theresi-enstadt which ended with most of the inmates being bund-led on to a train for Auschwitz, I felt a strong impulse to rush in and join them. I wanted to paint myself into their picture, and yield finally to something I'd always regarded as hovering and imminent, rather than past and gone.

Group members also came up with telling insights. When I was five months pregnant I was due to go to Paris to give some lectures. I'd consented, foolishly, to give an address in French to a large gathering which included Mitterrand's adviser on science, and I was getting terribly nervous at the prospect, panicking as to whether I could perform adequately. It was to be P's and my last time in Paris together sans child, but now the trip had turned into something to be dreaded; it persecuted me (like so many events and situations I found myself in). One evening, after a meeting, as I stood in the street talking about it with a member of the group, she said, 'It's the kind of thing which would scare most people, but for us these things become matters of life and death – survival issues.' Her words gonged like the Rank Cinema opening titles: they crystallised the bursts of panic and bouts of overwhelming anxiety which I kept experiencing and which louringly obliterated any sense of good.

It was a state to which I still regularly returned, with an almost gravitational force. A situation of intense pressure would arise – an accumulation of deadlines, a series of urgent tasks. Then anxiety would abduct me and normal life close down, suspended until the completion of the job, whereupon, vastly relieved, I'd resume daily living with a triumphant sense of having escaped. And so the cycle would continue, the bad displaced by the good which ceded again to the bad, the good unstable and somehow never sustainable. My life seemed to shape itself inexorably around duress and escape, around imminent catastrophe. Driven by a compulsive need to imprison and then release myself, I made an internal concentration camp of my own, and acted as both commandant and inmate. With an awful involuntary mimetic obsession, I constantly replayed the act of surviving.

Lists were one way I tried to muster the good; they were also a gauge of my anxiety. On them each second was earmarked, every possible chore logged (P quipped that my lists should start with 'breathe'), each amoebic particle of life fixed, controlled, arrested. My Gestapo was time.

Invariably, before long, the lists themselves became

another source of torment: like some sci-fi inversion, what started out as a means of exerting control mutated into something punitive which controlled me. In order to accomplish the itemised tasks my body braced – breath held, shoulder-blades locked, neck tightened into a vice, my whole person turned into an agent of coercion and propulsion (returning me, said the therapist, to my safe place, the place where I felt awful) – leaving me with no alternative but to sabotage the list and liberate myself . . . with a fresh one.

In *Angst!*, a 1993 Australian film about three comedians who are children of Holocaust survivors, one of the participants said she had constantly to remind herself that she was not in a concentration camp, 'because I think in those terms when I feel angry or anxious'. I watched P, who became my benchmark of normality, and saw that while he had his crises and struggles, these didn't throw into question his own perpetuation; he didn't exult triumphantly over his every success, nor feel persecuted by his every failure. He understood that good and bad things happened which were beyond our control; he didn't feel the need to make sure, constantly, vigilantly, that life continued.

Yet despite everything, pregnancy suited me; I was one of those who antenatally bloomed. It also brought me closer to my parents. The day before my amniocentesis my mother gave me a large red cardigan she'd knitted for herself. I loved it right away and wore it the next day: it seemed like a portable embrace, a bright red placenta to nourish me as I was nourishing the baby. It must have been the first thing I'd been able to accept from my mother in a long time.

While I was physically well in pregnancy, and thrilled to have finally joined the normals club – no longer would I have to look enviously at women with children – I was also buffeted by great new gales of anxiety. Would I be able to cope with a baby, could I survive its demands and dependency – common enough concerns in pregnant women (if routinely downplayed or ignored in medicalised childbirth), but my fears themselves produced another persistent terror, that of damaging the baby. I was certain that my bouts of panic were powering their way down the umbilical cord, annihilating all the advantages I was pouring into the baby through healthy food and exercise, and I needed constant reassurance that my anxieties wouldn't blight and spoil. I also worried about how I would manage to supply a baby with any sense of safety and security, given that these were so foreign to me and that, despite my parents' best efforts, I'd experienced little of them (or so I surmised) in my own babyhood.

After an interminable three-week wait for the result of the amniocentesis (in which period I underwent not less than three dozen imagined terminations) there came the good result. To celebrate, P and I took a short holiday in Wales, and on the drive there I finally allowed myself to admit the baby's reality and no longer anticipate inevitable loss through miscarriage or as a consequence of prenatal diagnosis. Then, immediately, I couldn't understand why I'd be having this baby in England, a country in which I just happened to have fetched up and with which I had no genealogical connection. I felt punched by the lack of continuity and by the realisation that I had no object to bequeath my child which had been bequeathed to me – there was no silver spoon or lace shawl. I'm not even sure if Jews use such things – they seem rather the accoutrements of christening – but their absence stood for the rupture which, at that moment, I felt so keenly. In Tenby, in a restaurant full of old objects, I saw a child's antique highchair and became obsessed with the idea of buying one. I shlepped P with me round all the town's antique shops in search of such a piece until I realised that it was a pathetic gesture – like buying a coat-of-arms, or simulating an heirloom – you couldn't drum up or wish into being an authentic mark of continuance. No such object belonging to my family survived the war (we counted ourselves lucky among survivors' families even to have pre-war photos) and I was surprised how suddenly bereft I felt for I'd always known that we had none of those – it was one of the givens of my childhood.

(And now I look at my six-year-old and see abundant continuity which doesn't require material corroboration: heirloom or no heirloom she's absorbed some of the culture of my parents, and feels as comfortable dancing to klezmer music as watching Power Rangers. This is osmosis through generations and happens to some extent of its own accord, though in my untrusting way I give it a regular push.)

Our baby was due on 1 September 1989 – fifty years after the Nazi invasion of Poland. A close friend declared with absolute certainty that it would be born either then or on 3 September (fifty years after the start of World War II): no child born into such family, she insisted, could resist such symbolic dates. B was duly born on 3 September.

Her first weeks dashed each comforting habit and anchor, leaving instead a dark dis-order, a primitive and alarming chaos. The split between good and bad was made flesh, in nipples so cracked that a ravine ran through them, and even the vastly experienced hospital breastfeeding counsellor hadn't seen the like. Yes, there was a physiological cause – grossly bad advice from midwives – but also a failure of trust in my ability to mother. When B sicked up milk, there were traces of my blood in it, and I read them as my badness. I couldn't even say the word 'milk': whenever it cropped up in a sentence, it amazingly came out as 'blood'. B cried incessantly – she was hungry – and I fed her incessantly, in pain and flinching; sensing my reluctance, she fed poorly and lost a lot of weight. It all seemed to be turning out wrong.

In those early months, motherhood struck me as almost wholly a matter of loss: I'd only just gained a self (however rudimentary), and it seemed as though already I was expected to relinquish it. The baby became confused for me at some level with my mother, and required me to cede to her my entire being in order for her to survive. Looking back at my mother's experiences, I felt much more generous than before. If it was this hard to parent in unexceptional circumstances, how impossible must it have been for her – freshly discharged from a concentration camp, in a strange country without the language, friends, a network or money? I felt like asking the therapist for a refund.

When B was three weeks old the hospital persuaded us to supplement breastfeeding with a bottle. But I was determined to vanquish that rubbery rival and a month later began to breastfeed her almost hourly to build up a decent milk supply. Through six weeks of this regime I gained confidence and she gained weight. Jubilant, I threw away the bottles, and when she was nearly three months old my breasts finally healed. I ended up feeding her for almost two years.

It was only when B was a podgy three-year-old that I realised I'd unwittingly turned into an 'eat, eat' Jewish mother – not that I'd ever used those words to her, except self-mockingly. But in those early months, the weekly visit to the clinic, with its triumphant recording of her upwardly soaring weight, had assumed a supreme importance because it reassured me that she'd survive. She was a wonderful eater – delighting in food and happily experimental – and we threw dishes at her until she was well sated. But one day, when she was three, I fantasised about how I'd feel if she were average or below average weight (as I'd been), rather than above. The resulting anxiety was insupportable: she might slip away. I saw then that I'd been assuming that her hold on life was tenuous and that I'd been trying to keep her alive with food.

We loosened up after that and she found her own natural weight, sturdy but slim, though feeding her remained highly charged for me, a conduit through which to pass good things. It was a matter of some pride to us that, as a baby,

257

she'd never once eaten bought baby food, as if the merest taste of Heinz carrot purée might have polluted her. (It scarcely needs saying that now, though still happy eating healthy and ethnic food, her idea of culinary heaven is a trayful of junk.)

Though our endeavours to prevent the adulteration of her taste-buds were based on sound dietary principles and the wish to share our pleasure in food, they were also about keeping her perfect. I got terribly anxious whenever she wasn't, regularly scanning her for signs of damage passed on, until I was struck by how familiar this sounded: in fact, by obsessively trying to avoid her inheriting any of my problems, I'd reproduced my own mother's belief that one could seal one's children against one's own life experience.

Five years later, after half a term at school, B began to wet her bed. This text-book example of separation anxiety appalled me, though the GP came up with an effective behaviourist solution and the thing soon played itself out. Just before it ended I had a fantasy of her raging at me, in the way that teenagers do about boyfriends and make-up: 'Everyone else has a separation problem – why can't I have one?' It had been so imperative that she should be different from me that I hadn't even wanted to concede her an ordinary little separation problem of her own.

On the other hand, one day, when she was two and a half, she got so angry with me that she threw a clog at me, and I thought I'd end up immortalised in the matricide statistics as the first death by clogging. But the therapist put a splendid spin on the incident, saying that because I'd acknowledged my own sadism (which had gushed out like a manic geyser since her birth), she was able to express her anger too.

Another time, not long after, she said to P, 'Everyone wants me to be sweet, but I want to be bad. At home I can be bad.' I regarded this as the *Good Housekeeping* Seal of Mental Health. She wasn't me. Indeed, she struck me as far more emotionally literate at two and a half than I'd been at thirty; certainly, the spectrum of emotions she could identify and express was far broader. (However, one day when she was six and we were having a row – she being particularly uncooperative and me being in a foul mood – she complained that I'd hurt her feelings. Whereupon I retorted, 'You've got far too many feelings' and immediately felt chagrined that I of all people could say such a thing, until it struck me that this might be a sign of my own psychological development, no longer so impelled to compensate for my own past wants.)

But there were many ways in which I mothered her just as I'd been mothered. Whenever she fell over, she immediately reassured me with an 'I'm all right'. When I drew her attention to it, she replied, 'But you're always so worried.' And in her early years, I often found myself in possession of absurd expectations of her, quite inappropriate for a child of her age. It was as if I had no conception that children couldn't, and shouldn't have to, behave as adults (or perhaps just no experience of it). I noticed, for example, that I was constantly urging her to look after her toys; I wanted them treasured and protected – frankly, unused. I'd always been preternaturally careful with my own belongings, which consequently had unusually long lives, and although we couldn't afford (nor indeed wished) to buy her vast quantities of things, I was never happier than when she had ample toys but they were all put away, safe and unblemished. Even while I was exhorting her to be careful I knew it was wrong, and one day the therapist gently put it to me that toys needed to be used and perhaps even broken, rather than treated as fragile and therefore not fully enjoyed. After that I tried to inhibit my words of restraint. Now B just declares, 'It's mine and I can do what I want with it', leaving me proud, and envious.

From the first, my parents were totally besotted; it seemed miraculous that they'd lived to see her born at all, given the odds against their surviving the war, as well as their and my late childbearing. I left B with them twice a week while I went to the therapist. When B was about three, I noticed that the television was often on when I came back to collect her, and mentioned to my mother that I was uncomfortable about this. About a week later, as I turned the key in the lock of my parents' home, I heard the television being quickly switched off. If there is a God, He or She is a cheeky deity who delights in mischievous transpositions, and plays the poltergeist with our transgressions and obsessions. Never, in all those years when my sister and I guiltily hid the television adaptor from our parents, did I imagine that I'd suffer a similar (or equivalent) subterfuge by them.

When B was three and a half and alone with my mother, she asked her what the tattoo on her left arm was. My mother replied, 'There was a war and there were good people and bad people. The bad people were called Germans, and they put the tattoo on, but there were some good Germans too.' B apparently sighed and said, 'Oh dear'; later she passed an unsettled night. Four days after, she asked my mother to show her the tattoo again and then declared, 'I don't want one and I want to blow your one away.' Though we felt that my mother had been right to respond to B's question, we asked her to mention the war as little as possible in front of B: we wanted to be the ones to explain it to her, as and when we saw fit. But when and how, without instilling a sense of persecution or an image of Jews as eternal victims? It wasn't a task I looked forward to.

B's birth completed the healing process between my parents, P, and me; I can even identify the exact moment when this became apparent. It was Christmas 1989 and we were all gathered together at my sister's house. B was almost four months old, I was happy, and my parents had been impressed by P's enthusiastic sharing of childcare (he'd swapped a full-time job for part-time work to do so). He also spent hours, when she slept in his shift, carefully transferring old Ferrograph recordings (made by my father) of my mother's many BBC broadcasts from reel-to-reel tape on to cassette. Now he presented my mother with a large box of the tapes (with similar collections of dubbed copies for my sister and me). She was touched and delighted; she told him he deserved a knighthood. Instantly, he replied, 'I've got one – a sleepless nighthood.' Everyone laughed and, in the relief of that shared laughter, the past was let go. P was now effectively absolved and welcomed into my family – my mother even recanted her former poor opinion of him to her bridge friends. Greater love hath no Jewish mother than to kvell about her daughter's partner to her bridge companions.

My family had always held big, celebratory Seders – one of my parents' best friends, Rafael Scharf (Felek as he was known), later called them an almost ecumenical institution. Non-Jewish friends were included, along with several of my parents' fellow survivors (most of whose religious observance was otherwise minimal). Felek, in concert with my father, conducted the religious side: his speciality was a miraculously truncated service (complete with comic gloss and astringent asides which invariably had us in fits), which happily meant that we could proceed swiftly to the food.

(The Seder, as a story of escape and survival celebrating the Jews' exodus from Egypt, has an obvious special resonance for Holocaust survivors. Yet I was never comfortable with the passage enjoining all Jews to imagine the exodus as if they personally were there and involved – such a confusion between real participants and empathetic descendants violated a distinction which had been critical in my own life.)

As my parents aged and my sister became increasingly uninterested, our Seder shrank to a nominal affair – just P, B, me, my parents, and the odd friend. But in 1992 my mother decided to revive it – she wanted B to experience a Seder in its full glory, just one last time. (So certain was I of its finality that I wrote in my diary 'the last Seder'.) Once again we congregated in my parents' front room around the resplendently-laid table. Once again Felek managed comically to compress the prayers. But this time the event fairly pulsated with meaning.

When the meal and prayers were over, Felek traditionally would initiate a stimulating discussion, once about whether Auschwitz's crumbling crematoria should be restored, another time about Primo Levi – the first time I'd heard of him. But this night he told a particularly poignant story. He'd been to the same Hebrew gymnasium (school) in Kraków as my mother, and they'd shared a very learned teacher named Benzion Rappaport. Each day, when he was thirteen, Felek was late for school because, before he set out, he had to lay tefillin and pray. Eventually his despairing mother consulted Rappaport, who took the young boy aside and told him some things he never forgot. Learning at school, suggested Rappaport, was also a form of worship, and perhaps therefore the morning prayers needed to be shortened for a schoolboy. The most important question which Felek should ask himself instead each day was, 'Ma chovato be'olamo?' – 'What is your duty in this world?' Since that day Felek never laid tefillin again and, under the influence of this instruction in morality, turned towards the more ethical, and less liturgical, questions of Judaism. (Perhaps we therefore have Rappaport to thank for our compressed Seders.)

But this story has a coda. In June 1945, Felek finds himself in Warsaw: having spent the war years in London, now, a sergeant in the British army, he's returned to collect his mother who miraculously survived the war in Poland. In the lobby of the Hotel Polonia, one of the few buildings in Warsaw still standing and with a roof and where the British embassy is located, a crowd mills around. Suddenly Felek spots an old schoolfriend, recently arrived from Palestine in search of survivors. They embrace and feverishly exchange information about mutual friends, when a Polish peasant,

262

who's been observing them for a while, comes up and asks, 'You are Jews?' 'Indeed we are,' they reply, whereupon he takes from his breast-pocket a bundle of papers, pages from an exercise book covered in Hebrew handwriting in fading ink. With it a scrap of paper, scrawled in Polish: 'Pious soul,' the message reads, 'this is a man's life's work. Give it into good hands.'

They look at the Hebrew manuscript and can hardly believe their eyes. It's the work of Benzion Rappaport, which he threw into a Polish field from the window of the train taking him to the death-camp in Bełzec. A man, the one who stands before them now, found it, deciphered the Polish message, and safeguarded the manuscript. When the war is over, he travels to Warsaw to look for Jews to hand it to. Jews in Poland in 1945 are hard to find, but in the crowded lobby of the Hotel Polonia he spots two – former pupils of Benzion Rappaport.

Felek and his friend saw to it that Benzion's book, a collection of essays on the glories of German philosophy (Hegel, Kant, and Schopenhauer), as well as his own thoughts on religion and ethics, entitled 'Nature and Spirit', was published in Israel.

As it happens, that wasn't the last big Seder in my parents' house in Langland Gardens. There was another the following year, but for my father it was torture – he'd fallen and hurt his back the day before and was longing to get back into bed. His hearing was also by now very poor so he couldn't participate in the conversation. Most symbolically of all, he displaced himself from his traditional seat at the head of the table. That year, for the first and last time, he sat at the other end, where my mother usually sat.

9

If death is separation, albeit the final one, no wonder my father did it so slowly. It was the only way he knew and the only way we'd let him.

By 1992 he'd become frail and his hearing had deteriorated until only twenty per cent remained. My mother determinedly called in almost every hearing-aid on the market for him to try, but none worked – the Ménières Disease he'd acquired in the Russian forced labour camps was now firmly in command.

14 September 1992 My father looks up at me imploringly, like a dog begging to be put out of its misery. I kiss him and look away. A few weeks later he becomes temporarily confused: he can't remember the dates when the Holocaust began and ended (though they'd seemed etched on his soul when he was younger) and asks me to remind him. When I do, he can't believe it was so short.

17 May 1993 Today he can't fathom what pyjamas are for or how they differ from day clothes. I try a couple of times to explain to him, but after the second unsuccessful attempt we both agree that it doesn't matter. He returns once more to the subject and then says, 'It's hard getting old and not being able to stop it or prevent it affecting those around you.' I hold his long thin wrist and try not to cry. The idea of him slipping away, lying there like some smiling old person fading resignedly, is grotesque – better the brittle old struggler whom I've often found so oppressive. I find it tremendously reassuring when he returns after episodes of confusion; I want to pretend they never occurred.

Later, when he's getting back into bed after being downstairs, I look at his feet and feel inordinately pleased that mine are so like his. I have his feet.

Most of the time he's lucid but he's now spending a lot of time in bed. At ninety-three he's finally acceded to the role of old person but I never agreed to it, never gave him permission. He isn't complaining any more because he isn't comparing his present life to his former one. It's no longer a deteriorated life, it's a prelude to death. Today, for the first time, when I sit in his room (which used to be my sister's and my room, the nursery), I feel I'm with a person who will die. Also for the first time I understand the meaning of the phrase 'heavy heart' – I'd always thought it a metaphor but now realise that it's a precise, physiological term. I think I believed that we should be magically exempted from any human misery, as if our family had already used up their allocation. Their survival during the war had made them seem invincible. Other people died, we didn't.

30 June 1993 P and I are going to the first night of David Mamet's *Oleanna* at the Royal Court, which I'm to review for BBC Radio. We've arranged to take B round to my parents where she'll have dinner and go to bed. When we arrive Iwonna, the young Polish woman now living with them, opens the door. We go into the dining-room, which is unaccountably quiet – something is amiss. 'Where are my parents?' I ask anxiously. 'Your father had a fall,' she replies. So, it has begun.

My father, who hitherto had showered and dressed himself and even walked down the long flight of stairs unaided, had fallen at the bottom of the stairs and, it transpired, broken a hip. My mother had taken him to hospital, and the evening is studded with my phone-calls from the theatre to Iwonna, the hospital, and my sister. The next day, my father has an operation to insert a pin; the following day he suffers a mild stroke but largely recovers. Yet he's in constant pain, and terribly angry that he's 'allowed himself' to get into such a situation by living so long.

30 August 1993   With my father's fall and stay in hospital, my mother is no longer denying the possibility of him dying. I think I preferred it when she did. I visit him in hospital, and we talk about the possibility of my mother selling their house, which my sister is urging her to do. My father judges such a move, in his words, precipitous, and I rejoice at this sign of masterfulness. I sit on the bed in an uncomfortable, twisted position, holding his hand, clenching it, and chatting to him. When I leave, I feel completely drained, as if I've poured all my strength into him.

My father is moved to another hospital and, at my mother's insistence and since he seems to be improving, we go away on holiday. When we return, my mother reveals that while we were away my father had another fall in hospital, breaking the other hip, and has had to have another operation to put in another pin. Before this second fall he'd been up and beginning to walk again. Now any movement is agonising, but everyone keeps trying to get him to move and walk, no one will let him give up and just get back into bed. He's furious.

15 September 1993   B, P, and I go to Langland Gardens for Rosh Hashanah, the first one without my father there. It has a quite different meaning, as if we're playing at it. First we can't find the prayer book, then we can't find the prayers. I stumble over the Hebrew and am so flustered that

I decide to read it in English, but it sounds hollow and the ornate English text seems unevocative. Jewish ritual for me is so steeped in my parents: there were a whole lot of things about it which I never needed to know before – my parents knew them for me. Now I'll have to make it my own. Perhaps having B to do it for will help.

30 September 1993 I visit my father in hospital; this week he's hardly talked. The consultant arrives. My father has been losing weight; they suspect some cancer but can't find it. We tell them to stop looking. The consultant estimates that he has two to three months left.

Some of the time this week my father looks very glazed. He who was always so emphatic and insistent now looks as if he's not there and I find the absence intolerable. At other times he looks innocent, bewildered, searching. This isn't the look of a paterfamilias; I can't bear its vulnerability. As his wish to communicate with words diminishes (some confusion but also the after-effects of the stroke, and perhaps sometimes as well a desire not to bother), so his eyes become more eloquent: always large, pale blue, with a film of sadness (which probably has some ophthalmological origin), they've now become dreadfully eloquent and full of reproach.

8 October 1993 I take B to synagogue for Simchat Torah, and the sight of a multitude of white-haired old men in their yarmulkes and tallises, along with the sound of the zesty songs, makes me cry. When the friend I'm with notices, she says she goes to synagogue to be reminded of her late father and to feel connected with him.

9 October 1993 We bring my father back home, to Langland Gardens. My mother has arranged for a young Pole named Jósek to come and look after him. My father is delighted to be home and seems to have rallied. He's very lucid and sweet; we talk about the underpinning of the house. Then he says, 'Whatever happens, I love you,' and I burst into tears.

I spent my childhood terrified that my parents would die and here, thirty years later, in my old room, this drama is being played out and it's just a normal part of life. Every time I went away on holiday he'd give me a special look as if asking, 'Will I ever see you again?' and now I'm finally having to face permanent parting. I'm so pleased I had the chance to vent all my spleen, bile, and rage towards him while he was alive – there's nothing unfinished here.

Because I've spent so much of my life envisaging my father's death (and fearing it), he's had hundreds of imagined funerals – he must be the most buried man in the West. But now that it's actually happening I rue all that anticipation and those days of pre-emption, I feel angry and bitter at them, jealous of them because then he was still alive. I could have just lived those days.

My father is inching his way towards the grave as if by stealth, as though he might be challenged and ordered to stop if anyone sees him.

I visit him and he sleeps and doesn't respond. I lavish kisses on him, stroke his hand, and his breath quickens. I have contact.

I want everyone else's father to die so that I won't feel I've been singled out, or persecuted by his death.

Whenever my father has died in my imagination before, he's always come back. This time will there be a reprieve?

I feel as if after his death I'll go limp, like a ragdoll: my whole fight was keeping my parents alive, and now that one of them is going . . . I wanted to cram as much as possible into my life before he died, as if I'd die with him. His death was always the boundary I was pushing at.

19 October 1993 The doctor puts my father on morphine, and I have recurring pains in the region of my heart. In this culture it's unseemly to grieve so for your father – for a child or partner yes, but for a parent, no – it causes other people a frisson of discomfort. (But then this culture wasn't ever really mine.) My mouth fits snugly into his sunken cheeks; I want to sever one of his liver-spotted hands to keep as a relic. Maybe after my father's death I won't be such a fearful person any more – the worst will have happened, I'll shed my attempts to control everything and let life play itself out over me. My sister keeps talking bustlingly about how life must go on, as if she thought it might not, and as if grief weren't a part of it. I try to remind myself that I already lost my father some time ago with his increasing withdrawal from life and that (in the idiom of comfort which people use around death) I'll always have him.

But will I remember his smell? My father was a great sniffer. For years now he's been sniffing us, or kiss-sniffing, as if he wanted to inhale us whole. My mother was desolate last week when he ceased to sniff, and I was thrilled when I thought I faintly detected one more.

My mother says to me, you must be strong, and she is. She cries privately.

The next day I hold his hand and peel his grapes for him. Then my mother and I talk about what I'll do after with my old books (which still sit on shelves surrounding him), as if he isn't there.

22 *October 1993* To the funeral of the husband of my mother's best friend, with whom she was in Auschwitz. I try to control my noisy sobs and feel guilty that only some are for him and the rest for my father, yet another dress rehearsal.

On Sunday at six-thirty a.m. I wake in a panic and think, 'It ought to be stopped – how can my father die?' The next day, sitting in my kitchen late at night when everyone else is in bed, I feel as if the final, really intense stage of mourn-

ing has begun. Late at night turns out to be my best time
to grieve.

31 October 1993 My father is agitated (as so often these
days); I sit with him and try to soothe him. 'Co szukasz?',
'What are you looking for?' he asks me suddenly. 'Nothing,'
I reply. 'Me neither,' he says.

1 November 1993 In my fear of my parents' dying I always
assumed that life was fragile and precarious, death omnipresent and menacingly imminent. But now, watching my
father, I see that dying isn't so easy.

My mother is having a terrible time at night when he cries
out and moans. It's now quite clear that I can't take the
pain of it away from her, nor the death away from her.

In the late afternoon my father starts to gasp and struggle
for breath, his hands trembling, his heart thumping. My
mother and I sit either side of him, certain he is about to
go – I phone P to come and collect B. But later he calms
down. I want him to die peacefully, but how can he when
he didn't live. peacefully and has had such difficulty in life
letting go? He hasn't lost his cursed will to survive.

3 November 1993 My father is better – he recognises their
friend Hanka when she visits him. So I begin again to believe
that he'll never die; I need the respite of a little denial.

5 November 1993 The GP visits my father, says he was
shaking because he's caught the flu virus that's doing the
rounds. I drive to a late-night chemist to buy him some
paracetamol.

13 November 1993 B is ill, has a fever. She sweats a lot
and talks in her sleep. I find her standing up in bed saying,
'Let's die, let's die a bit more.'

My father says to my mother, 'I'm dying' – a statement of

fact, almost of surprise, as if to say 'it's finally here'. A few days later he calls out for Marcus, his father.

17 November 1993   My father says to me, 'Your hands are cold.' I remember a friend at his wife's funeral saying that some parts of a person die later than others: caring for us is one of the last parts of my father to go. I can't believe that soon he'll never again ask me how I am, did I sleep enough, have I eaten enough? (Is there a law of human maturation which says that what once you struggled against you'll eventually come to yearn for?) He'll never again ask me about my work either, though it's ages since I wrote primarily for him, and for quite a while he hasn't even read what I've written. In June, he tried to read an interview with Edward Said that I wrote, and put it down, saying for the first time that he found it too demanding.

24 November 1993   Will I feel a sense of relief or even freedom when my father dies? People often say they do after the death of a parent, but I feel as though I freed myself while he was alive from some of his more tyrannical aspects. The only thing from which his death will free me is my fear of his dying. He will be dead safe.

25 November 1993   Sometime in the last week my mother rearranged my father's bed to allow easier access. It no longer lies with its side along the wall but, now that he's too weak to move and hence fall out, it's standing in the middle of the room, with only the headboard adjacent to the wall. It looks so awful – unmoored, like a bier in transit. Only an inert person would be positioned like this; it's another sign of diminishing life. I fear that it might disorient him, but he probably has no external sense of orientation left. It's as if each sense, each layer of personhood is being relinquished one by one. My images of death are so sudden, violent, and unnatural, as if death were an act, but this is most definitely a process – of life being slowly, painstakingly unpicked, with as much effort as it took to acquire, its mirror image. The move from life to death which I always thought so enormous now seems slight.

I don't know what to wish for, and no one else knows what to wish me. The only people who comfort me are those who acknowledge that there is nothing which can readily be wished.

It's so bizarre that my father is dying and yet we're not doing anything about it. After all these years of doing, now we can do no more – there's nothing to be done other than wait. We three live in a bubble of intensity, shared by Jósek, who's cared for him so tenderly – washed him, turned him, fed him, held his hand. But now that it's apparent that there's nothing more that can be done for him and he will surely die, Jósek goes a little crazy. He starts getting acute psychosomatic symptoms, a throbbing in his head, palpitations in his heart. My mother sends him to the doctor, who can find nothing wrong. Almost our only moments of comic relief occur when we're congregated round the dining-room table, with Jósek on duty upstairs, and my mother imitates him graphically acting out his symptoms. Jósek's father died when he was five and I think he's re-experiencing some of the panic he must have felt at being unable to keep him alive. Tending my father so sweetly was a way, for him, of retrospectively caring for his own, and now that the game is up he feels overwhelmed. He has confused my father with his – or maybe only I have. My mother and sister pooh-pooh my theory, and it's decided that, for his sake and ours, Jósek should return to Poland. He feels bad about leaving but also more than a little relieved, and we reassure him that he's done all he could, more than anyone else could or would have, and now there's nothing left for him to do.

Everyone seems to accept my father's dying except me. People keep saying, 'Let's hope it happens quickly,' but I don't. Of course I don't want him to suffer, but I'm immersed in my own suffering and still greedily squeezing every last bit of life and love from him that I can, still savouring every flicker of recognition. My mother and sister seem to be finding his reduced state more intolerable, but I haven't felt any less connected with him now than before, perhaps because of the strong physical bond forged when I had eczema as a baby, and he held and bathed me. Or perhaps it's all just an unresolved Oedipal complex.

As my father declines, each previous stage which had seemed so intolerable appears retrospectively bearable and relatively vigorous. I feel that he might sit up abruptly in bed like a stage phantasm, full of life.

The fear of loss, which has always accompanied me so doggedly, grew from a need to control: this death is a slow painful yielding up of control, and brings a recognition that the process can't be stopped but also that we're not being persecuted. I keep gravitating to newspaper stories about murdered children to remind me of the normalness of my father's dying. Lately, I've hardly had any fantasies about dying when my father does; I understand that my task is to allow him to die and me to live.

His body is emaciated; nothing more can be squeezed from it.

26 *November 1993* My father has pneumonia; he will surely die this weekend. I try for the millionth time to imagine it, picture myself saying to people, 'My father's just died.' How will it ever become a dissociated phrase and not epitomise catastrophe? But here I am, again trying to leapfrog the whole process – he hasn't even died yet and I'm already trying to imagine being in a position where his death is no longer agony. Perhaps I'm trying to convince myself that that day will come.

My father has his last meal.

An old friend of my parents, another survivor of Auschwitz, who lost her husband many years ago, says to me, 'You're young, the person who suffers most is the wife.' I'm enraged by her dismissive comment and tell her so.

27 November 1993 P says, 'Your father has had such a habit of struggling against extinction that he can't let go.'

28 November 1993 My father lost consciousness yesterday. I was shocked to see him – he looked as if he'd already died. He hasn't drunk anything all day, and seems so removed. He was almost too weak to lift his arm, though he did a few times; he grimaces when moved. My vigorous father has become utterly frail. Yet when my cousin's son, a doctor, came to visit, he found his pulse still strong and his circulation good. His hand was very warm and gripped mine. My mother, sister, and I took turns to sit next to him, kissing and stroking him. We cried, talked, laughed, and remembered – no one could die more swathed in love. His death now seems inevitable and imminent.

Sometimes I can't bear to look at my mother – she's so forlorn, so sad. None of us can believe what's happening, that we sit and eat, joke even, while my father is upstairs, dying. Mostly I feel less frightened than I'd imagined I'd feel, despite occasional bursts of panic. He still smells sweet, even in extremis.

29 November 1993 I didn't dare phone today to find out if he'd survived the night, P had to do it. He had.

The district nurse comes to change my father's dressing and undresses him. It's been months since I've seen him naked and I'm terribly shocked by how thin he is, with protruding hipbones and folds of superfluous skin, like an Auschwitz survivor, as if somehow, extraordinarily, a concentration camp has claimed him in the end, after all. I can't bear to look at his face either, it's so dying. The GP comes and marvels at his strength, his formidable heart, his kidneys, his swallowing reflex, and the circulation in his pulse. I feel triumphant – for a few moments I too glory in his endurance as if it were a disinterested feat, and try to enlist the GP's remarks as reassurance, the way I used to when my mother would proudly report back to us how the doctors had extolled his heart or blood pressure. But when I look at his tortured expression any comfort evaporates; he's so redolent of Ethiopian famine victims that I half expect to see a fly settle on his face. Perhaps now I can let go of him.

30 November 1993–1 December 1993 It's clear that my father's body has outlived its usefulness, but still dying seems such a selfish, at best indifferent thing for him to do. B and I make a list of all the other people besides my father whom I have left to kiss.

In the evening, when B is asleep and P out at his choir, my sister rings and says that my father is declining fast and will die tonight. Unlike me, she's never said this before, so I believe it. I wash up, tidy the flat, and pack my bag, all in a kind of manic excitement – here it is. I phone my mother to alert her that I'm coming and I write a note for P to give B in the morning, telling her where I've spent the night so that she won't fear that I've died, too. Later, I think it might have been myself I was trying to reassure. P returns at eleven: as he comes in, I go out.

My father is breathing heavily, with difficulty. I sit by the bed, kiss him and talk to him. His mouth is open, it seems as if he wants to shut it but can't, he has to breathe. My father is dying as he lived, in struggle. I wait for every breath, suspending mine until his comes; I treat each of his breaths as if it's the last, but at the same time a sign of continuing life. I'm getting more and more tired. At about one thirty a.m. my mother comes in and urges me to come to sleep. As she's walking out of the room she wobbles alarmingly, gripping the doorpost, and I'm not sure whether to run to her or stay with him. I stay. Soon I'm so exhausted I can hardly stay awake, but still my father is breathing. I want to get into the bed with him so that I can sleep and he can die but the bed isn't big enough. I start to worry that he'll survive the night and I'll be too tired to function the next day; I imagine him imploring me to get some sleep. So at four a.m. I lie down on the sofa in his room and doze off, and am dimly aware at four thirty of my mother coming in and covering me with a blanket. He's still alive. At just after five I wake up, shoot up from the sofa, and touch him – he feels cold. I rush round to the other side of the bed and put my hand in front of his mouth – there's no breath. He has died. While I slept.

Jósek, who hasn't left yet, comes in. 'Koniec,' I tell him, 'It's over,' and he kneels over the bed, kissing my father and sobbing. Soon my mother comes in.

After, we sit on my mother's bed: 'He had a strong heart,' she says, 'and a big one.' I phone my sister at six to tell her.

My mother tells me that Jewish men are buried with their tallis, and she goes and gets it out of the drawer of his desk.

I feel terribly upset that I was asleep when he actually died – cheated: I wanted somehow to participate in his death; also to see if I could have borne it – now I'll never know. In the early hours of the morning I'd felt his hand getting colder but hadn't realised that it meant he was dying – absurdly, I'd thought that descriptions of the dead being cold were metaphorical, somehow I hadn't known that people really lost their body heat or I'd have stayed awake. But then maybe I'd have gone mad at the moment of his death.

I phone P, who says my father and I were so connected that he could only die when I was asleep. The thought comforts me. Later, the therapist says I wanted to die for him; she also judges my obsession with my exclusion Oedipal (no surprise this), yet curiously I find the notion soothing, too. Anyway, says a close friend, dying is a private business. And then, a few days later, still struggling to come to terms

276

with the fact that when I awoke he was dead, I realise that I hadn't actually been sitting with him to keep him company while he died. I'd been sitting with him because I still thought I could keep him alive. But I couldn't.

P phones, upset because B (aged four) has announced that she wants to come to see my father to say goodbye. I talk to her on the phone and suggest that she could close her eyes and send him imaginary kisses, but she insists she wants to see him in person and says she'll give him imaginary kisses after the funeral. She's so certain that this is what she wants that we accede. She arrives at lunchtime after nursery and goes straight upstairs; my sister is leaning over the bed. I pick B up and she has a good look. In the event she decides not to kiss him; satisfied, she goes downstairs.

All day I keep returning to my father's bedside and his cold, increasingly dead body, but can no longer find anything I need.

My mother's best friend and fellow survivor (whose husband died six weeks ago) arrives. They embrace and weep together, for themselves, for each other and, I imagine, for the many past losses. Death must be very familiar. Someone in my children of survivors' group says that the death of survivors is especially powerful because life and death are particularly intense for them and their families.

The undertakers arrive. My mother silently goes to fetch my father's tallis. After they leave I go into his bedroom and sniff the tidy pile of freshly laundered pyjamas. They still smell of him.

2 *December 1993* I tell B that her grandfather was a wonderful father. She says, 'He still is, even though he's dead.' I talk about the fact that he wanted to die, and she says, 'He was searching for peace for a year.'

I remember once, when I was a schoolgirl, my mother telling me that orthodox Jews walk in stockinged feet only after they've lost a parent and not while their parents are alive. After this, because I thought that somehow it might precipitate their death, I always tried to avoid walking in stockinged feet, sometimes going to great lengths at school, though never giving the true reason because I would have felt ashamed of being found in possession of such a superstition. (And also because it seemed absurd to have lighted upon this one odd piece of orthodoxy to observe when I ignored almost all the others.) Today I found myself walking around in tights and burst into tears.

I chide P for his coolness. He says he comes from such a different culture, where people are scarcely able to cry: he's never seen such terrible, overwhelming grief, and he doesn't know what to do or how to behave around it. I tell him that I just need holding.

3 December 1993   Dislocated and inconsolable.

5 December 1993   My father's funeral. In the morning, for the first time, I light a Jahrzeit (memorial) candle, something I've seen my parents do so often on the anniversaries of their parents' deaths, and one of those rituals of adulthood which I used endlessly to try to imagine myself doing. I walk over to Langland Gardens and pin a whole display of photos of my father on to a board for people to see after the funeral (an idea I've borrowed from P, who did it for his mother's funeral). It's wonderful to bring the robust younger man back into view, and there are terrific photos of my parents newly married (my mother gloriously Greta Garboish in a picture hat), though there's nothing before 1930 – everything earlier was destroyed in the war. The most telling change occurs between 1938 and 1946: the war hollowed his cheeks and bestowed on him a premature gravitas, adding to that bequeathed by his father's death. On the other hand, my father at seventy looks to me now as if he were in the pink, though at the time I must have been awash with anxiety about him dying.

The first surprise of my father's funeral is its venue. Every time I'd been to Golders Green crematorium I'd thought that one day I'd be back there for the funerals of my parents. But I hadn't realised that the building was only used for cremations: my father was never going to be cremated, and his funeral takes place in the tiny synagogue opposite. I'm filled with relief. This isn't going to be that often-imagined funeral after all.

His coffin lies on an old-fashioned cart with large wheels, a cloth draped over it and flowers on top. I find myself feeling relieved that he's back. Since his death he's been tended by the Chevra Kadishah, who prepare Jews for burial. Washing and dressing the body is considered an important mitzvah (meritorious act) and an honour, but I've felt confused as to where he was; now he's been returned to us.

Officiating at the funeral is Dr Louis Jacobs, the distinguished rabbi and scholar, whose Talmud lectures my father attended with great relish. I've asked him to acknowledge the hardship in my father's life and he does, but also points out that my father, like many Polish Jews of his generation, felt at home in both the artistic/intellectual and the practical worlds.

B is agitated during the funeral and I try to quieten her, but otherwise I feel very little, and though I cry on a friend's shoulder when it's over, this is as much from relief as anything else. My father's funeral wasn't the ordeal I'd anticipated so often; my grief is more private.

My father always claimed that most of his friends had died and he was the last to go: 'I feel as if I'm in a waiting-room but the train has already departed,' he'd say. (He also declared that, 'Living for me is a bad habit.') But there are over 100 people at his funeral (it's standing-room only, as one of my friends declares), about 80 come back to Langland Gardens afterwards, and forty for prayers in the evening. I'm heartened by this display of affection for him, and can just imagine him shaking his head saying, 'Cos takiego'

(Well, I never), with a mixture of surprise and bashful pleasure.

One of the things I'm feeling the keenest is the end of a certain strand of Polish-Jewish culture which my father so embodied for me. I feel a yearning for Yiddishkeit in any form and for my parents' pre-war lives. My mother talks so unsentimentally and acceptingly about the people she's lost – her grandfather, her parents, her brother, her two sisters, her nanny, her best friend. She says, 'I cherish the memory of all those people, but it's history, you can't keep thinking of them or you'd go mad. You have to live for the future.' That's how she's survived. But I'm upset that my nephews can't remember who Nusia, my father's sister, was; it's the passing of time I can't brook. I resolve to draw up a family tree.

(Eleven months later the memorial stone for my father misspells his first name as Joseph, instead of Josef. I'm so upset at this anglicisation, this obliterating of his cultural difference, that I meet part of the cost of having it re-engraved.)

6 December 1993   I feel most peculiar and spaced out, as though some kind of insipid external normality is returning to my life. But how can everything just resume? I find the idea literally sickening, and talk about death to everyone.

My sister and I have spent our lives worrying about how our mother would cope with the death of our father (the therapist says we were projecting our own fears on to her). Certainly, my mother is distraught but her capacity to withstand it is never in doubt. And then I realise that, having endured the loss of so many people close to her, she's now experienced at surviving loss. What's more, she understands the difference between losing someone violently in their prime and, after forty-seven years of marriage, losing someone who now wants to die. She keeps stressing those forty-seven years and I see why they comfort her – this is the first natural death in old age in her family that she's witnessed.

1 January 1994 December was very hard. Even so, I thought I'd find it difficult to leave 1993, as if I were leaving my father behind in it, but I didn't. On impulse I phoned his brother in Jerusalem, and felt reconnected.

11 January 1994 To Langland Gardens: my father's smell has disappeared. B says, 'This house smells of Nata' – but not Grandpa, I want to add (though I don't). I think that's why she's remarked on it – she's noticed it, too.

7 June 1994 'My father's death' is an oxymoron – how can my father and death sit together in the same sentence? I used to describe him as Houdini: whatever awful situation he fetched up in, whatever disease ensnared him, he always managed to escape – no wonder he seemed immortal. Yet over the last two years of his life I found I couldn't remember what he'd looked like before he was thin and stooping – every earlier image seemed to have been effaced. They'd return after his death, my brother-in-law maintained. I silently discounted this as just one of those things people say, but he was right: my father's death has begun to restore a raft of earlier images.

My mother is angry with me when I cry about my father in front of her. She's either stonily silent or says, 'Don't. You mustn't.' But I must. Yet now that I see how agonising it is to lose a parent who's ninety-three and wants to die, I can't imagine how losing relatives and friends in their prime, and children, was survivable.

Looking back to the second chapter of this book, it seems absurd that I imagined reading it could kill my father. He never did read it and died eventually anyway.

On holiday in summer I have more space for intense grieving and it makes me feel better, though my level of anxiety about my health rockets and I worry frantically about P dying. Even though he understands its origins, he still finds this irritating. I also come upon a book of poems about the death of her alcoholic father by the American poet Sharon Olds and find myself gratified by the equal intensity with which she experienced it. Her poetry also confirms what I'd always known: that the difficulties I had in letting go of my father didn't only result from my being a child of survivors. Most people find the loss of a parent painful and symbolic; my particular obsession was only another instalment in the problems I'd had separating from my parents – problems certainly not unique to children of survivors, but common to us, and perhaps with extra resonance.

1995 I've changed so much over the past year. The fear that my father might die has been replaced by the knowledge that my mother – and P, and me, and even B – undeniably will. I even feel reassured by the fact that I'll die too – it confirms that my father wasn't singled out or specially selected for death. For the first time, I recognise the meaning of the term 'a natural death'; death to me no longer seems necessarily unnatural.

10

As the months and years since I had begun therapy passed there were obvious signs of change. I became less promiscuous with my smile. I learned to ride a bike, and became genuinely fond of a German woman who came to stay now and again. I could sometimes allow myself to be surprised by the world, without always associating change with disaster. And I could allow myself to feel depressed (and recognise that I had been so for some not inconsiderable portion of my childhood and adult life) without the whole cavernous vault of the universe collapsing on my head. Depressed, what's depressed? It's just depressed.

Other changes were less defined but still palpable. I became intellectually more rigorous, more willing (I noticed) to cross-examine my own and other people's assumptions, able to speculate and hypothesise rather than always requiring certainty. At school, the only flaw regularly identified in end-of-term reports (apart from my wilful refusal to enjoy hockey and record-breaking lateness – forty times in one term) was that I was sometimes superficial. Though this mystified me at the time, now it made sense, for how could psychological rigidity not be accompanied by a similar unwillingness to dig intellectually? The intellect, after all, isn't some discrete free-floating zone, unconnected with the rest of the mind and the emotions.

Nevertheless, there were still great swathes of despair and despondency, and the old recurring patterns. On one occasion I went for an interview with a Jewish charity which funds research to whom I'd applied for a grant to help me write this book. A member of the interviewing panel asked me pointedly why anyone should be interested in children of Holocaust survivors when there were so many other current claims on our sympathy and concern, like Bangladeshi flood survivors. I found myself floundering in assent and unable to make a case – in the hierarchy of importance the Bangladeshis incontestably rated higher. It was only later that I recognised that he probably expected, and certainly should have got, a robust rebuff: there isn't – or shouldn't be – a hierarchy of concern, though in my own childhood and that of other children of survivors such a hierarchy had been established early on. I'd been unable to answer him because he was only expressing a variant of what I'd grown up believing.

In February 1994, Steven Spielberg's *Schindler's List*, set in the Płaszów camp where my mother had been an inmate, arrived in London. The city was almost immobilised by thick, freezing snow the afternoon we attended a screening together. I was nervous. The film, though it hadn't yet opened, had been so hyped and its veracity so praised that I almost felt as if I were going to Płaszów itself rather than to only a film about it, and hoped I'd be able to stomach it. During the screening, my mother, sitting next to me, kept leaning over and urgently glossing its authenticity, so that soon I began to think that I was watching a newsreel about the actual camp and had to keep reminding myself that it was a recreation – albeit, according to her, an accurate one.

There they were – the villa on the hill where she was summoned to play, the young cook, Goeth himself – people and places which made up the key mythologies of my childhood; Spielberg had supplied concrete images finally in which to situate them. My mother said later that the film had made her choke, but 'the faces [of the inmates] were all Polish faces, not Jewish'. There can't be enough young Jewish faces to be found in Poland any more.

When it was over we repaired to a café where I was to interview my mother about her reactions to the film for an article which I was writing (at her suggestion). There, once again, she gave me an account of her time in Płaszów and this time for me it had more reality, paradoxically because I'd just seen the camp represented in a film. Yet the ubiquitous media discussion and debate about Płaszów after all these years also angered me, for when had anyone ever mentioned the place before? Amon Goeth, too: when my mother had talked about him during my childhood I'd always thought she was mispronouncing Armand but I didn't like to press her – I did not see the name in print until *Schindler's Ark* was published. And now here were pages and pages about Płaszów and Goeth in every newspaper and magazine – it had taken an American feature film to confer reality on them and arouse public interest. My mother shared my anger.

Later that week we both took part in a Radio 3 programme about the film. She talked about her time in the camp in a way I'd never heard before, softly, almost disbelievingly, and with a simple, direct truthfulness. It seemed as if the film, and the raw emotion she was feeling in the aftermath of my father's death, had made this possible. She ended the programme by playing the Chopin nocturne she'd played to Goeth. Everyone was deeply moved, and the interview and nocturne were repeated on Radios 3 and 4 three times over the next three days.

Soon after, I gave the first Seder in our house; my sister and her family, my mother, Felek, and Recia came. It was our first Seder without my father, though for the most part I was too busy to feel his absence. When I later announced that I'd do it each year, my mother told me to keep the ceremonial artefacts she'd lent me – Elijah's cup, the special plate, and the cloth to cover the matzos. It was as if she'd passed me the baton of Jewishness; I felt unfamiliarly adult.

And then Langland Gardens, the home into which my family had moved when I was three, was finally sold. The house seemed to embody my connection with England; I'd invested it with any sense I had of belonging here – without it, I might as well be in Prague or Paris. It was also like my father dying all over again – I seemed to have elided the sturdiness and solidity of the house with his sturdiness and solidity, and both had now turned out to be finite, at least insofar as I was concerned. I spent weeks sorting through the clothes, records, and books I'd left for decades in its cupboards and on its shelves: the symbolism of the process was inescapable, taking back things of mine which my parents had stored, deciding which to keep and integrate into my adult home, and which to get rid of. I felt as if we were dismantling not only the contents of the house but the structures of feeling embedded in it.

The removal men delivered to me fourteen boxes, plus sundry pieces of furniture, among them a cabinet my mother had brought from Poland which until then she'd used to store her music – it had belonged to the parents of her first husband and had stood in the Kraków flat where she'd spent the early months of the war. And my father's desk. The desk, a massy piece of walnut which his brother had bought for him in Poland after the war, was absolutely identified with my father, and I wanted it above anything else from my parents' house. It soon became apparent that it wasn't going to get through the front door, but in the face of my entreaties the removal men kindly persisted. After twenty minutes' prising off its squat legs ('They don't make 'em like this at MFI,' as one of them remarked), they got it in. His desk became my desk.

On the day my mother moved from Langland Gardens,

the sight of its cold, empty lounge made me cry. My mother, though, said, 'It served us well, but it's time to move on.' I don't think I ever admired her more.

That year, 1994, saw a frenzy of interest in the war: a few months after the première of *Schindler's List* came the fiftieth anniversary celebrations of D-Day. I was well into my twenties before I had any inkling of what 'D-Day' and 'the Allies' meant. But then from where would I have gleaned that information? I'm not sure that my parents had known much at all about D-Day when I was a child – they obviously didn't have first-hand knowledge – and I can't remember 'doing' it at school (although perhaps it was so far from my family experience that it didn't register). D-Day was one of the many things I grew up knowing that I didn't understand – it sat alongside Yorkshire pudding and mince pies (evidence to my childish mind of English culinary barbarism, else why would you eat a pudding alongside meat and mincemeat as a pudding?), Lent, Good Friday (good for whom?), and countless English idioms – indices of my social bewilderment, part of the arcane cultural code I'd haplessly failed to acquire. (Public humiliation was exacted when I took part in the children's TV programme *Crackerjack*, and couldn't complete the saying 'Every dog has its . . .'. 'Dinner?' I ventured; 'master?' I hazarded wildly. One of the earliest, and most touching presents P gave me was a dictionary of English idioms.) No, I knew instead about gefilte fish, Lebkuchen, pickled cucumbers, and the Jewish mother's uniquely resonant expression of disgust – 'feh'. But none of this was of any use in the wider culture.

I learned properly about D-Day for the first time during the fiftieth anniversary celebrations, but the event left me (along with many other Jews) feeling uncomfortable. It seemed an encomium to Britishness, a jingoistic celebration of the war. B, P, and I went down to P's prep school (which had close connections with Monty) for a D-Day celebration, and I was dazed by the eruption of nostalgia, as if the war had largely engendered not Jewish suffering but British longsuffering, and had given rise to a typically stalwart display of packing up your troubles in your old kit-bag with nothing for comfort but Vera Lynn (and doubtless the occasional Yorkshire pudding made with powdered egg). I knew it was unfair not to acknowledge the genuine hardship Britain had suffered in the war, but the invisibility of Jews once again made me feel resentful.

One woman in my children of survivors' group said she felt so angry that Britain had done so little for so long that she couldn't watch the celebrations at all. Other British Jews remarked bitterly that the Allies fought to defeat Hitler and not to save the Jews. (It was a while before I was able to recognise that my dismissal of the British wartime experience was not dissimilar to the way my parents had downplayed those non-life-threatening miseries which came lower in the hierarchy of suffering than concentration camps – and almost everything did. Only then was I able to acknowledge the hardship of the British experience in its own right, without comparing it to anything else.)

This sense of exclusion from a national 'we' came up strongly at the first British conference for Children of Survivors and Refugees of the Holocaust, organised by a group of psychotherapists in London in June 1994. Asked to give the keynote address, I spoke in public for the first time about some of my childhood experiences. A few minutes after I'd started speaking someone in the front row began to sob. There was such palpable relief that the issue was finally being addressed in Britain that it probably wouldn't have mattered if I'd gone on to read the telephone directory – for many of the people there the event's very existence was hugely meaningful. The conference also threw up endless stories of other people's agonising assimilation, and their struggle to integrate Britishness with Jewishness. When I sat down after having spoken, I was shaking, as if I'd broken some magic family taboo by admitting that things had been less than perfect. The experience left me exhausted and drained.

In January 1995, the fiftieth anniversary of the liberation of Auschwitz was the occasion for an eruption of British and international media interest in the Holocaust. Suddenly, Holocaust survivors living in Britain became visible for almost the first time (a process which the release, a year earlier, of *Schindler's List* had initiated). They were interviewed on the news, profiled in newspapers, and quoted in an extraordinary, extensive public debate about the concentration camps.

Something seemed to have changed in my own reaction to the subject, too. Hitherto, I'd felt an ambivalence towards Holocaust literature, mostly avoiding it on the grounds that I'd been raised on Holocaust stories and consequently had had a surfeit. But now I watched, listened, and obsessively read every television and radio programme and each article on the subject. When, at the beginning of it all, I watched Claude Lanzmann's *Shoah* for the second time, I seemed really to hear and (insofar as anyone is able) take in the accounts, as if I were hearing them for the first time. I even viewed my father's bronze sculpture about Auschwitz with fresh eyes.

There were several reasons for this change. One was the unprecedented scale of the discussion, which served to place the Holocaust clearly in the public and social realms and thereby endowed it with another layer of reality, this time shared: the Holocaust, in a sense, became everyone's and not our family's alone. Second, my father's dying had not only acquainted me with the reality of loss but brought home the difference between annihilation and natural death – a distinction which previously I'd known intellectually but never actually felt. It was as if only now, having at last understood that not all deaths were aberrant, could I begin to appreciate the greater horror of those that were.

And finally, and perhaps most importantly, after years of

work on my relationships within the family, the Holocaust no longer primarily connoted a bundle of personal injunctions and reproaches – 'Be good,' 'You think you've got problems?' 'Don't upset them' – freeing me instead to struggle to try to make sense of the historical event in the same way as everyone else. My sense of persecution certainly rocketed during that month, but I was also able to perceive the Holocaust beyond its concatenation with my parents. As a result, I was devastated for weeks.

After each new television or radio programme I would phone my mother to check that she was all right and had survived the grisly reminders (being especially aware, both during this time and when *Schindler's List* was released, that she no longer had my father to support her through them). Her survivability astonished and moved me – properly, perhaps only for the first time – and made me think more sympathetically of the qualities it must have required. No longer obliged by family pressure to remember what she'd been through, I did so now through choice.

During the fiftieth anniversary of the liberation of Auschwitz we also gently inducted B into the next stage of knowledge about the Holocaust, giving her some notion of its scale but not of the means of death. She immediately connected it with my mother's tattoo, and made me roll up both my sleeves to make sure that I didn't have one too. She also swiftly projected herself backwards. 'Would they have put me into prison? I'm glad I wasn't alive then so that they could.'

11

I'd never felt any real desire to visit Poland, except by time travel. The only Poland I'd ever had any streak of interest in was old and past and seemed almost mythological – contemporary Poland bore no relationship to it at all. Yet when, at the stone-setting for my father, Felek invited me to join him on a trip to Kraków the following July, I had no hesitation in accepting. After the death of my father my interest in both Polish Jewry and the Holocaust had intensified, and I felt the urge somehow to integrate these two Polands – the past and the present – in my mind. The war seemed so close now, as if I could almost touch it, no longer the stuff of myth or old people's ramblings. I harboured the hope that after visiting Poland it might recede, and I might be able to let it go. With mounting excitement I pored over a map of Poland for the first time: Kraków, Tarnów, Jasło – these places actually existed, beyond my family narratives, and their physical relationship to each other seemed, for the first time, full of meaning. I also decided to visit Auschwitz-Birkenau, again something I'd never previously wanted to do.

As the trip drew nearer, however, I began for various reasons to get anxious. One factor was that, after a second visit to Israel – this time I did get to insert a slip listing my wishes into the Wailing Wall – I returned to London to discover that I was pregnant again. (Since both babies were conceived just before leaving for Israel, I told P I thought we'd better not go back there for a while.) While I was thrilled to be expecting another child, my moods in the first trimester were very volatile, and the prospect of a visit to Auschwitz seemed guaranteed to send my anxiety levels rocketing further. I tried to calm myself by allowing that such a visit wasn't mandatory – after all, one of my family had been there already – and that I could postpone the decision of whether to go or not until I was actually in Poland.

Another reason for my ambivalence about the trip was the reading I'd been doing about Poland. A couple of weeks before my planned departure my cousin Ludek faxed me from Chicago, where he lived, a six-page testimony by a former classmate of his at the Jasło gymnasium and now Professor Emeritus at the Kraków Polytechnic. The document, headed 'Liquidation by Germans of Jews in Jasło and Environs in 1942', recounted what the young Pole had witnessed as a fifteen-year-old high school student. (Ludek had lodged copies of the testimony both at Yad Vashem in Israel and the United States Holocaust Memorial Museum in Washington.) Martin Gilbert, in his *Atlas of the Holocaust*, chronicles the deportation of 16,000 Jews from Jasło to the Bełzec death-camp in August 1942,[1] but Ludek's friend described the arrival of the Gestapo in Jasło in May 1942, when it established its seat in the gymnasium dormitory, and ordered all the students to gather in a clearing in the forest the following day to build a mass grave. On that day and several further occasions, the Germans, with the help of Ukrainians, brought the Jews of Jasło to the grave, shot them in the back of their heads, and obliged the young Poles to cover the corpses with earth.

I found the testimony devastating: it brought home what would have been the fate of my father had he just stayed put during the war. My family, for obvious reasons, had always focused on my mother's wartime experience – in some sense, I'd always thought of her as the only Holocaust survivor in the immediate family – but now it was obvious to me that my father, too, had been a Holocaust survivor in no uncertain terms.

The day I booked Felek's and my flight to Poland I was plunged into an almost uninterrupted vortex of panic. I couldn't think what had caused it until, filling in my diary in the evening, I recalled that the day had started with me finally committing myself to going to Poland. I'd clearly come to associate the country, over the years, almost entirely with death: now I had a strong if irrational sense of 'See Poland and Die'.

As soon as I understood the cause of my panic it subsided and when, the following day, I got a fax from the British Council in Warsaw agreeing to give me a grant to help pay for my trip, I felt inordinately better – as if, absurdly, I'd be protected by a magic ring of British custody.

My mother came to tea the day before my departure, and wrote down in my notebook the addresses of her school, various homes and hiding places, so that I could visit them. Neither my mother nor sister yet knew that I was pregnant: I wasn't intending to tell them before the amniocentesis result, for although my mother seemed to treat my Polish trip with remarkable equanimity, I felt certain that the idea of my going, fourteen weeks pregnant, to Birkenau would have horrified her. (She later said that I was right.) But by the time the trip was imminent, I was into the second trimester and felt ready and excited. The evening before I left a close friend dropped in and pressed her Prague golem into my hand to take with me as an amulet.

It was a baking hot July day when Felek and I arrived in Warsaw. The first shock was that the country really did exist – after all those years as a mental category, an abstraction, its materiality astonished me. Immediately, both my connection and lack of connection with it became apparent: as I scanned the faces of people in the airport and the railway station, I saw only Polish faces – no Jewish ones at all. Yet when I looked up at the advertisements on the giant billboards, I found to my amazement that I could both read (after a swift lesson in pronunciation from Felek) and understand them.

In some sense, this wasn't surprising: both my sister and I had learned Polish before we'd learned English. Apparently, we only really began to speak the new language when Eve started school, and insisted on being spoken to exclusively in English. I was then two and must have just been becoming properly verbal. But our parents continued to talk Polish between themselves and to address us in it, though we replied in English. Polish, therefore, became for me almost entirely a passive language, one I could understand but couldn't speak beyond a crude pigeon Polish, and purely an oral one. And now here, for the first time, I was reading signs and advertisements, and soon beginning to speak (albeit with horrendous grammar), with phrases suddenly emerging from the deep sediment of childhood. It was thrilling.

I spent my first twenty-four hours in Poland, as we travelled by train to Kraków and I got my first sight of that bosky city, in a state of near manic excitement. Felek and I had arranged to meet the next day in the Rynek Główny, the market square, which looks so much like an Italian piazza that I suddenly understood why my parents had repeatedly taken us on holiday to Italy – it must have reminded them of Poland. But as we sat in the outdoor café, the Noworolski, frequented by my mother, the tears arrived. How could she have borne the loss of this language and her culture, for cold and café-less London? I kept thinking that, had it not been for the war, this would have been one of my cafés and this my life. (My life had always seemed full of the subjunctive.) Felek said perhaps not: perhaps, like him, I would have found a small town like Kraków confining. Already I couldn't imagine that. Yet just when I felt myself on the brink of being overwhelmed by sentiment (to the schmalzy accompaniment of nearby accordion music, a fixture, it seems, of café-fringed squares everywhere), it rudely dawned on me that had the war not occurred, I probably wouldn't have existed at all: my mother would have remained married to Julius Hubler and given birth to a different set of children.

Felek walked me to Kazimierz, the Jewish quarter, which, before the war, was home to most of Kraków's 65,000 Jews, over a quarter of its 250,000 population. Now there are 200 Jews left in Kraków – there must be more Jews in London's Stamford Hill. One of the chief surprises was how dilapidated it all looked: my mother had spoken, if not of wealth, then of evident bourgeois comfort, but here were only peeling façades and an inner-city abandoned look. (Of course Kazimierz *had* been abandoned: there can scarcely be a comparable European example of so many inner-city properties being simultaneously and involuntarily emptied. I later learned that the post-war Communist government had housed social undesirables in the area and it had fallen into disrepair. Though there's now a Kazimierz Action Plan, supported by the Prince of Wales Business Leaders Forum, neither the state nor the relatively new private sector had hitherto dared touch many parts of this prime site, lest descendants of the original owners returned to make claims.)

Felek's tour (interspersed with impassioned quotations from Polish literature) was an extraordinarily vivid evocation of the past, every corner, each building inspiring an anecdote or reminiscence. Here was a large yellow building: it had been the Hebrew gymnasium where both my mother and he were pupils, taught by Rappaport. And 'There lived the Einhorns, there the Danzigers . . .' and so on. 'I can name a Jewish family living in every single building in Ulica

Józefa Dietla (the longest avenue in Kazimierz). They all died in the camps. How does one accommodate oneself to that?'

Felek turned into a side street and stopped. With a shock I realised that we were standing in front of my mother's home, the house where she'd been born and had lived both before and after her stay in Berlin. The contrast between my charged fantasy and the pedestrian reality (I'd somehow imagined something of at least nineteenth-century antiquity, not this relatively modern-looking block) was enormous, and yet to me the building was extraordinarily totemic, as if its pores had soaked up parts of my family's past which were now preserved in its very fabric. I fumbled with the new camera P had lent me – I'd always lacked confidence with them – and cursed myself for not having asked him to explain how to use it, for now I wanted urgently to decant this building into my camera, to bank as many images of it as possible. This feeling recurred throughout my stay in Poland: every booklet, each receipt and postcard seemed imbued with a value far in excess of what they might actually sustain, as if they were archaeological relics encoded with meaning and potential clues. They were my booty which I hoarded anxiously, keen to steal it away to a safe place, back home. So I snapped the building, and its gorgeous art nouveau light and house-number from every angle until I felt as if I'd sucked it dry.

Yet after a snack at the new Centre for Jewish Culture, like a homing pigeon I was compelled to return, alone, to the house. Uncertain if I'd really captured the images on film (in the meantime I'd worked out how to take close-ups), I took more photos. A young man was washing his car outside. As he saw me try the handle of the building's main door, he asked if I was looking for someone. I stumbled no, but that my grandfather had owned the building and my mother had been born there (as at other emotional times in my trip, I found that virtually all my Polish deserted me).

Perhaps, he ventured, the old woman sitting by the open window knew her – she'd lived here a long time, fifty years.

The old woman invited me in, and I entered her cramped, ground-floor, two-room apartment. She'd only moved in after the war and so knew nothing of my family, but I learned that she was eighty-four, lived with her son, her legs weren't good, and her husband (who'd been a waiter at the Hotel Royal, where I was staying) had died three years ago. Not for the last time during my trip, I was forced to consider the paradoxes in my parents' lives. My mother had probably suffered more during the war than this woman could have imagined, but compared with her, living in a different country, my mother was elegant, affluent, and mobile. She certainly wasn't a victim, and I felt no sense that this pitiable old woman in a dressing-gown had appropriated anything of ours.

And yet it was around this point, after I'd left my mother's street (Ulica Berka Joselewicza – its name so melifluously Polish-Jewish that I kept wanting to repeat it), that I began to cry. Walking round Kazimierz, reading and thinking about it as it was, the other dimension of the Holocaust emerged – the richness and vibrancy of the culture which was snuffed out. This was the heart of Polish Jewry, indeed of European Jewry, not an anonymous mass but stuffed with individual scholars, artists, musicians, and ordinary people who treasured learning.[2] Now there was only an absence so loud that I found it deafening: all I could see was what was missing. Jews.

A youngish-looking woman in short black shift, red-brown lipstick and smart tortoise-shell sunglasses walks down the street crying. She looks at the names on the doorbell of every house just in case the odd original inhabitant might have incredibly rematerialised, and makes a pact with the streets: neither of them would advance beyond 1942 or '43. The buildings wouldn't be permitted a what-is, but would stay locked for ever in a what-was and what-now-isn't, a what-will-never-be-again. Other people hurry by but they're in a different time zone and occupy an adjacent, unconnected reality – a present without a past, while she's unable to relinquish a past without a present. The woman sobs as if the sheer unexpected extent of the tears of a stylish young woman for the dead might somehow revive them.

I cry like I've only ever cried twice in my life before, when P and I split up and when my father died – tears which don't bring the relief which normally comes with crying, only further tears. That night I go to sleep crying; the next morning I wake up crying. I cry as if I may be crying for ever.

I'm shocked by how much I cry and why: shouldn't I be celebrating my mother's survival? But, of course, I'm not only crying about her, and if one cries this much for someone who survives, then one has much more crying to do for those who didn't. Finally, twenty-four hours after I started crying, I stop and begin to enjoy myself: I visit, talk, interview, shop. And then it's time to go to Auschwitz-Birkenau.

It's the hottest day yet, absolutely sweltering. I've joined one of the many daily tours to the camp. There are only six other people on the bus besides the guide – a Norwegian family of four, and a young American couple. As we get nearer my anxiety level rises, but the Norwegians still laugh and giggle. I'm appalled, but what do I want – for them to die in sympathy for what we're about to see? Soon we pass the smoking chimneys of Silesia; it seems insolent to have chimneys of any kind near such a place. And again I ask myself: should the whole world freeze, and organise itself entirely around this one piece of history? My answer, I suppose, is yes, for that's how so much of my own world has been organised.

We arrive and as I get out, I'm taken aback by the sheer force of my sobs. As the others photograph each other under 'Arbeit Macht Frei' and in front of pictures of camp inmates, I regret my decision to come and dread the tour.

But soon I calm down, and in Auschwitz I (the main camp, as opposed to Auschwitz II, known as Birkenau) I'm relatively unmoved: the place looks like a film set, small and full of billowing poplars, and I know that much of what we see is a post-war addition – during the war there were no crematoria in Auschwitz I.[3] Indeed, Auschwitz I still seems to focus largely on the non-Jewish experience (we're led round the shrine of Father Kolbe, a Catholic martyr but also author of pre-war virulently anti-Semitic writings – this they don't tell you in the guided tour). But most of the Jews who were gassed were taken straight to Birkenau and never even saw 'Arbeit Macht Frei', which has subsequently become the emblem of their murder.[4] Yet despite the signs of the marginalisation of Jewish experience in Auschwitz, it's still in some curious way a relief to be here, where absence is so present – in Kazimierz, it's just absent.

We have a Polish guide whose father, it turns out, was killed in Auschwitz in 1941 for being a member of the resistance. I find this both comforting and disconcerting: it forces me to acknowledge that I'm trying to assert my difference to the other tourists in this place, as if I belong higher up than them in the hierarchy of sensitivity, and am entitled to borrow that old aura of martyrdom. But this woman, being the daughter of a victim rather than a survivor, necessarily comes even higher than me, and therefore collapses the endeavour.

The others are due to see a film about the liberation of Auschwitz, but I ask to be directed instead to the archive, where I enquire if they've information about my mother and my aunt. Within a couple of minutes the archivist has found index cards for both of them, revealing that the third camp to which they were sent, Lichtewerden, was one of the forty or so camps which made up the Auschwitz III chain – I'm not sure that even my mother knows this. The archivist photocopies the cards for me.

After the film, we're taken to Birkenau, vast and still one

of the most desolate places on earth. It's midday and the sun is blasting down unforgivingly; there's virtually no shade. The guide tells us that pregnant women were among the first to be sent to the gas chambers. When I see the ramp, I finally understand Claude Lanzmann's preoccupation with it in *Shoah*: this marked another stage in the technology of killing, enabling the victims to be brought as close as necessary to their place of death. It seems like the furthest point in the world from the human civilising impulse. I can't believe that the other tourists are photographing each other smiling on the ramp – but perhaps this is the only way they can deal with it all, by trying to contain it within an ordinary touristic experience.

I also see that (like many others before me) I've confused time and place, history and geography, as if coming in person to the site of terrible events which occurred fifty years ago could somehow yield them up for us to transform them – they might actually extrude through the stones and earth and be mitigated by modern sorrow. But it's time which has enfolded and buried those events, not place, and it was their contemporaries on different continents who had the possibility of intervening, not those of us standing here now. In fact in Auschwitz I, I get a sense not so much of having come to a place where over a million of the doomed were brought fifty years ago, as one where millions of tourists have visited subsequently, and it's only in the relatively neglected and decayed Birkenau that the effects of time more aptly give off ravage and abandonment.

I urgently want us to leave, and finally we do. On the coach I cry again, this time with relief. I think I had some ridiculous fantasy that at Auschwitz I might die.

After visiting Birkenau I shopped until I dropped. I suppose it was some sort of expression of the life-force. In the shower later I found myself yearning for the continuation of this pregnancy (which feels provisional, and will continue to do so until after a benign amnio result), needing another

Jewish child to emerge from all the loss and replace missing Jews, and hoping that, if it does, the baby might signal the end of some of my obsession with death and herald a new chapter of life. And then I realised that this was exactly what my parents and their fellow survivors had hoped for from their children; I mustn't charge another foetus with such a burden.

I'd been brought up on stories of the 'numerus clausus' and ghetto benches (both ways of limiting Jewish participation in higher education and the professions), but with so few Jews left in Poland – about 5000 out of a pre-war population of three and a half million, the largest Jewish community in Europe and one-third of world Jewry – I was shocked to find that the subject of anti-Semitism was still so electric and so current. I knew that the whole issue of Polish anti-Semitism had only really been opened up for debate in 1987, when Jan Blonski, a Professor of History, had written a highly critical article on the role of the Poles during the Holocaust for a Catholic weekly. 'The Poor Poles Look at the Ghetto' had provoked an enormous amount of mail, including many defensive and grossly anti-Semitic responses as well as a substantial number in support. Everyone agreed that all six of the extermination camps (Belzec, Birkenau, Chelmno, Majdanek, Sobibor, and Treblinka) had been situated on Polish soil not because of Polish antipathy to Jews, as was sometimes suggested, but because that was where most Jews lived. And while there's a continuing difference of opinion about the number of 'smalcownicy' (extortionists who blackmailed Jews in hiding) during the war, Blonski argued that the Poles nevertheless shared responsibility for the Holocaust because many, if not most, of them were not only indifferent to the fate of the Jews but even felt some gratitude to the Germans for ridding them of this pestilential presence.[5]

An American anthropologist has claimed more recently that the whole development of Jewish tourism to Poland is a form of what has been called 'negative sightseeing' (visiting sights of destruction rather than places of pleasure), and is designed merely to confirm young American and Israeli Jews' prejudice about the extent and ferocity of Polish anti-Semitism. They come to engage not with Poland as it is today, but with Poland as it was and, in a sense, as they need it to be, to legitimate their own countries as havens for Jews and remind themselves of past suffering by becoming surrogate Holocaust survivors rather than the successful, privileged Jews they feel a little uncomfortable about having become.[6]

There's something in this, and yet I found myself surprised by the anti-Semitic attitudes I found in present-day Poland. I met up with a delightful Polish Catholic woman in her fifties, whose only surviving family live in London and are Jewish. She comes to the screening of a TV film about Felek, and after asks me, 'Can one say the word "Jew" in English without it sounding pejorative?' I had to make her repeat the question because I thought I'd misunderstood or misheard. It only made sense when Felek explained that 'Żyd' in Polish has such negative connotations that liberal Poles try to circumvent it by using 'żydek', little Jew. (To which Felek invariably replies, 'Why, is he little?' And when, under the mistaken assumption that Polish Jews only speak or spoke Yiddish, Poles compliment him on the excellence of his Polish, Felek retorts, 'This is how Jews from Kazimierz speak Polish.')

The Polish woman was also astonished to learn that prewar Felek had been a Zionist but that he didn't, so to speak, wear horns. 'We were taught that they were the worst, the most violent,' she told me, and seemed inclined to want to touch him, as if disbelieving that the cultivated man with whom she'd swapped literary references from Mickiewicz and Wyspianski in the gorgeous art nouveau Jama Michalika café the morning before could really have also belonged to that species.

I felt uncomfortable around some of the signs of the current Polish interest in Jews. The two adjacent Café Ariels in Kazimierz, a pair of rival Jewish restaurants owned by non-Jews, were awash with random Judaica – menorahs, mezuzahs, as well as cassettes of music both Yiddish and Hebrew – and in the main market grotesque wooden Chassidic dolls were on sale. Poles, as well as foreigners, stopped to smile fondly over sepia postcards of pre-war Chassidic Jews in Kazimierz, but to me there was something kitsch about these artefacts that arrested and idealised pre-war Jewry, which wasn't a homogenous world of the devout but richly diverse, often fractious, both obscurantist and scholarly (and, Felek reminded us, often dreadfully anti-feminist), and included Zionists, Bundists (Jewish socialists), as well as the assimilated and partly assimilated. There was also great poverty and hardship.

Nostalgia does violence to the lived experience of pre-war Polish Jews, severs any identification with them, instead folklorising them and reducing them to a collection of mementoes and trinkets. I couldn't help feeling that some of the Poles peddling this stuff never, to put it at its mildest, particularly cared for the Jews, but were now happy to make money out of them. The Chassidic dolls on sale might equally be effigies.

And yet wasn't I guilty of that same process, of reducing Judaism to tearfully-recollected Chassidism, klezmer music, and gefilte fish, by crying about the demise of the shtetl although I almost certainly would have hated to have lived in one, and by 1910 almost three-quarters of Galician Jews didn't but lived in medium or large towns instead?[7] Indeed, some say that the unchanged life of the orthodox would have crumbled by now even without the war. (Nevertheless, the shtetl remained for me, as for so many others, an icon of pre-war Jewry, and a year earlier I'd been appalled when, after I'd included a reference to the shtetl in an article I'd written for the *Guardian*, a sub had phoned to ask me what a shtetl was. At first I'd thought he was joking; then it had become clear that he wasn't, and that no one else on the arts desk knew what it was either. How could I live in a country where educated young people didn't know what a shtetl was?)

The sentimental memorialisation of the shtetl was actually a product of post-war American anthropology and reached its apogee in *Fiddler on the Roof*.[8] Since then the Chassidim – *qua* Israeli settlers, Brooklyn messiahs, or as recalled from the old shtetl – seem to have become the prevailing emblem of Judaism. Indeed, so prevalent is this conception of Jews that when, following my trip, I wrote an article about Polish Jewry stressing that there were no religious Jews left in Poland today, the *Guardian* illustrated it with absolutely classic photos of visiting young American orthodox Jews, under a caption which suggested that they were members of Kraków's ageing Jewish population. Just as Muslims have become wholly elided with, and invariably depicted as fundamentalists, so it seems hard for non-Jews to think of ways of representing contemporary Jews in all their variety without recourse to the ultra-orthodox stereotype.

In reality, even before the war, there were many different ways in Poland of being Jewish. I couldn't understand, on discussing Kraków with my mother after I'd returned to London, why she refused to acknowledge that she'd lived in Kazimierz, when it seemed self-evident, having seen the street, that her birthplace lay in the Jewish quarter, albeit on its very fringes. It seemed absurd to insist on my superior knowledge of this, and I did appreciate that the boundaries of the area might have actually been different then, or been conceptualised differently. In fact, my mother seemed to see the main road separating her part of the cross-street from the rest as highly symbolic, and eventually I came to understand that this was less a question of geography than of affiliation. It expressed a reluctance to be identified with Kazimierz proper and its clear connotations of orthodox

Jewry: if Kazimierz connoted Chassidic Jews, then of course she didn't live there.

A couple of days after going to Auschwitz, I set out on another trip in the beating sun, this time with my first cousin Zygmunt (who lives in Bytom, a couple of hours north-west of Kraków) as guide. As we talked eagerly in Polish and English, he took me to the part of the Kraków ghetto where, before the war, my uncle Milek had had a chemist's shop; to Płaszów, almost without signs of the concentration camp except for the vast, brutalist memorial to the dead (which, as others in Poland, omitted to mention that most of the dead were Jews – that was left to a much smaller plaque with an anguished inscription erected by Kraków's surviving Jewish community). To Wieliczka, where my cousins were born: Zygmunt drove round the town glossing its ownership – 'That's ours. And that's ours. And that's ours,' the tenses somehow getting altered in description or translation. He'd recently been pressing his family's claim to the car park and, though he'd made some headway, the whole process seemed fraught with problems and a resolution some way off.

Then to Tarnów where we could find virtually no reminders of the ghetto where my mother and her sister were confined in 1942: finally, we came upon a memorial to the first deportees from Tarnów to Auschwitz, mostly non-Jewish Poles who in 1940 had had the distinction of becoming Auschwitz's first inmates. But no one seemed to know in which part of town the ghetto had been situated. Eventually, we found an elderly gentleman who, though he'd only moved there after the war, knew something of Tarnów's wartime history, and led us to the town's two minimal plaques marking the burning of the synagogue and indicating the vestiges of its bimah. After leaving Tarnów and as we drove from small town to town, Zygmunt's commentary summoned the world of pre-war Polish Jewry: between thirty and fifty per cent of the inhabitants of these places were Jewish, and Jews owned all the major shops.

And yet in these towns now there were scarcely even traces or glancing references to this thriving pre-war life: an entire culture had been spirited away.

And then, with a feeling of disbelief, to Jasło – a very ordinary small town surrounded by verdant countryside. Again my father's house was nothing like my decades-old fantasy. And how could all these people who weren't my father be walking round Jasło? To me, the town barely existed beyond its links with him, yet those citizens moved about as if the town belonged exclusively to the modern world, with its own pressing imperatives. It was nineteen months since my father's death and my sense of grief, now far less intense and continuous, was temporarily reanimated by the whole trip. I longed in that hot summer to discuss Poland with him, and rued the fact that it was only after his death that my interest in Polish Jewry had been properly excited, until I realised that it was *because* of his death that I'd become so fascinated by it – partly as an enduring connection with him but also because, if I'd been this interested in Polish Jewry earlier, I might never have managed to separate from him and them: I needed my own independent oxygen before I was able voluntarily to sniff some of theirs.

I wanted to take something tangible with me from Jasło, but it was too unremarkable a place (and knew it) even to have produced postcards of itself, so instead I asked Zygmunt if I could keep the stubs of the car-park ticket. (After returning to London I got upset when I realised that I'd forgotten to search for the Jewish cemetery in Jasło where my paternal grandparents had been buried, or to look for my grandfather's factories and estate. My mother comforted me, saying that I'd done more than enough – I couldn't have waded endlessly in death. And my cousin Ludek wrote to me that the estate had been divided and now belonged to a number of peasants, while the cemetery had been desecrated by the Germans, it's gravestones used to pave nearby streets. After the war, the cemetery had been recon-

structed, but it had proven almost impossible to match headstones to graves – Ludek himself had tried – and many of
the inscriptions had been worn away.) On the journey back
to Kraków, Zygmunt asked me if I wanted to phone my
mother. So there I sat, in the middle of the Galician countryside, having just visited my father's birthplace, talking to my
mother in London on my cousin's car-phone; I could almost
hear the disbelief of my father (b.1900), at say the age of
ten, over such a scenario.

Zygmunt took me wherever I wanted to go (which was
the past) but he himself seemed zesty and full of the present.
As we'd headed out of Kraków, practically my first question
to him had been, 'How could you have remained in Poland
after the war?' He answered patiently and by the end of the
day the reasons seemed obvious. A few days later, I felt
ashamed of having posed the question at all, as if he were
required to justify his place of residence but I wasn't. A
couple of young Jewish women I met in a bar in Kazimierz
told me how enraged they got when foreigners invariably
asked them endlessly about the war, as though Poland were
purely a cemetery, whereas they were engaged in trying to
build some contemporary Jewish presence. And when, after
a service in the tiny Remuh synagogue where the different
nationalities (chiefly American and Israeli) far overwhelmed
the native congregants, I shared a Friday night meal with
over twenty others at the new Jewish Youth Club in Kazimierz, I learned that the regular local attenders stay away
when there are Jewish visitors in town: they don't like to be
gawped at like some anthropological specimen, 'the last
Jews of Kraków'. Yet even knowing this and appreciating it,
I couldn't help crying yet again as the youth club leader led
the remnants of the community alongside the larger
number of foreign visitors in a boisterous rendition of
Hebrew songs, as if the volume and energy of the singing
might somehow compensate for the numbers. They wanted

to assert the resilience of Jewish life; I still needed to mourn its destruction.

Past scuffled with present each day in this way. For most Poles, I could appreciate that the tyranny uppermost in their minds was of course the Communist one. And I saw how hard their current lives were: before, under the Communists, everyone had been similarly bereft, but now sharp divisions were opening up, and their standard of living seemed pitiful. Street stalls were crammed with inviting fruit, at prices utterly beyond most of them. I brought back a couple of beautiful dresses which cost a fraction of what they would in London, but which to the Poles were the equivalent of a month's average salary. This buying wasn't entirely a comfortable experience: if anyone was the predator now, it wasn't the Poles, but visiting Westerners like me. I also didn't like the idea of being the kind of person who was oblivious to the hardships of others, caring only for the suffering of her own kind, and during my last few days in Poland I felt relieved to be able to avert my gaze a little from my own family biography and notice in equal measure the world around me – contemporary wounds and not old scars.

On my final day in Kraków I visited the Jewish cemetery. The names on the graves were familiar and resonant: Liebeskind, Rosenthal, Spiro, Kon – these were the kinds of names all my parents' friends had; they seemed to me not like the dead but a living community. I'd gone to the cemetery at my mother's request, in search of the graves of Adam, my late aunt Hela's husband, and, more importantly, of my mother's nanny, Mania. First, at the headquarters of the tiny residual Jewish community in Kazimierz, I'd scanned the makeshift post-war register of those graves which had been salvaged and restored (many had been destroyed by the Germans, along with the records). I couldn't find Mania in either of their two logs but I did find Adam, and was given a crude map of the cemetery to help me locate the grave.

Yet when I searched the grounds I couldn't connect the map with the plots and, though I trudged tirelessly up and down the aisles, over broken and newer graves, and rummaged around overgrown thickets, I was finally forced to give up. (I'd been terribly excited about the possibility of finding the two headstones, even though Adam meant little to me beyond someone who'd bequeathed his name and a lot of grief to my late aunt, but I'd clearly been nursing some kind of fantasy of retrieving those graves back from untended anonymity, and somehow restoring them to my mother. My failure gave me some inkling of how those whose families died without any graves must feel, with no precise place to attach their sense of loss.) So instead I settled upon a random unmarked grave, put some pebbles on it (Jews aren't meant to place flowers on gravestones, using pebbles instead as a sign of having visited) and said the few words of Kaddish I knew. Then, only a little self-consciously, I spoke to Mania in English, told her what had happened to my mother during and after the war, and introduced myself as her daughter.

And so, sobbing, I left the cemetery, and couldn't wait to leave Kraków. I'd done what I'd come to do, and announced to any who'd hear me that I'd had 'Dosc ze smiercia', enough already with death. I hoped that this might close the door on my obsession with the subject and with Jewish suffering, or at least transform it, the way that seeing the dead body of a loved one is meant to help you realise that they're dead. I didn't want to be a so-called 'Catastrophe Jew', or a purveyor of what's been variously described as 'ghetto nostalgia' and 'lachrymose history', especially since Judaism is firmly oriented towards life rather than death, and discourages a preoccupation with the morbid. As I left Poland, it seemed to me that I had done the right thing, that my trip, though painful, had been a healing experience rather than a self-indulgent one. I also felt much more sympathetic to my parents' worldview: their hostility to my relationship with P had been scarcely surprising since in pre-Holocaust Poland intermarriage didn't exceed one per cent,[9] and most Poles had been totally uninterested in the Jewish community,[10] and had looked down on Jews, considering themselves superior. Now I also understood that when my mother used to ask us if someone was English (and therefore by implication non-Jewish), she had in fact been extrapolating from her pre-war life, when you assumed that if someone was described as Polish they weren't therefore also Jewish.

Yet it wasn't so easy to forsake my obsessions. Back in London I felt like a visitor from another planet and listened endlessly to lacrymose Yiddish melodies. My preoccupation with the past became so intense that I even began to feel nostalgia for the Jewish hospital in Stoke Newington where I'd been born (and had never felt the slightest interest in revisiting). Seized suddenly with a desire to see it, though I knew that it had been closed down, I ran to the phone-book to see if I could find it entered there. It wasn't, and at that point I realised that I'd gone too far: I was now dusting everything in the past with dolour, as if what was prior demanded reverence simply by virtue of its irrecoverability. I'd caught myself out in embarrassment with this fixedly retrospective gaze.

A few days after returning to London, I went round to my mother's with my Polish spoils – postcards, books, photographs, and cassettes. I recounted incidents and observations, and showed her photos of all the homes she'd lived in, which she pored over with pleasure and interest, as if they were fascinating historical documents belonging to someone else's life. And then I put on a cassette of a song by Mordechai Gebirtig. Gebirtig was a poor Jewish carpenter who lived at No.5 Ulica Berka Joselewicza with his wife and daughters: my mother was close friends with one of them, Siwka, with whom she went to school, and sometimes heard the father humming a tune as he worked. The whole family was murdered by the Germans in 1942 and it was only after his death that he was discovered to have been one of the finest composers of Yiddish music; since then his folksongs have been recorded around the world. One 'Unser Shtetl Brennt' (Our town's on fire) which he wrote in 1936 after a pogrom in Przytyk is as plangent and evocative a piece of music as one's ever likely to hear, and I'd been playing it and crying to it for days. A few bars into 'Unser Shtetl Brent' my mother crumpled into a terrible shocked sadness and began to sob. (Why was I surprised that the music could penetrate where the pictures and words could not?)

I switched off the cassette-player immediately, and apologised again and again for upsetting her, but already she'd begun to talk: 'When I think of all the people I lost – my brother, my father [and she named a long list], I don't know why I didn't hang myself. How could I survive, go on living after all that, and after losing Josef too?'

Later, I wonder why I did it. Why did I try and force her to reconnect with all that she'd lost? Sadism, or revenge for all those years of feeling impelled to look after her? A wish for her to take back some of the grief which I'd carried for her, and which now felt intolerably burdensome? Or some perverse desire to see her whole, inhabiting not only the triumphant but the sad parts of herself as well? Or all of these? Whatever the reason, the moment it had occurred and I glimpsed the sheer drop of her grief, its awe-inspiring dimensions, I regretted it deeply, but already she'd recovered, saying, 'Yet I get up and I'm happy to be here in this lovely flat, and to live.' I also reminded her, unnecessarily, of all she had to live for – her children, friends, music, and grandchildren.

I urgently wanted to tell her that there might be another of these last on the way, but stuck to my resolve to say nothing until after the amniocentesis result. The idea of her having to go through yet another loss didn't bear thinking about, especially since, for a few weeks after I returned from Poland, my mother had become for me exclusively a Holocaust survivor – I couldn't relate to her in any other terms. (It was quite a relief, about a month later, to feel exasperated with her once more, and see the other dimensions to our relationship restored.) The wait for the amnio result was even worse the second time round than the first: this time in trying to anticipate the worst I kept confusing 'termination' with 'extermination' – they'd become horribly elided in my mind. But the worst never materialised, only the best, to the evident delight of my mother.

And as the pregnancy advanced I began to return to the present, propelled there too by my little B's boisterous engagement with life. One day, a couple of months later and some weeks into her second year at school, she said to me, 'I'm not getting told off so much now as at the beginning of term. And I'm not getting praised so much either. I'm just normal.' And I could hear from the pride in her voice how great an achievement that must have been for her in this particular family.

12

I am not a case-history: no one wants to be a case, especially one with a history, or be reduced to a cluster of symptoms. In professional literature, the case-history sets out to prove the professional's diagnosis: it retrospectively shapes the patient's history, which seems to move inexorably towards a therapeutically 'worked through' resolution, free of any recurring messes or imperfections. Reading this kind of literature, with its 'finished' endings (as if the patient's journey is concluded once she's no longer in the professional's orbit) is always for me an exercise in disappointment and envy: by comparison my own accommodations seem flawed and contingent.[1] I am not a case-history – my own path is far more bumpy and circuitous, and this story doesn't end with all problems neatly solved, although through the process of transcribing my parents' tapes I do feel some kind of resolution. I now know and can retain their stories.

A book invariably skews a life too: by focusing on one subject, it implicitly downgrades others. Here, I've tried to sift from the soup of my past only those ingredients which seemed in some way related to my parents' wartime experiences and their aftermath – already a highly speculative venture, since those aspects are invariably pulped in with all the others. (Perhaps, too, I've understated some of the more positive traits with which my parents' histories have endowed me.) What's more, by concentrating for the purpose of the book on those ingredients alone and not on the many others which have helped to shape my life, I run the risk of over-stressing them, and appearing to suggest that they've been its main or only influences: by (necessarily) organising this book around my parents' Holocaust experiences, it may seem as if my life too revolves around them. I appear to be even more obsessed with the Holocaust than I actually am, someone whose preoccupation with loss is relentless and total. (Yet, paradoxically, I and other children of survivors seem to feel much greater ambivalence at drawing on the iconography and metaphor of the Holocaust to describe our own personal experience than non-Jews like the poet Sylvia Plath, who metamorphosed herself in her poetry into a concentration camp victim without apparently worrying about the ethics. While the Holocaust is culturally available as a reference for most post-war writers and citizens, we who are and yet aren't so intimately connected with it police the distinction between survivor and the rest with care.) But, of course, like every life, mine is a nexus of many different factors, choices, and identities – I laugh, eat, shop, dance, kiss, work, as well as ponder and mourn and moan (though from this text you'd probably never guess it).

What's also disturbing is that when you take your life as your text, you invite it to be read and judged like one. But I'm not a book, and don't relish the idea of being identified with the confessional school of psychobabble – those senti-mental, prurient authors who seem to derive a unique grati-fication from publicly venting their most private feelings. Indeed, some of the time I can't quite believe that I've embarked upon such a public act of self-exposure. To discuss one's feelings so unrestrainedly is a breach of British social etiquette: this, after all, is the culture where the anticipated reply to the question 'How are you?' remains 'Fine', where a preoccupation with self is deemed indulgent and unseemly, and the prevailing view is that most people 'just get on with it' (as if pondering one's life and living it were somehow incompatible). Though everyone may have a story to tell, only exhibitionists – the thinking goes – actually tell it. My father, un-English though he remained, subscribed to that view and certainly would have been scathing about this text's obsession with self. (Perhaps that's why it's been so necessary – and hard – for me to write it.) And, of course, it is all too easy in a personal memoir to overstate one's own uniqueness. Clearly all Jews, and not just I alone, nor only children of survivors and refugees, have been profoundly affected by the Holocaust,[2] and all post-war Jews are stalked by a sense of 'what if'.

But then, being Jewish in Britain (let alone being the child of survivors) is very different today from when I was a child. Certainly, my daughter, despite going to a church school (as I did), is already confident about her Jewishness in ways I never was, and which seem to me more American than British. I'm delighted but also a little disconcerted hearing her talk so breezily in public about being Jewish – she hasn't yet discovered that it isn't quite done, and I want to preserve her state of ignorance for as long as possible. Friends whose child goes to the same synagogue Sunday school rang recently to ask if we were as dismayed as they were when their child came back singing a song they thought disturbingly exclusive. The song began, 'I'm proud to be a Jew, I want for you to know.' We, on the other hand, on the Jesuitical principle of the earlier the better, and considering how Christian and non-multicultural the environment remains, didn't mind at all – it was rather the song's grammatical ghastliness which appalled me.

If being Jewish has changed, so too has being English, not just for me but also for the wider culture. Of course, the idea of Englishness as cricket and Noël Coward, public schools and tea, was only ever part of ideology and mythology, though these images have proved peculiarly enduring and go to make up what Audre Lorde (writing about America) called the 'mythical norm' – 'white, thin, male, heterosexual, Christian, and financially secure'.[3] Jews, on the other hand, were always seen as epitomising those who lived on the borderlines of various cultures, at the point where social influences cross-fertilised.[4] In Western countries today, the baton of rootless outsider has been handed to members of other, more obviously distinct cultures, often Muslim or Arab, and Jews more frequently appear as insiders.[5] While black people have long confronted and challenged dominant, excluding definitions of Britishness, marginalised whites are now increasingly adding dissident voices of their own. Indeed, in these postmodern times, suddenly everyone is interested in diasporas and displacement, in the marginalised and 'les exclus'. Eva Hoffman, in her fine memoir about being uprooted in 1959 from Poland to Canada, recalls struggling with her sense of foreignness and alienness until she went to university, only to find a whole generation defining themselves by their sense of dislocation.[6]

Today, especially in popular culture, being of mixed race or possessing other culturally hybrid characteristics is a social asset, while the state of dispossession is seen as a template for the modern condition: the transgressive seems to exert a powerful fascination and the very notions of home and homeland are endlessly post-colonially critiqued and dismantled. Today, it seems, we all believe ourselves creole, causing deep anxiety to the dominant culture which strikes back with proposals to teach children to be British. Indeed, the greatest postmodern irony is that it's the offspring of immigrants – the Portillos and Michael Howards – who strive hardest to assert their Britishness and keep the stock unpolluted, producing the paradox of the son of a pre-war Jewish refugee (Home Secretary Howard) introducing punitive asylum laws.

Sometimes my own endless self-dismantling feels as if it's produced a greater rather than lesser sense of struggle, though I no longer find myself (except in extreme crisis) so routinely feeling that all sense of the good has been obliterated. And, after decades of expending such large quantities of energy in resisting death that there often wasn't enough left for living, trying not to die is no longer quite so central to my existence. Having put death at the centre of life, it's finally becoming apparent to me that it belongs at the end.

All in all, surveying things now, I can't believe how much connectedness and separateness I've attained.

It's a windy day and I'm going out with B. 'Put your coat on,' I plead, 'you'll be cold.' 'No, mama,' she replies, 'I'm not cold. You are.'

Notes

Chapter 2

1 Płaszów, as Eugeniusz Duda describes in 'A Guide to Jewish Cracow' (*Our Roots*, Jewish Information and Tourist Bureau, Poland, 1992), was divided into two sections – A, a camp for compulsory labour, and B, for those who were to be exterminated straight away by beating or execution. Though it had no gas chambers, by the middle of 1943 Płaszów had been transformed into a sub-camp of the Majdanek concentration camp.

Chapter 5

1 Quoted in Anton Gill, *The Journey Back From Hell*, p.76, Grafton, 1988.

2 Ibid., p.154. Several other survivors interviewed by Gill refer to their continuing anger over both the Jewish and non-Jewish apparent indifference to their wartime experience.

3 Linley Boniface, 'Saved from death by Schindler's list', *Hampstead and Highgate Express*, 5 May 1995.

4 Esther Bronstein, *Open Space: Bringing the Holocaust Home*, BBC2, 19 January 1995.

5 Primo Levi, *If This is a Man*, p.66, Abacus, 1987.

6 Primo Levi, *The Truce*, p.227, Abacus, 1987.

7 Robert Wistrich, *Anti-Semitism: The Longest Hatred*, Methuen, 1991.

8 David Feldman, *Englishmen and Jews: Social Relations and Political Culture, 1840–1914*, Yale University Press, 1994.

9 Quoted in ibid., p.76.

10 Quoted in Bill Williams, 'The Anti-Semitism of Tolerance: Middle-Class Manchester and the Jews 1870–1900', pp.86, 88, in A.J. Kidd and K.W. Roberts (eds), *City, class and culture*, Manchester University Press, 1985.

11 Quoted in Bryan Cheyette, *Constructions of 'the Jew' in English literature and society*, p.16, Cambridge University Press, 1993.

12 H. G. Wells, *The Shape of Things to Come: the Ultimate Revolution* (1933), quoted in ibid., p.144.

13 Quoted in ibid., pp.145, 157.

14 T.S. Eliot, *Selected Poems*, p.31, Faber and Faber, 1961.

15 Ibid., p.35.

16 Quoted in Cheyette, op. cit., p.116.

17 Quoted in Cheyette, op. cit., p.146.

18 Feldman, op. cit., p.332.

19 Zygmunt Bauman, 'The Homecoming of Unwelcome Strangers: Eastern European Jewry Fifty Years After the War', p.18. *Jewish Quarterly*, no. 135, Autumn 1989.

20 Zygmunt Bauman, *Modernity and the Holocaust*, Polity Press, 1989.

21 Isaac Deutscher, *The Non-Jewish Jew*, Merlin Press, 1981. Sartre broke with Moscow by declaring that 'The authentic Jew abandons the myth of the universal man', Jean-Paul Sartre, *Anti-Semite and Jew*, p.136, Schocken Books, 1965.

22 Alain Finkielkraut, *The Imaginary Jew*, pp.69,70, University of Nebraska Press, 1994.

23 Ibid., p.68.

24 A similar process had taken place in France when French Jews had gained emancipation in 1791: as Count Stanislas Clermont-Tonnerre asserted in his famous declaration to emancipate the Jews: 'We must refuse the Jews everything as a nation and give them everything as individuals; they must constitute neither a political group nor an order within the state; they must become citizens as individuals,' Quoted in Judith Friedlander, 'Anti-Semitism in France, 1978–1992', p.64, in Lawrence D. Kritzman (ed), *Auschwitz and After: Race, Culture, and 'the Jewish Question' in France*, Routledge, 1995.

25 Richard Bolchover, *British Jewry and the Holocaust*, p.78,

Cambridge University Press, 1993. Bolchover suggests that it's unlikely that most non-Jews ever saw the emancipation of the Jews in contractual terms: 'The emancipation contract thus existed only in the minds of British Jews; it was in this sense a delusion albeit based on an interpretation of some statements of nineteenth-century British political thinkers,' p.181.

26 Quoted in Rickie Burman, 'The Jewish Woman as Breadwinner: The Changing Value of Women's Work in a Manchester Immigrant Community', p.36, *Oral History*, vol. 10, no. 2, Autumn 1982. For an unforgiving portrayal of the snobbishness and materialism of the upper-class nineteenth-century English Jew, see Amy Levy's angry short novel *Reuben Sachs: A Sketch* in Melvyn New (ed), *The Complete Novels and Selected Writings of Amy Levy, 1861–1889*, University Press of Florida, 1993.

27 Quoted in Rosalyn Livshin, 'The Acculturation of the Children of Immigrant Jews in Manchester, 1890–1930', p.81, in David Cesarani (ed), *The Making of Modern Anglo-Jewry*, Basil Blackwell, 1990.

28 Williams, 1985, op. cit., p.92.

29 Bill Williams, ' "East and West" in Manchester Jewry, 1850–1914', p.21, in Cesarani, op. cit.

30 Livshin, op. cit.

31 Williams, 1990, op. cit.

32 Livshin, op. cit.

33 Steven Cohen, *That's Funny, You Don't Look Anti-Semitic*, Beyond the Pale Collective, 1984.

34 Livshin, op. cit.

35 Quoted in Howard Cooper and Paul Morrison, *A Sense of Belonging*, p.76, Weidenfeld and Nicolson, 1991.

36 Bolchover, op. cit. The Jewish philosopher Franz Rosenzweig usefully distinguished between assimilating into someone else's culture, causing the extinction of one's own distinct identity and history, and assimilating into one's own culture the most valuable and enriching aspects of someone else's (Cooper and Morrison, op. cit.). Assimilation has also been contrasted unfavourably with integration, with the former implying incorporation and the disappearance of difference, while the latter is based on mutual respect (Claire Pajaczkowska and Barry Curtis, 'Assimilation, Entertainment, and the Hollywood Solution', in Linda

Nochlin and Tamar Garb (eds), *The Jew in the Text: Modernity and the Construction of Identity*, Thames and Hudson, 1995).

37 Feldman, op. cit.

38 Ibid.

39 Quoted in ibid., pp.302–3.

40 David Cesarani, 'Communal Authority in Anglo-Jewry, 1914–40', in Cesarani, op. cit.

41 Louise London, 'Jewish Refugees, Anglo-Jewry and British Government Policy, 1930–1940', in Cesarani, op. cit.

42 Ibid.

43 Ibid, p.166.

44 *Jewish Chronicle*, 28 October 1938, quoted in ibid., p.185. This conflict between German Jews and the Ostjuden was so durable that it was reproduced even among pre-war Jewish refugees in Bolivia (see Leo Spitzer, 'Andean Waltz', in Geoffrey H. Hartman (ed), *Holocaust Remembrance: The Shapes of Memory*, Basil Blackwell, 1994).

45 Tony Kushner, *The Holocaust and the Liberal Imagination*, Basil Blackwell, 1994.

46 Bolchover, op. cit.

47 Jewish Women in London Group, *Generations of Memories: Voices of Jewish Women*, The Women's Press, 1989.

48 London, op. cit.

49 Quoted in ibid., p.175.

50 In 1938 the Medical Practitioners' Union declared that 'All men know that there is one race which is never absorbed, a race to which claims of "business" always come before any consideration for those who are unwise enough to give them hospitality.' Quoted in Kushner, 1994, op. cit., p.84.

51 Barry Turner, *The Long Horizon: 60 Years of CBF World Jewish Relief*, CBF World Jewish Relief, 1993.

52 Kushner, 1994, op. cit.

53 Norman Bentwich, *They Found Refuge*, The Cresset Press, 1956.

54 Quoted in Tony Kushner, *The Persistence of Prejudice: Anti-Semitism in British society during the Second World War*, p.153, Manchester University Press, 1989.

55 Ibid.

56 Quoted in Kushner, 1994, op. cit., p.114.

57 Quoted in Kushner, 1989, op. cit., p.155.

58 Bolchover, op. cit.

59 Quoted in Cohen, op. cit., p.74.

60 Quoted in Bolchover, op. cit., p.50.
61 Quoted in Kushner, 1994, op. cit., p.57.
62 George Weidenfeld, *Remembering My Good Friends*, p.91, HarperCollins, 1995.
63 Bolchover, op. cit., p.51.
64 Louise London, Wiener Library conference, 'Family/ History: Survivors, Refugees and their Children', London, 29 January 1995.
65 Kushner, 1989, op. cit.
66 Kushner, 1994, op. cit. gives many examples of unhappy employer/domestic relationships.
67 Quoted in Bolchover, op. cit., p.72.
68 Bertha Leverton and Shmuel Lowenson (eds), *I Came Alone:. The Stories of the Kindertransports*, Book Guild, 1990.
69 Helga Wolff, *No longer strangers*, The World of Books, 1995.
70 Herbert Levy, *Voices from the Past*, p.39, Book Guild, 1995.
71 Wolff, op. cit., p.40.
72 Ibid., pp.41–2.
73 Quoted in Kushner, 1989, op. cit., p.68.
74 Ibid.
75 Bentwich, op. cit.
76 Kushner, 1994, op. cit.
77 Quoted in Kushner, 1989, op. cit., p.149.
78 Ibid.
79 Quoted in Ruth Gorb, 'An enemy alien in Britain', *Hampstead and Highgate Express*, 5 May 1995.
80 Levy, op. cit., p.44.
81 Tony Kushner, 'All Quiet on the Home Front?', p.12, *Jewish Quarterly*, no.135, Autumn 1989. (Kushner, 1989, op. cit., refers from here on however to *The Persistence of Prejudice: Anti-Semitism in British society during the Second World War*, Manchester University Press, 1989.)
82 Quoted in Kushner, 1989, op. cit., p.98.
83 Ibid., p.92.
84 Ibid., p.2.
85 Quoted in ibid., p.96.
86 Ibid., p.92.
87 Angus Calder, *The People's War*, quoted in ibid., p.99.
88 Quoted in ibid., p.115.
89 Ibid., p.133.
90 Ibid.
91 Levy, op. cit., p.88.

92 Quoted in ibid, p.107.
93 And wasn't confined to Britain: a similar nexus of beliefs was current in France. See Lawrence D. Kritzman, op. cit.
94 Kushner, 1989, op. cit.
95 Ibid.
96 Bolchover, op. cit.
97 Kushner, 1989, op. cit., p.180.
98 Quoted in Bolchover, op. cit., pp.10–11.
99 Zalman Shazar, quoted in Haim Gouri, 'Facing the Glass Booth', in Geoffrey H. Hartman, op. cit.
100 Bolchover, op. cit.
101 Quoted in ibid., p.58.
102 Quoted in ibid., p.66.
103 Ibid.
104 Yehuda Bauer, quoted in ibid., p.99.
105 Ibid., p.156.
106 Ibid.
107 Quoted in ibid., p.115.
108 Quoted in Kushner, 1989, op. cit., p.177.
109 Kushner, 1994, op. cit., pp.131–2.
110 Kushner, 1989, op. cit.
111 Ibid.
112 Quoted in Jean Seaton, 'The BBC and the Holocaust', p.71, *European Journal of Communication*, vol. 2, 1987.
113 Quoted in Kushner, 1989, op. cit., p.117.
114 Quoted in ibid., p.157.
115 Ibid., p.157.
116 Quoted in Martin Gilbert, *Auschwitz and the Allies*, p.99, Mandarin, 1991.
117 Quoted in Kushner, 1989, op. cit., p.160.
118 Ibid., p.159.
119 Ibid.
120 Ibid., p.160.
121 Kushner, 1994, op. cit., p.200.
122 Ibid.
123 Michael R. Marrus, *The Holocaust in History*, Penguin Books, 1989.
124 Quoted in Antony Polonsky (ed), *My Brother's Keeper? Recent Polish debates on the Holocaust*, p.92, Routledge, 1990. A high official in the Foreign Office, Frank Roberts, rejected pressure from the Polish ambassador to London who, having met Karski, suggested action which the British

government could take on behalf of the Jews. Hitler, Roberts warned, 'seems to be in a very difficult mood about prisoners of war. It therefore seems to me inadvisable to irritate him more than is necessary, particularly on a Jewish issue.' (Quoted in Louis L. Gerson, 'The Reaction of the Polish Government-in-Exile and the Allied Governments to the News of the Endlösung: the Role of Jan Karski', p.315, in Andrzej K. Paluch (ed), *The Jews in Poland*, vol. 1, Jagiellonian University, 1992.)

125 David Cesarani, *Justice Delayed*, Mandarin, 1992.
126 Kushner, 1994, op. cit.
127 Seaton, op. cit., p.57.
128 Quoted in ibid., p.61.
129 Anthony Smith, quoted in ibid.
130 Seaton, op. cit.
131 Quoted in ibid., p.66: an ell was one and a quarter yards.
132 Ibid., p.66.
133 Stephen Ward, 'Why the BBC ignored the Holocaust', *Independent on Sunday*, 22 August 1993.
134 Seaton, op. cit.
135 Kushner, 1994, op. cit.

Chapter 6

1 Tony Kushner, 1994, op. cit.
2 Ibid.
3 Quoted in Tony Kushner, 1989, op. cit., p.199. In America, one month after the end of the war, fifty-eight per cent of people said that they thought Jews had too much power in the United States (Leonard Dinnerstein, *America and the Survivors of the Holocaust*, Columbia University Press, 1982.)
4 Quoted in Martin Gilbert, op. cit. p.133.
5 Quoted in Kushner, 1994, op. cit., p.199.
6 Gilbert, op. cit.
7 Kushner, 1994, op. cit.
8 Seaton, op. cit.
9 Henning Krabbe (ed), *Voices From Britain: Broadcast History 1939–45*, George Allen and Unwin, 1947.
10 Leonard Cottrell, 'The Man from Belsen', in Laurence Gilliam (ed), *BBC Features*, Evans Brothers, 1950.
11 Ben Helfgott, personal communication, 13 January 1995.
12 Tony Kushner, 1994, op. cit.

13 Ibid., p.216.

14 'France remembers Pétain's trial for collaboration – Fifty years on', *Jewish Chronicle*, 11 August 1995.

15 Lawrence D. Kritzman, op. cit.

16 Robert Wistrich, 1991, op. cit.

17 Iwona Irwin-Zarecka's pointed observations are quoted in Debórah Dwork and Robert Jan van Pelt, 'Reclaiming Auschwitz', in Hartman, op. cit.

18 A process of which no visitor to contemporary Poland can fail to be aware – see Chapter 11.

19 Jill Tweedie, 'The silent byways of the righteous gentiles', *Guardian*, 17 December 1990.

20 Anton Gill, op. cit.

21 Barry Turner, op. cit.

22 Quoted in Sarah Moscovitz, *Love Despite Hate: Child Survivors of the Holocaust and Their Adult Lives*, p.6, Schocken Books, 1983. Some of those later housed in a Sussex home also thrived through the interest and warmth of local people who showed them their animals and gardens, and gave them flowers. See Gill, op. cit.

23 Gill, op. cit. See Martin Gilbert's stirring new book about the child survivors, *The Boys: Triumph over adversity*, Weidenfeld & Nicolson, 1996.

24 Bentwich, op. cit.

25 Kushner, 1994, op. cit., p.232.

26 Bentwich, op. cit.

27 Quoted in Kushner, 1994, op. cit., p.232.

28 David Cesarani, 1992, op. cit. See Dinnerstein, op. cit., for an account of the parallel process taking place in the US.

29 Quoted in ibid., pp.78–79. In 1945, General Patton, in charge of Displaced Persons camps, declared that the Jews 'are lower than animals' (Dinnerstein, op. cit., p.17).

30 Cesarani, 1992, op. cit.

31 Ibid. Tom Bower, *Blind Eye to Murder*, Little, Brown, 1995, also charts the process, showing, too, how the British allowed ex-Nazis to regain power in Germany with their enormous wealth intact. Britain only passed war crimes legislation in 1991.

32 Ben Helfgott remarks that 'they admitted war criminals – Lithuanians, Latvians, and Ukrainians – but the last thing they wanted to do was admit Jews' (personal communication, 13 January 1995).

33 David Cesarani, personal communication, January 1995.

34 Kushner, 1994, op. cit.

35 Again, this experience wasn't exclusive to Britain: Janine Chasseguet-Smirgel recounts that 'supervisions . . . show that many analysts – both Jewish and non-Jewish for that matter – are unable to recognise material connected with the Shoah. For instance, for a Jewish patient, a train is seldom an excursion train . . .' Janine Chasseguet-Smirgel, ' "Time's White Hair We Ruffle." Reflections on the Hamburg Congress', *International Review of Psycho-Analysis*, no. 14, 1987, p.434. See Chapter 7 for a history of the debate about the psychological after-effects of the Holocaust, and a discussion of survivors' hostility to psychoanalysis.

36 Cesarani, personal communication, January 1995.

37 Rudolph M. Witenberg, 'Children under the Nazi System', *American Journal of Orthopsychiatry*, vol. 15, no. 3, July 1945.

38 Editha Sterba, 'Emotional Problems of Displaced Children', *Journal of Social Casework*, vol. 30, no. 5, May 1949.

39 Zelda S. Wolpe, 'Readjustment of the Child in the Post-war Era', *American Journal of Orthopsychiatry*, vol. 15, no. 3, July 1945. But see Chapter 7 for two exceptions – Bruno Bettelheim and Paul Friedman.

40 Anna Freud, 'An Experiment in Group Upbringing' (1951) in *The Writings of Anna Freud, Vol. 4: Indications for Child Analysis and Other Papers, 1945–1956*, International Universities Press, 1968.

41 A. M. Meerloo, 'Psychological war experiences in the second world war', *Overgedrukt uit de Psychiatrische en Neurologische Bladen*, no.5/6, 1946.

42 All titles of papers in vol. 15, no. 3 of the *American Journal of Orthopsychiatry*, July 1945.

43 H. A. Thorner, 'The Treatment of Psychoneurosis in the British Army', *International Journal of Psychoanalysis*, vol. 27, parts 1 and 2, 1946.

44 Hansi Kennedy, who worked closely with Anna Freud, personal interview, 13 January 1995.

45 Pearl King, personal communication, 13 January 1995.

46 Ibid.

47 Geoffrey Cocks, *Psychotherapy in the Third Reich*, Oxford University Press, 1985. Some German psychoanalysts joined the Nazi party while a few, like John Rittmeister,

joined the resistance (Rittmeister died working for them). But most collaborated to a greater or lesser degree, unlike the Dutch psychoanalytic society, which dissolved itself in 1941 in protest at the ban on Jewish members.

48 Martin Wangh, 'The Working-Through of the Nazi Experience in the German Psychoanalytical Community', and Volker Friedrich, 'The Internalisation of Nazism and Its Effects on German Psychoanalysts and Their Patients', in Hella Ehlers and Joyce Crick (eds), *The Trauma of the Past: Remembering and Working Through*, Goethe-Institut, London, 1994. See also Janine Chasseguet-Smirgel's interesting article on the Congress, op. cit., in which she incidentally mentions the extraordinary number of German non-Jewish analysts who, in the years before the Congress, would volunteer information about their Jewish grandmothers – 'so many [Jewish grandmothers] that the idea that Germany was pervaded with Jews seemed to be not so far-fetched after all', p.435.

49 Ernest Jones, *The Life and Works of Sigmund Freud*, Pelican, 1964.

50 André Haynal, 'Central European Analysis and Its Move Westwards in the Twenties and Thirties', in Ehlers and Crick, op. cit.

51 Phyllis Grosskurth, *Melanie Klein*, Karnac Books, 1987.

52 Ibid.

53 Pearl King, personal communication.

54 James Young, *Writing and Rewriting the Holocaust*, p.37, Indiana University Press, 1988.

55 Isaac Deutscher, op. cit., p.37.

56 Heinrich Himmler, quoted in Alexander and Margarete Mitscherlich, *The Inability to Mourn*, Grove Press, 1975.

57 Dori Laub, 'Bearing Witness', in Shoshana Felman and Dori Laub, *Testimony: Crises of Witnessing in Literature, Psychoanalysis, and History*, p.68, Routledge, 1992.

58 Helen Fein, quoted in Zygmunt Bauman, *Modernity and the Holocaust*, Polity Press, 1989.

59 James Young, op. cit., quoting Gerd Korman.

60 Cesarani, 1992, op. cit., p.162.

61 Tony Kushner, 'Survivors in the 1940s and beyond', paper given at the Institute of Contemporary History and Wiener Library conference, 'Family/History: Survivors, Refugees and Their Children', London, 29 January 1995.

62 Cesarani, 1992, op. cit. Kushner has suggested that, since the little interest which there was in the concentration camps in the 1950s and '60s focused on the sexual maltreatment of women, it's scarcely surprising that many survivors were reluctant to talk about their experiences. Kushner, 1995, op. cit.

63 Philip Norman, 'A cosy British dose of the same old anti-Semitic poison', *Independent on Sunday*, 25 August 1991.

64 Kushner, 1994, op. cit.

65 Cesarani, 1992, op. cit.

66 Kushner, 1994, op. cit.

67 Mark Arnold-Forster, *The World at War*, Book Club Associates, 1974.

68 Kushner, 1994, op. cit.

69 James Young, *The Texture of Memory*, Yale University Press, 1993.

70 Madeleine Bunting, 'Holocaust centre "long overdue" ', *Guardian*, 19 September 1994.

71 'Holocaust Centre opens in House of Peace' on Beth Shalom in Nottinghamshire, *Holocaust Survivors' News*, The Holocaust Survivors' Centre, September 1995.

72 *Anti-Semitism World Report 1994*, Institute of Jewish Affairs, 1994.

73 See, for instance, *Where Shall We Go?*, Swing Bridge Video, 1991, in which Holocaust survivors living in Britain talk to young people about the effect of the Holocaust on their lives, and Carrie Supple's *From Prejudice to Genocide: Learning about the Holocaust*, Trentham Books, 1992.

74 Kushner, 1994, op. cit.

75 Geoffrey Alderman, 'Agenda: Holocaust Studies', *Guardian Education*, 1 November 1994.

76 Gill, op. cit.

77 *Voices of the Holocaust*, British Library, 1993.

78 Journal of the Anne Frank Educational Trust UK, 1995.

79 Helfgott, personal communication.

80 Aaron Hass, *The Aftermath: Living with the Holocaust*, p.90, Cambridge University Press, 1995. See also Helen Epstein, *Children of the Holocaust: Conversations with Sons and Daughters of Survivors*, G.P. Putnam's, 1979.

81 Arthur H. Samuelson, 'A Writer, Not a Celebrity', *Jerusalem Post Magazine*, 13 January 1989.

82 Bjorn Krondorfer: *Remembrance and Reconciliation: Encounters between Young Jews and Germans*, Yale University Press, 1995.

83 Nelly Furman, 'The Languages of Pain in *Shoah*', in Lawrence D. Kritzman, op. cit. See in the same volume Kritzman's introduction, and Naomi Greene's interesting paper, 'La vie en rose: Images of the Occupation in French Cinema'.

84 Kazimierz Brandys, 1984, quoted in Antony Polonsky, op. cit., pp.182–3, which reprints Blonski's original article and includes many of the responses to it.

85 Tom Segev, *The Seventh Million: The Israelis and the Holocaust*, Hill and Wang, 1994.

86 Dan Bar-On, *Fear and Hope: Three Generations of the Holocaust*, Harvard University Press, 1995.

87 Segev, op. cit., pp.471–2. The Israeli writer David Grossman, born in the 1950s, recalled that 'at school we learned more about the French revolution than we did about the Holocaust'. (Robin Lustig, 'Dreams written on his palm', *Observer*, 21 January 1990.)

88 Rafael Moses, 'An Israeli Psychoanalyst Looks Back in 1983', in Steven A. Luel and Paul Marcus, *Psychoanalytic Reflections of the Holocaust: Selected Essays*, Ktav Publishing House, 1984.

89 Akiva W. Deutsch, *The Eichmann Trial in the Eyes of Israeli Youngsters*, Bar-Ilan University Press, 1974.

90 Segev, op. cit.

91 Hass, op. cit.

92 Segev, op. cit.

93 Deutsch, op. cit., p.18.

94 Segev, op. cit.

95 Ibid.

96 Deutsch, op. cit.

97 Haim Gouri, 'Facing the Glass Booth', in Hartman, op. cit.

98 Eva Fogelman, 'From Mourning to Creativity: Second Generation in Different Continents', paper given at the First International Jerusalem Conference of Children of Holocaust Survivors, 21 December 1988. An Israeli Professor of Mental Health suggested to Fogelman that she was trying to import into Israel an American phenomenon: Israeli children of survivors felt more integrated, he claimed, and joining her group would have separated them from their Israeli peers.

99 Michal Yudelman, 'The Week That Was', *Jerusalem Post*, 20
 April 1995.
100 Mitscherlich and Mitscherlich, op. cit., p.65.
101 Krondorfer, op. cit.
102 Elena Lappin, *Jewish Voices, German Words: Growing Up Jewish
 in Post-War Germany and Austria*, Catbird Press, 1994.
103 Susan Neiman, quoted in Krondorfer, op. cit., p.33.
104 James E. Young, 1993, op. cit., p.25.
105 Quoted by Krondorfer, op. cit.
106 Nancy Wood, 'The Holocaust: historical memories and
 contemporary identities', *Media, Culture, and Society*, vol.
 13, 1991.
107 Lawrence L. Langer, *Admitting the Holocaust*, Oxford
 University Press, 1995.
108 As Kushner, 1989, op. cit., calls it. In 1957, allegations that
 Finchley Golf Club excluded Jews from membership
 turned out to be true, and were followed by revelations of
 Jewish quotas at other London golf clubs – see Geoffrey
 Alderman, 'Political Attitudes and Voting Patterns' in
 Robert S. Wistrich (ed), *Terms of Survival: The Jewish world
 since 1945*, Routledge, 1995.
109 A view vigorously challenged by David Rosenberg, 'Racism
 and Anti-Semitism in Contemporary Britain', *Jewish Quarterly*,
 vol. 32, no. 1, 1985.
110 See, for instance, Wistrich, 1991, op. cit.
111 Runnymede Trust Commission on anti-Semitism, *A very light
 sleeper*, Runnymede Trust, 1994.
112 Annual Report 1994, the Board of Deputies of British Jews.
 According to one newspaper report, Peter Popham, 'Stalked
 by the shadows of history', *Independent*, 14 November 1995,
 in 1994, for the third year running, Britain had the worst
 record of any country in the world for anti-Semitic attacks.
113 Rosenberg, op. cit.
114 Quoted in Cesarani, 1992, op. cit., p.204.
115 Feldman, op. cit., p.11.
116 Ena Abrahams, 'I Had This Other Life . . .', p.101, in Jewish
 Women in London Group, *Generations of Memories: Voices of
 Jewish Women*, The Women's Press, 1989.
117 Lesley Hazleton, *England, Bloody England*, p.48, The Atlantic
 Monthly Press, 1990.
118 Cooper and Morrison, op. cit. Lord Young remembers his
 parents discussing the rise of Hitler. 'They did not want to

display the outward signs of Jewishness. My own title, if that had not happened, should really have been Lord Yankelovitch' (Ruth Bloomfield, 'Jewishness in UK "fading away" ', *Hampstead and Highgate Express*, 15 September 1995).

119 Sue Hubbard, 'Inheritance', p.87, in Sonja Lyndon and Sylvia Paskin (eds), *The Dybbuk of Delight: An Anthology of Jewish Women's Poetry*, Five Leaves Publications, 1995.

120 Elena Lappin, 'Between the Lines', *Jewish Quarterly*, vol. 42, no. 1 (157), Spring 1995.

121 See Rosalyn Livshin, 'Acculturation of Immigrant Jewish Children, 1890–1930', in Cesarani, 1990, op. cit., and Ena Abrahams, op. cit., p.101, who, when she was a class teacher, was encouraged by an inspector to apply for a deputy headship but advised 'to think . . . seriously . . . (about) changing your name. Because it might be a great hindrance to you'.

122 Anna Freud, 'Special Experiences of Young Children Particularly in Times of Social Disturbance', p.155, in Kenneth Soddy (ed), *Mental Health and Infant Development*, Routledge and Kegan Paul, 1955.

123 See Bryan Cheyette, op. cit.

124 Rosemary Friedman in 'The Meaning of Anti-Semitism', *Jewish Quarterly*, vol. 38, no. 1 (141), Spring 1991.

125 William Cash, 'Kings of the Deal', *Spectator*, 29 October 1994.

Chapter 7

1 Helen Epstein, op. cit.

2 Quoted in Henry Krystal (ed), *Massive Psychic Trauma*, p.8, International Universities Press, 1968.

3 Bruno Bettelheim, *The Informed Heart*, Penguin Books, 1986.

4 Hillel Klein quoted in Paul Marcus and Alan Rosenberg, 'A Philosophical Critique of the "Survivor Syndrome" and Some Implications for Treatment', in Randolph L. Braham (ed), *The Psychological Perspectives of the Holocaust and of Its Aftermath*, Columbia University Press, 1988.

5 Leslie Berger, 'The Long-Term Psychological Consequences of the Holocaust on the Survivors and Their Offspring', in Braham, op. cit.

6 Paul Marcus and Alan Rosenberg, 'Treatment Issues with

Survivors and their Offspring: An Interview with Anna Ornstein', in Paul Marcus and Alan Rosenberg (eds), *Healing Their Wounds: Psychotherapy with Holocaust Survivors and Their Families*, Praeger, 1989.

7   Robert Krell, 'Alternative Therapeutic Approaches to Holocaust Survivors', in ibid.

8   Quoted in Arlene Steinberg, 'Holocaust Survivors and Their Children: A Review of the Clinical Literature', in ibid.

9   William Niederland, 'The Problem of the Survivor', in Krystal, op. cit.

10 Eva Fogelman, 'Therapeutic Alternatives for Holocaust Survivors and Second Generation', in Braham, op. cit.

11 Robert Krell, 'Holocaust Survivors and Their Children: Comments on Psychiatric Consequences and Psychiatric Terminology', *Comprehensive Psychiatry*, vol. 25, no. 5, September/October 1984.

12 Martin S. Bergmann and Milton E. Jucovy, *Generations of the Holocaust*, Columbia University Press, 1982.

13 Robert J. Lifton, 'The Survivors of the Hiroshima Disaster and the Survivors of Nazi Persecution', in Krystal, op. cit.

14 A. Russell, 'Late Psychosocial Consequences in Concentration Camp Survivor Families', *American Journal of Orthopsychiatry*, vol. 44, no. 4, July 1974.

15 William Niederland, 'The Clinical After-effects of the Holocaust in Survivors and Their Offspring', in Braham, op. cit.

16 1974 paper quoted in Jack Terry, 'The Damaging Effects of the "Survivor Syndrome" ', p.137, in Steven A. Luel and Paul Marcus, op. cit.

17 Terry, op. cit.

18 Bergmann and Jucovy, op. cit.

19 Myra Giberovitch, 'Formulating an Agenda to Meet the Needs of Elderly Holocaust Survivors', in John Lemberger (ed), *A Global Perspective on Working with Holocaust Survivors and the Second Generation*, JDC-Brookdale Institute of Gerontology and Human Development, 1995.

20 Hillel Klein, 'The Survivors Search for Meaning and Identity', in *The Nazi Concentration Camps*, Proceedings of the Fourth Yad Vashem International Historical Conference, Yad Vashem, 1984.

21 Shamai Davidson, 'Human Reciprocity Among Jewish prisoners in the Nazi Concentration Camps', in ibid.

22 Janice F. Bistritz, 'Transgenerational Pathology in Families of Holocaust Survivors', in Braham, op. cit.

23 Dan Bar-On, op. cit.

24 Davidson, op. cit.

25 See, for instance, John J. Sigal and Morton Weinfeld, 'Mutual Involvement and Alienation in Families of Holocaust Survivors', *Psychiatry*, vol. 50, August 1987.

26 Shamai Davidson, 'The Survivor Syndrome Today: An Overview' in *Group Analysis: The Survivor Syndrome Workshop*, Trust for Group Analysis, 1980.

27 Dov R. Aleksandrowicz, 'Children of Concentration Camp Survivors', in E. James Anthony and Cyrille Koupernik (eds), *The Child in His Family: The Impact of Disease and Death*, John Wiley and Sons, 1973.

28 Davidson, 1980, op. cit.

29 Krystal, op. cit.

30 Robert Krell, 'Alternative Therapeutic Approaches to Holocaust Survivors', pp.216–7, in Marcus and Rosenburg, op. cit.

31 Primo Levi, *The Drowned and the Saved*, pp.62–3, Abacus, 1989.

32 Rafael Moses, 'Discussion of Dinora Pines' Paper on Transmission of the Holocaust Trauma to the Second Generation', p.108, in *Holocaust Trauma: Transgenerational Transmission to the Second Generation*, special issue of the *Journal of Social Work and Policy in Israel*, vols. 5–6, 1992.

33 Terry, op. cit.

34 Ludwig Haesler, 'Modes of Transgenerational Transmission of the Trauma of Nazi Persecution and their Appearance in Treatment', p.53, in *Journal of Social Work and Policy in Israel*, op. cit.

35 Paul Handel quoted in Aaron Hass, *The Aftermath*, p.41, Cambridge University Press, 1995.

36 Terry, op. cit., p.136.

37 Moses Laufer, 'The Analysis of Child Survivors', in Anthony and Koupernik, op. cit.

38 Sarah Moscovitz, *Love Despite Hate: Child Survivors of the Holocaust and Their Adult Lives*, p.237, Schocken Books, 1983.

39 John J. Sigal, 'Resilience in Survivors, Their Children and Their Grandchildren', *Echoes of the Holocaust*, no. 4, June

1995 (Bulletin of the Jerusalem Center for Research into the Late Effects of the Holocaust).

40 Daniel Goleman, 'Holocaust Survivors Had Skills to Prosper', *New York Times*, 6 October 1992.

41 Leo Eitinger, quoted in Fogelman, op. cit.

42 Bergmann and Jucovy, op. cit.

43 Vivian Rakoff (cited by Epstein, op. cit.), who went on to conduct studies with John Sigal. Interestingly, most of the early work in this area was done in Canada, with Bernard Trossmann another pioneering researcher.

44 Krystal, op. cit.

45 Milton E. Jucovy, 'Therapeutic Work with Survivors and Their Children: Recurrent Themes and Problems', in Marcus and Rosenberg, op. cit.

46 Russell, op. cit.

47 See for example John J. Sigal et al., 'Concentration Camp Survival: A Pilot Study of Effects on the Second Generation', *Canadian Psychiatric Association Journal*, vol. 16, 1971; Stanley L. Rustin and Florence S. Lipsig, 'Psychotherapy with the Adolescent Children of Concentration Camp Survivors', *Journal of Contemporary Psychotherapy*, vol. 4, no. 2, Spring 1972; and J.J. Sigal et al., 'Some Second-Generation Effects of Survival of the Nazi Persecution', *American Journal of Orthopsychiatry*, vol. 43, no. 3, April 1973.

48 Harvey A. Barocas and Carol B. Barocas, 'Wounds of the Fathers: The Next Generation of Holocaust Victims', *International Review of Psycho-Analysis*, no. 6, 1979.

49 Epstein, op. cit.

50 Rustin and Lipsig, op. cit.

51 Barocas and Barocas, op. cit., p.331.

52 Dori Laub and Nanette C. Auerhahn, 'Reverberations of Genocide: Its Expression in the Conscious and Unconscious of Post-Holocaust Generations', in Luel and Marcus, op. cit.

53 Bergmann and Jucovy, op. cit., p.312.

54 Moshe Halevi Spiro, 'Editor's Preface', p.8, in *Journal of Social Work and Policy in Israel*, op. cit.

55 Aaron Hass, 'In the Shadow of the Holocaust', p.57, I.B. Tauris, 1991.

56 Rustin and Lipsig, op. cit.

57 Harvey A. Barocas and Carol B. Barocas, 'Separation-

Individuation Conflicts in Children of Holocaust Survivors', *Journal of Contemporary Psychotherapy*, vol. 11, no. 1, Spring/Summer 1980.

58 Barocas and Barocas, 1979, op. cit.

59 Joan T. Freyberg, 'Difficulties in Separation-Individuation as Experienced by Offspring of Nazi Holocaust Survivors', *American Journal of Orthopsychiatry*, vol. 50, no. 1, January 1980.

60 Barocas and Barocas, 1980, op. cit.

61 Freyberg, 1980, op. cit.

62 Yael Danieli, 'The Heterogeneity of Post-war Adaptation in Families of Holocaust Survivors', in Braham, op. cit.

63 Nanette C. Auerhahn and Ernst Prelinger, 'Repetition in the Concentration Camp Survivor and Her Child', *International Review of Psycho-Analysis*, no. 10, 1983.

64 Bistritz, op. cit.

65 Hillel Klein, in 'Discussion', in *The Nazi Concentration Camps*, op. cit.

66 Hass, 1991, op. cit., p.51.

67 Epstein, op. cit., p.307.

68 Judith S. Kestenberg, 'Transposition Revisited: Clinical, Therapeutic, and Developmental Considerations', in Marcus and Rosenberg, op. cit.

69 Judith S. Kestenberg, 'Psychoanalyses of Children of Survivors from the Holocaust: Case Presentations and Assessment', *Journal of the American Psychoanalytic Association*, vol. 28, no. 4, 1980.

70 Bergmann and Jucovy, op. cit.

71 Barocas and Barocas, 1979, op. cit.

72 Danieli, op. cit.

73 Yael Danieli, 'The Impact of Holocaust Experience on Families of Survivors Living in the United States', p.607, in *The Nazi Concentration Camps*, op. cit.

74 Hass, 1991, op. cit., p.59.

75 Dina Wardi, *Memorial Candles: Children of the Holocaust*, p.6, Routledge, 1992.

76 Art Spiegelman, *Maus II*, p.15, Penguin Books, 1992.

77 Danieli, 1988, op. cit., p.116.

78 J.J. Sigal et al., op. cit.

79 Danieli, 1984, op. cit.

80 Dinora Pines, 'The Impact of the Holocaust on the Second

Generation', in Dinora Pines (ed), *A Woman's Unconscious Use of Her Body*, Virago, 1993.

81 Joan T. Freyberg, 'The Emerging Self in the Survivor Family', in Marcus and Rosenberg, op. cit.

82 Bergmann and Jucovy, op. cit.

83 Eva Fogelman, 'Group Treatment as a Therapeutic Modality for Generations of the Holocaust', in Marcus and Rosenberg, op. cit.

84 Aleksandrowicz, op. cit.

85 Shamai Davidson, 'Psychosocial Aspects of Holocaust Trauma in the Life-Cycle of Survivor-Refugees and their Families', p.23, in Ron Baker (ed), *The Psychosocial Problems of Refugees*, The British Refugee Council, 1983.

86 Judith Kestenberg, 1980, op. cit.

87 Natasha Burchardt, 'Transgenerational Transmission in the Families of Holocaust Survivors in England', in Daniel Bertaux and Paul Thompson (eds), *Between Generations: Family Models, Myths, and Memories*, Oxford University Press, 1993. In *Maus II*, op. cit., Art Spiegelman's father says, 'Ever since Hitler, I don't like to throw out even a crumb.'

88 Florabel Kinsler, 'Second Generation Effects of the Holocaust: The Effectiveness of Group Therapy in the Resolution of the Transmission of Parental Trauma', in *Journal of Psychology and Judaism*, vol. 6, no. 1, Fall/Winter 1981.

89 Laufer, op. cit.

90 Krystal, op. cit., p.192.

91 Epstein, op cit., and Hass, 1991, op. cit.

92 Danieli, 1984, op. cit.

93 J.J. Sigal et al., op. cit.

94 Howard B. Levine, 'Towards a Psychoanalytic Understanding of Children of Survivors of the Holocaust', p.80, *The Psychoanalytic Quarterly*, vol. 21, no. 1, 1982.

95 Hass, 1991, op. cit., p.61.

96 Vivian Eskin, 'The Impact of Parental Communication of Holocaust-related Trauma on Children of Holocaust Survivors', p.382, in John Lemberger, op. cit.

97 Russell, 1973, op. cit.

98 Nadine Fresco, 'Remembering the Unknown', *International Review of Psycho-Analysis*, no. 11, 1984 – a very sensitive piece interviewing eight French children of survivors.

99 Levine, op. cit.

100 Danieli, 1988, op. cit.

101 Ibid.

102 Davidson, 1983, op. cit.

103 John J. Sigal, 'Hypotheses and Methodology in the Study of Families of the Holocaust Survivors', in Anthony and Koupernik, op. cit.

104 Bergmann and Jucovy, op. cit.

105 Wardi, op. cit.

106 Kestenberg, 1980, op. cit.

107 Levine, op. cit.

108 Norman Solkoff, 'Children of Survivors of the Nazi Holocaust: A Critical Review of the Literature', *American Journal of Orthopsychiatry*, vol. 51, no. 1, 1981.

109 Elana Kuperstein, 'Adolescents of Parent Survivors of Concentration Camps: A Review of the Literature', *Journal of Psychology and Judaism*, vol. 6, no. 1, Fall/Winter 1981.

110 Aleksandrowicz, op. cit.

111 Davidson, 1983, op. cit., p.25.

112 See, for example, L. Rosenberger, 'Children of Survivors', in Anthony and Koupernik, op. cit,; Aleksandrowicz in ibid.; Moshe Almagor and Gloria R. Leon, 'Transgenerational Effects of the Concentration Camp Experience', in Marcus and Rosenberg, op. cit., as well as Dr Gloria Leon's study, cited by Robert Krell, 1984, op. cit.; Uriel Last and Hillel Klein, 'Holocaust Traumatization: The Transgenerational Impact', in *The Nazi Concentration Camps*, op. cit,; Arie Nadler et al., 'Transgenerational Effects of the Holocaust: Externalization of Aggression in Second Generation of Holocaust Survivors', *Journal of Consulting and Clinical Psychology*, vol. 53, no. 3, 1985; John J. Sigal and Morton Weinfeld, 'Mutual Involvement and Alienation in Families of Holocaust Survivors', *Psychiatry*, vol. 50, August 1987; and see Berger, op. cit., for details of similar conclusions in other studies.

113 Anthony and Koupernik, op. cit. Berger, op. cit., cites clinicians who think that parental communication of their Holocaust experiences is beneficial, and those who think it isn't.

114 Eskin, op. cit.

115 Hass, 1991, op. cit.

116 Dori Laub and Nanette C. Auerhahn, 'Knowing and Not Knowing Massive Psychic Trauma: Forms of Traumatic

337

Memory', *International Journal of Psycho-Analysis*, no. 74, 1993.

117 See, for instance, Barocas and Barocas, 1979, op. cit.
118 Hass, 1991, op. cit.
119 Giberovitch, op. cit.
120 Fogelman, 1988, op. cit.
121 Krystal, op. cit.
122 Levi, 1988, op. cit., pp.32–3.
123 Bergmann and Jucovy, op. cit.
124 Gill Pyrah, 'The survivor syndrome', *Listener*, 16 August 1979.
125 Judith S. Kestenberg, 'Children of Survivors and Child-Survivors' in *Echoes of the Holocaust*, no. 1, April 1992 (Bulletin of the Jerusalem Center for Research into the Late Effects of the Holocaust).
126 Davidson, 1983, op. cit.
127 Krell, 1989, op. cit.
128 Terry, 1984, op. cit.
129 Dinora Pines, 'Working with Women Survivors of the Holocaust', in Pines, op. cit.
130 Krell, 1984, op. cit.
131 Freyberg, 1989, op. cit.
132 Krell, 1989, op. cit.
133 Bergmann and Jucovy, op. cit.
134 Haim Factor, 'The Need for Long-term Care Services Among Elderly Holocaust Survivors Living in Israel', in Lemberger, op. cit.
135 Bar-On, op. cit.
136 Florabel Kinsler, 'Group Services for Holocaust Survivors and their Families', in Lemberger, op. cit.
137 Aaron Hass, 'Survivor Guilt in Holocaust Survivors and their Children', p.179, in Lemberger, op. cit.
138 Lifton, p.184, in Krystal, op. cit.
139 'Jewish Women', *Fireweed*, no. 35, Spring 1992.
140 Danieli, in *The Nazi Concentration Camps*, op. cit.
141 David Grossman, *See Under Love*, Jonathan Cape, 1990. Avi Erlich's *Short Eternity*, published by his family in Israel, also tackles the theme of a child of survivors avenging his parents' tormentors, while Gila Almagor's *The Summer of Aviya*, Collins, 1991, is a powerful autobiographical short story about the daughter of a disturbed survivor mother, which was later made into a film.

142 See, for instance, Flora Hogman, 'Memories of the Holocaust', and John J. Sigal, 'Resilience in Survivors, Their Children and Their Grandchildren', both in *Echoes of the Holocaust*, no. 4, June 1995 (Bulletin of the Jerusalem Center for Research into the Late Effects of the Holocaust); and Bjorn Krondorfer's fascinating and sensitive book *Remembrance and Reconciliation: Encounters between Young Jews and Germans*, op. cit., based on the workshops he runs for third generation Jews and Germans.

143 Bar-On, op. cit.

144 Ibid.

145 Bergmann and Jucovy, op. cit.

146 Tom Segev, op. cit., p.169.

147 Aleksandrowicz, op. cit.

148 Krystal, op. cit.

149 Hillel Klein, 'Children of the Holocaust: Mourning and Bereavement', in Anthony and Koupernik, op. cit.

150 See, for instance, Gerald Posner's riveting *Hitler's Children: Inside the Families of the Third Reich*, Mandarin, 1992; Peter Sichrovsky, *Born Guilty: Children of Nazi Families*, Basic Books, 1988; and Dan Bar-On, *Legacy of Silence: Encounters with Children of the Third Reich*, Harvard University Press, 1989.

151 See, for instance, Volker Friedrich, 'The Internalisation of Nazism and Its Effects on German Psychoanalysts and their Patients', in Ehlers and Crick, op. cit.; Ludwig Haesler's powerful paper, op. cit.; and two impressive volumes – Barbara Heimannsberg and Christoph J. Schmidt's *The Collective of Silence: German Identity and the Legacy of Shame*, (Jossey-Bass, 1993), in which German therapists sometimes very personally confront with mixed feelings the Nazi past; and Krondorfer, op. cit., in which third generation Jews and Germans attempt to deal together with their different experiences of the Holocaust.

152 Peter Sichrovsky's *Strangers in Their Own Land: Young Jews in Germany and Austria Today*, (I.B. Tauris, 1986), includes an anguished interchange between a married couple in which the husband is the child of survivors and the wife a non-Jewish Austrian. In Elena Lappin's anthology *Jewish Voices German Words: Growing Up Jewish in Postwar Germany and Austria*, op. cit. contemporary German-Jewish writers bridle at being constantly made to deal with the past rather than being allowed to live in the present.

153 See, for instance, Bergmann and Jucovy, op. cit., and Dinora
   Pines, 'The Impact of the Holocaust on the Second
   Generation', in *Journal of Social Work and Policy in Israel*, op.
   cit., where Rafael Moses, op. cit., expresses unease with
   the juxtaposition.
154 Maria Orwid et al., 'Psychosocial Effects of the Holocaust
   on Survivors and the Second Generation in Poland:
   Preliminary Report', in Lemberger, op. cit.
155 J. Lansen, 'The Second Generation: Dutch Examinations
   and Professional Care', in *Echoes of the Holocaust*, no. 2,
   April 1993 (Bulletin of the Jerusalem Center for Research
   into the Late Effects of the Holocaust); H.G. Vuysje, 'A
   Model for Integrated Psychosocial Support of the Jews in
   the Netherlands', in Lemberger, op. cit.
156 Pines, op. cit.
157 Burchardt, op. cit.

Chapter 11

1 Martin Gilbert, *The Dent Atlas of the Holocaust*, J.M. Dent,
   1993.
2 Felek has written movingly about the amateur scholars who
   made up Eastern European Jewry and perished in the
   Holocaust. He quotes the writer Yitzhak Katzenelson's
   tribute to his father:

   When did he learn the Bible by heart?
   The Commentaries of Onkelos and Martin Luther?
   The Talmud, the Codes, the Midrash, Shakespeare and
   Heine?
   When did he read Gogol, Thucydides and Plutarch?
   When did he study the Holy Zohar?
   When did he sleep?

   and the Polish poet's description of the shtetl as 'a place
   where the cobbler was a poet, the watchmaker a
   philosopher and the barber a troubadour' (Rafael F. Scharf,
   'A Beloved Teacher: A Vanished Human Landscape', p.31, in
   Judaism Today, no. 1, Spring 1995).
3 Debórah Dwork and Robert Jan van Pelt, 'Reclaiming
   Auschwitz' in Geoffrey H. Hartman, op. cit.
4 Ibid.
5 Jan Blonski, 'The Poor Poles Look at the Ghetto', in Antony

Polonsky, *My Brother's Keeper? Recent Polish Debates on the Holocaust*, Routledge, 1990, where other contributions to the subject are also to be found. Already in 1946 Isaac Deutscher was quoting a Polish paper which, at the height of the Holocaust, wrote 'The Nazis are solving the Jewish problem in our favour in a way in which we could never have solved it' (Isaac Deutscher, op. cit., p.88). While liberal organisations like Żegota, the Council to Aid the Jews, tried to give the Jews support, right-wing underground papers like *Barkada*, (*The Barricade*) were arguing in an editorial in March 1943 that 'The liquidation of the Jews on Polish soil . . . will free us from several million parasites' (quoted by Lucjan Dobroszycki, 'The Jews in the Polish Clandestine Press', p.292, in Andrzej K. Paluch (ed), *The Jews in Poland*, vol. 1, Jagiellonian University, 1992).

6 Jack Kugelmass, 'The Rites of the Tribe: The Meaning of Poland for American Jewish Tourists', YIVO Annual 21, 1993.

7 Tomasz Gasowski, 'Jewish Communities in Autonomous Galicia: Their Size and Distribution' in Paluch, op. cit. By the late 1920s a large proportion of rural Eastern European Jewry had migrated from the shtetl to the cities in search of work.

8 As Barbara Kirshenblatt-Gimblett relates in her fascinating introduction to Mark Zborowski's and Elizabeth Herzog's *Life is with People: The Culture of the Shtetl*, Schocken Books, 1995, the sentimental memorialisation of the shtetl was actually a product of post-war American anthropology under the aegis of Margaret Mead. Mead, supervising a research project on pre-war Jewry, inappropriately grafted some of the techniques used to study small communities on Pacific Islands on to much vaster East European societies. The 1952 publication in America of the resulting seminal book, Zborowski's and Herzog's *Life is with People: The Culture of the Shtetl*, celebrated the lost world of a timeless and idealised Eastern European shtetl which didn't square with the pre-war reality – the shtetl wasn't a cultural island but far more heterogeneous and changing.

9 Robert Wistrich, 1995, op. cit.

10 Rafael Scharf in Polonsky, op. cit.

Chapter 12

1 See Dorothy Smith's 'K is Mentally Ill: The Anatomy of a Factual Account', *Sociology*, vol. 2, no. 1, 1978, for a discussion of how case-histories can assign an individual a 'career' as mentally ill.

2 In *Jewish Perspectives: Twenty-Five Years of Jewish Writing*, Jacob Sontag (ed), Secker and Warburg, 1980, various Jewish writers discuss the impact on their work of the wartime destruction of European Jewry.

3 Audre Lorde, 'Age, Race, Class, and Sex: Women Redefining Difference' in *Out There: Marginalization and Contemporary Cultures*, Russell Ferguson (ed) et. al., The MIT Press, 1990.

4 Isaac Deutscher, op. cit.

5 Robert Wistrich, 1995, op. cit.

6 Eva Hoffman, *Lost in Translation*, Heinemann, 1989.

Index

346